THE DEVIL'S DOUBLE

LATIF YAHIA

WITH KARL WENDL

THE DEVIL'S DOUBLE

~~~~~~~~~~~

*The true story of the man forced to be the
double of Saddam Hussein's eldest son*

arrow books

Published by Arrow Books in 2003

1 3 5 7 9 10 8 6 4 2

Copyright © 1994, 1997 Latif Yahia, Karl Wendl 2003
© of the German edition 2003 by Wilhelm Goldmann Verlag, Munich,
a division of Verlagsgruppe Random House GmbH
Translation copyright © Shaun Whiteside 2003

Latif Yahia has asserted his right under the Copyright, Designs and
Patents Act, 1988 to be identified as the author of this work

First published in the United Kingdom in 2003 by
Arrow Books Limited
The Random House Group Limited
20 Vauxhall Bridge Road, London sw1v 2sa

Random House Australia (Pty) Limited
20 Alfred Street, Milsons Point, Sydney,
New South Wales 2061, Australia

Random House New Zealand Limited
18 Poland Road, Glenfield
Auckland 10, New Zealand

Random House South Africa (Pty) Limited
Endulini, 5a Jubilee Road, Parktown 2193, South Africa

The Random House Group Limited Reg. No. 954009

www.randomhouse.co.uk

A CIP catalogue record for this book
is available from the British Library

Papers used by Random House are natural, recyclable
products made from wood grown in sustainable forests.
The manufacturing processes conform to the environmental
regulations of the country of origin.

ISBN 0 09 946555 8

Typeset by MATS, Southend-on-Sea, Essex
Printed and bound in Great Britain by
Bookmarque Ltd, Croydon, Surrey

This book is dedicated to the memory
of my father, Yahia Latif Al Salihi,
whose life was taken by the
Saddam Hussein regime in 1995.

ONE

At the Front

Twenty-third September 1987, in the morning. I'm sitting in a black Mercedes limo with mirrored windows. My chauffeur doesn't say a word. The car must be brand-new, the dark leather smells sharp and fresh. No dust, no stains, the carpets on the floor still have strong colours. The dashboard is made of fine, expensive wood, the air-conditioning runs in complete silence, the engine is barely audible. We glide majestically through the grounds of the Palace of the Republic in Baghdad, an area the size of the centre of a normal European city. Ministries, ministerial apartments, sports fields, theatres, cinemas, hospitals, an airport. In between are fabulous parks and fanciful fountains, turquoise swimming pools with marble rims. A city within a city. Saddam's secret nerve-centre. Impressive.

I have no idea where I'm being taken to, and I'm not about to ask. I'm frightened, because a second black limo is driving directly behind us. I was never frightened at the front, and now the sweat is suddenly trickling from my pores. I wipe my damp hands on my green uniform and think, 'Why me?' People are always disappearing in Iraq. They are arrested, tortured, imprisoned for life or executed immediately. No one knows the real reasons. All we have are suppositions, rumours.

But one thing we do know: a word out of place, a joke, an obscene gesture about the President or his family is enough, it could be your death sentence. I'm convinced that I've always been blamelessly loyal to the regime, but I still have an oppressive sense of insecurity. It's eating into me, growing more intense the longer we spend in the Mercedes. 'Have I ever criticised Saddam anywhere, at any time?' I wonder. 'Talking to friends, fooling about, talking to colleagues at the front. Have I ever made it known, for example, that I'm repelled by this war, that I feel it's only robbing me of my youth and my time? Have I ever carried out an order badly or even indirectly refused to carry it out?'

Nine months earlier, on the 6 January 1987, I had been called up into the Iraqi army. The Iran–Iraq war was still raging, and our forces had occupied 1800 square kilometres of Iranian territory. We had more than 40 divisions in the Iran–Iraq border area, on the Shatt Al-Arab, the estuary of the Tigris and the Euphrates in the south of our country. Apart from the missiles that sometimes fell on Baghdad and ended up destroying two shops in the city centre, I hadn't noticed much about this war, simply because I wasn't interested in it.

A few weeks previously I had graduated with a first in law from Baghdad University. It was a great day for me and my family. What I really wanted to do was work for my father's company. But a law stated that every student over the age of 18 who had finished or abandoned his university training had to join the army. Those who don't go to university, or who drop out for some reason, have to go to the front for 36 months. Graduates, the pride of Iraq, only have to serve for 21 months.

I hated the army from the first day, because I knew that

my 21 months of military service could turn into ten years as laws in Iraq don't mean a thing, and can be changed at any time on the presidential whim. If Saddam is short of soldiers at the front, the length of military service is simply extended. 'The fatherland needs you.' And at the time nobody at all, let alone an ordinary citizen like myself, could see an end to the Iran–Iraq border dispute. All we knew was that Saddam wanted the waterway, and Iran wanted it as well.

Friends of my family had been fighting the war against Iran for years. There was barely a family that had not sacrificed at least one son in this conflict. The war-wounded were everywhere in Baghdad. Young men with burned faces, amputated legs, amputated arms. Desperate people with empty souls and expressionless eyes. And healthy young men with Kalashnikovs over their shoulders, waiting for buses that would bring them back to their units.

When I drove in my car through the magnificent city of Baghdad I didn't talk to any of them because their war was of no interest to me, but I did sense that most of them no longer felt much like fighting. But they had to, whether they wanted to or not, because desertion or refusal to carry out orders were punishable by death. That was what Saddam Hussein had decreed for the duration of the war, which had now lasted for more than seven years. Thousands of deserters had already been killed, in the Al-Ameriya camps, in Prison Number 1, in the Al-Rashid camp in Baghdad. Mass executions that were not performed out of the public eye, behind prison walls or in killing cells, but in full view of the Iraqi people, and live on television.

Saddam's goal was one of deterrence and intimidation, which was why he ordered these public executions, before the eyes of the desperate families of the young soldiers.

Mothers, fathers, sisters and brothers had to watch as the traitors to the fatherland were hanged, so that they would feel the torments of their children and brothers as though they were happening to themselves. So that they too would be tainted by dirt and shame.

But that terrible torture was not enough in itself: on top of that, the families had to pay a fine, to the state, as compensation for their sons' guilt. And the bereaved were not allowed to give the dead a decent burial. 'A deserter has failed the president and Allah,' they sneered, 'he has lost his honour.'

Saddam never described this cruel treatment of the youth of Iraq as deterrence, which is what it was, but as 'just punishment for godless people'.

I joined a commando division, a special unit for university graduates. Our trainers were to turn these privileged recruits, the 'Ayad Saad', into officers as quickly as possible. Within four months we would have to be capable of assuming leadership tasks within the army.

I was given training number 23. Our course was called 'Saddam the Arab', and began on 16 January 1987 in the Al-Rashid barracks on the edge of Baghdad. For a month we had nothing but drill, to the point of exhaustion. Twenty-four hours of brainwashing, to excess: woken at four o'clock, roll-call inspection at five, then the issuing of orders. Physical training, exercise, physical training. Naked from the waist up, wearing only our uniform trousers, we were harried across the dusty barracks yard. Sit-ups, running on the spot, knee-bends. We crawled across the asphalt, hurried along the obstacle course. The worst of the trainers was Salim Al-Juburi, a massive, dark-skinned man from Southern Iraq. He yelled at us, hit us with a cable if we didn't carry out the exercises properly, treated us like animals. We hated him for it, but he was fair and had no favourites. He even drilled 200 Moroccan soldiers, our Moslem brothers, who were being trained in Baghdad, until they were dead on their feet.

Lunch was at two o'clock. After that it started all over again: drill, gymnastics, exercising, political training. No break, no down time, not a second to think of anything except the army and a soldier's duties. Anyone who refused to subordinate themselves was sent running across the parade ground until he couldn't stand. Our trainers had only one goal: to break our personalities, to turn us into will-less fighting machines. During our training we were forbidden to speak to our friends and relations on the telephone. Even letters were strictly forbidden. Nothing was be allowed to distract us.

It wasn't until after a month that we got two days' leave. forty-eight hours away from terror, forty-eight hours of being human.

Then came the second, properly military part of the training. We joined the Al-Saeka company, learned to use light arms, attack weapons. How to dismantle a Kalashnikov, how to load the magazine, how to clean the gun, how to remove a loading obstruction. Monotonous work. Dismantle, clean, reassemble. Dismantle, clean, reassemble. We practised until we could assemble and operate the weapons in our sleep. After that came a rapid course in karate and self-defence. How can I kill an opponent quickly and silently with a knife? We were trained in how to act in hand-to-hand combat and street-fighting, how to approach an opponent silently.

The course concluded with survival training: hours and whole days without food and water. They put us in an enormous room that would have held more than 1,000 people. The stench was terrible, disgusting: a throat-catching smell of urine, shit, sweat. Thousands of men had already been worn down here to the point where they forgot about God and the world.

We were locked in that hall, 500 of us. Our trainers sat on a kind of high chair, like umpires at a tennis match. The floor of the hall was made of stamped earth, with puddles of water with dead dogs and cats in them. The animals were half decomposed, some them practically skeletons. Everywhere there were cockroaches, beetles, horseflies. They had even brought in snakes and dumped them in the dirt.

We had to spend a week in that room. The trainers forced us to eat cockroaches, to throw ourselves into the puddles with the animal corpses and hold out in there. Anyone who refused to do so was beaten and kicked by his comrades 'for practice'. Solidarity and friendship ceased to exist. It was a battle for survival that some of us could barely endure. Sattar, a sensitive, lanky colleague of mine from university, almost died of revulsion when the trainer shouted at him from his high chair, 'Sattar, eat those creatures. Catch them and eat them.'

Sattar held the cockroaches, each as big as a matchbox, in his hand. He pressed them together until a milky-white liquid swelled out of their hard shells. 'Put them in your mouth and chew them until they crunch,' yelled the trainer. But Sattar couldn't do it. He retched, tried not to vomit, pressed his lips together. His gaunt face turned bright red, the veins on his forehead stood out as though they were about to burst. Sattar was able to conquer his urge to vomit two or three times; his body twitched, tears welled up in his eyes. Then it burst out of him. He fell slowly to his knees, retched, vomited, retched. 'Pick him up,' yelled the trainer, 'pick up the sack of shit!' and we knew what was to be done: two men gripped Sattar under the arms and hoisted up the vomiting man. A third held his head and a fourth shoved cockroaches into his mouth, from which vomit was still pouring. 'Bite them, you're an Iraqi soldier, bite them,' came the shouts from the high chair, and it sounded as though the trainer was actually enjoying the humiliating spectacle. Sattar chewed, then threw up, and once again they stuffed the cockroaches into his mouth. There was a crunching sound as he bit, and Sattar's whole body shuddered as he swallowed the creatures down.

Although the course took a lot out of me, I know now that the training did bring me on and made me a man. Afterwards I was in excellent physical condition. As my brain had been completely switched off, my body worked completely automatically in a way that was difficult to define: order, compliance, no backchat. By the end I was carrying out 60-kilometre route-marches with full pack with hardly any difficulty at all, because every muscle, every fibre of my body was reacting completely automatically, and my head was incapable of building up any resistance to the strain.

We were fighters, and the inhuman training had toughened our will to fight. 'The supreme goal,' the trainers would bellow at us, 'is for you to become brutal and inhuman, like animals. Even the Israeli secret service is frightened of you, and you can be proud of that. The world must be afraid of you, and you must forget your fear.'

We felt like an elite, and the system constantly imbued us with fresh self-confidence. 'You're a team,' they told us, 'you're young men who have been allowed to study, and who have therefore been chosen. You have every opportunity to become what we want you to be. You have the unique opportunity to serve your country in a way that is granted to very few. So far you are merely raw material for the army's elevated tasks. In the end you will be the most highly qualified soldiers in the world.'

On 5 April 1987 basic training came to an end. We were given four days' leave, and I went to Baghdad to see my family. My father was proud of me because when I was at home I acted as though the strain had made no difference to me, as though I enjoyed it all. But I was divided: deep within me I felt reluctant to fight, while at the same time I was fascinated by the use of weapons. In the Arab world weapons are part of being a man; a weapon is more than just a killing instrument, it's also an expression of strength and resolution, power and wealth. In Iraq it's customary for all men to carry a gun. There is no house, no family without a gun. Whether it's a pistol, a rifle or a Kalashnikov, a gun is a part of a man, and if you don't own one you're not a man. That's what Saddam has always taught us.

I didn't talk much to my father about the previous few weeks, and instead we talked about the coming month of training. The programme included parachute jumping. Within 30 days we were supposed to be able to jump out of aeroplanes and carry out guerrilla attacks behind enemy lines.

Our head trainer was coarse and rock-hard, of an ideological bent, but a soldier to the marrow. He stopped us being afraid of the first jump, and constantly suggested to us that we were something special. We were only allowed to think about our job and nothing else. 'You must learn fear,' he philosophised in a fatherly way, 'if you don't know fear, you won't be able to deal with it.'

In the middle of the barracks was the jumping-tower, about 120, 130 metres high. The iron steps to the top looked endless to us, but the trainers harried us recklessly. The first time I stood at the very top with my training parachute on my back, I gave a start. I was afraid, but I had no choice: 'Anyone who doesn't jump,' we were threatened, 'will repeat the whole course.' Through loudspeakers attached to the top of the tower, the jumping trainer shouted at me: 'Don't be afraid, be strong, concentrate.'

I tensed my muscles, took a deep breath, yelled 'Al-Saeka' and plunged into the void with that battle-cry.

Made it. I had overcome myself.

On 9 May 1987 the 'Saddam the Arab' course was over. Of the 500 men who had started at the same time as me, 60 had given up. They were eliminated as officer candidates, or had to repeat the course.

We collected our awards in our proud gala uniforms. We entered the parade ground in blocks of 200 men, an army band intoned the Iraqi national anthem, and even Army Commander Abd-Al-Jadbar Shanshal had come to hand us our certificates, and inform us that we were now full members of the Iraqi army.

It was a proud day. I was only 23, and already an officer.

I had now taken the first step on my career within Iraqi society, in which – apart from money – military achievements count for more than anything else. I was pleased, I felt proud and free, and also I was about to get another four days' leave. I went back to my parents' house, but this time my days at home were not so carefree as they had been before: I knew that I would have to return to the front after this short leave. I had received my marching orders at the same time as my decoration for successfully concluding my officer's training.

On 13 May 1987, a blazing hot day, we were taken on military buses from Baghdad to Moussa Ibn Nassir, the 35th

Division. The 35th Division was east of Basra in Southern Iraq. The commander of the group was Mohammed Taher Tawfik, an affable man whom I knew because he came from the same district of Baghdad as me. I was nervous, exhausted, I wasn't really sure what to expect. Mohammed Taher Tawfik noticed this, but the time of encouraging words was over: 'You have 24 hours to rest from your journey, and after that you'll be transferred, to the front,' he thundered, and there was to be no further discussion.

The barracks were like an underground car park and extended several storeys beneath the earth. I slept badly that night. The heat, the mosquitos, the dull detonations of shells that could still be heard down below all gave me pause. For the first time in my life I was hearing war. I felt the vibration when the enemy's fire was returned, and even imagined that I could smell war.

I was in it, there was no going back.

The next day I was transferred to Observation Station Number 5-2 in Al-Aazir. The post was in a marshy area, and our Iranian enemies, the Khomeinis, as we called them, were barely more than three kilometres away. If the wind was right we could even hear them talking in their positions, saying that they would cut our throats when they finally overran us. Sometimes they shouted 'Jaysh May-Akram'.

May Akram was a sleazy Iraqi bar singer who performed in the worst venues in Baghdad, and even in licentious Iraq, where alcohol and bars and night-clubs are just as prevalent as they are in the USA or Europe, she had a terrible reputation. As far as the Iraqi people were concerned, May Akram was basically a whore. So the Iranians' sneering cries meant: 'You're a godless army of whores.'

My job had none of the warlike romanticism that had

been described to us so often during our training: 'Observation of enemy troops and radio communication of coded results of observation to the unit' was the order that my superior had given to me. My position was a kind of raised stand on the top of six poles. All around my position there was nothing but marsh. The stand could only be reached by a little boat. Inside there were two tiny benches that also served as beds, a table on which our radio stood, and a little gas ring. The whole stand wasn't much more than three metres square in area. This was where I was to hold out – so this was the glorious war against the devil Khomeini.

My team consisted of the radio officer Ismail Taha, a hardened fighter who was hardly older than I was, but who had already spent several years at the front; Mohammed Mottasher, a simple soldier from a Baghdad suburb; and a cook. I had to keep that position for 22 days. Watching, watching, watching. Monotonous, dull. It was hard to concentrate all the time. If I noticed the tiniest change in the positions of the enemy, I had to pass the fact on immediately to my unit. The unit then responded with heavy artillery fire. We ourselves had only light arms, so we would have had no chance to respond to an enemy attack. 'Withdraw quickly and quietly' was the instruction if the attack were actually to come.

Nothing at all happened for weeks. My work consisted of waiting, observing, waiting. For hours, for days. And then there would be brief, intense artillery battles. Then, once again, tense and nervous waiting. Most of the time I didn't see anything but the little trucks bringing the food rations to the soldiers at the front. We generally saw only the dust thrown up by the trucks. Sometimes, especially at night, we thought we could hear the enemy breathing, they seemed so close. Then for days at a time we would see nothing of them, although we knew very well that they were there. The front had dug itself in; this was positional warfare that could have continued like that for ever.

Although I hadn't been there for long, I was thoroughly fed up with the job: sitting and waiting. Above you the deep blue sky, around you the killing heat, in front of you the endless water, the marshes of the Shatt Al-Arab. Admittedly I was an officer and thus better off than the ordinary soldiers. But what good did that do me? None at all. I ate the same things as everyone else, slept on the same wooden bed, was, like them, an insignificant cog in this vast war, for which there was no reason as far as I could see: I didn't hate my enemy, in fact I couldn't hate him, because I didn't know him. If the war had had a murderous dynamism, it would have been easier to hate our enemy. But like this? We simply had too much time to think, and 95 percent of our service consisted of waiting. Absurd.

The only advantage that I drew from my position as an officer was that I was given seven days' home leave every three weeks. So I was able to leave my position for the first time after 22 days. I went home. Baghdad, city of my dreams. My family lived in the district of Al-Aadamiya, a good part of the city. Our house was roomy, and my father was very enthusiastic when I told him about the front. But he quickly noticed that when I talked to him I was constantly trying to explain why the war was being waged in the first place. 'Look at our house, Father. We've got everything we need. People in Iraq live well. Why must we die at the front – why?' He avoided my questions and replied to each of my arguments against the war by saying, 'Military service is service for the fatherland, and desertion is paid for by death.'

There was no way out, I had to go back. My concern for my family forced me to do my duty.

Two days later, on 10 June 1987, the Khomeinis attacked us from all sides. A baptism of fire. They wanted to wipe out the 35th Division. I ordered my radio officer to contact headquarters. He yelled the alarm into the ether, and the instructions that came back from the officer in charge were brief and to the point: 'Abandon position, withdraw.' But it was already too late: when we climbed down from the stand into our boat, we saw the first Iranian helicopters appearing. First two of them, then a whole squadron. They put on a kind of deadly firework display. A shell exploded in our observation post, tearing the primitive iron construction apart. A few minutes earlier and we would have been done for, but the danger wasn't yet past: although our artillery units were covering the enemy with their fire, they were advancing further and further. We were encircled, and there was nowhere we could get to. Admittedly we could still fight our way to a different base, but there was no point: the commander of that base had had to capitulate.

The whole company was imprisoned. Officers and men were separated. They tied us by the hands, drove us into a primitive cellar, beat us. Only six men were set to guard us, because the battle was continuing undiminished.

Ghassan Hamud, the commander of the 10th Tank Brigade and a decorated war hero, had begun the counter-attack. His task was clearly to get us out of there and force the Iranians back. And he managed it: two hours later the Khomeinis were back where they had been before the attack. They left all their things behind, fled on foot, waded through the marshes. Including our guards. A crazy war.

*

Hundreds of Iranian soldiers were imprisoned in this counter-attack by the men of the 10th Tank Brigade. A day of triumph for the Iraqi army, and Saddam Hussein brought in his whole propaganda troop: television, newspaper reporters, photographers. We were celebrated as though we had won the war. Our whole unit received special awards, and I was promoted to First Lieutenant.

I should actually have been celebrating that day as well, but I felt miserable: First Lieutenant Nassem Tibn, a young soldier from the Anbar area of Baghdad, who had trained with me, had been seriously injured in the counter-attack. He wasn't injured by a bullet in battle, but by an Iranian soldier who had been taken prisoner. The recruit was already lying on the ground with his hands behind his neck, and it was Nassem Tibn's task to guard him. All of a sudden the Iranian leapt up like a coiled spring. He had a stone in his hand, and struck Nassem Tibn hard in the face with it. My friend cried out and collapsed bleeding to the ground, with a great wound gaping on his head. It looked terrible, and a large amount of blood flowed out of the wound into the sand.

One of my men reacted promptly, cocked his gun and shot the Iranian soldier who had left my friend in such a sorry state. It was the first time I saw anyone die. The Iranian was hit in the chest, toppled forwards, crept a few metres and fell on his face. He groaned, twitched and then lay there motionlessly in his torn, faded uniform. It was somehow undignified, inhuman, to see the boy dying like that, but I felt a deep inner satisfaction: he had deserved that punishment.

A few days later, on 25 July 1987, I was transferred to an artillery division, Unit 954, which was also right at the front. All of our equipment came from the Soviet Union. Very modern 85 mm mortars with a range of three to four kilometres. I was glad I had been assigned experienced officers: Squadron Leader Mohammed Ghaleb, a pleasant character who had already carried out hundreds of attacks in this war, and Lieutenant Nassir Baker and Lieutenant Saad Ahmad, who were both from Baghdad, both from good families, and more Western in their thinking than the average Harvard MBA student. They were both tall and slim, highly trained, and with the obligatory moustache.

I soon became their friend, although I could at first see no reason why they had taken me into their group so quickly and in such a friendly way. I was there when discussions of position were carried out, and ate with the other officers in the command post. Our position consisted of a network of underground passages, supported with wooden beams and reinforced with sandbags. The command post was small and stuffy, but it did have a certain atmosphere. We called it 'the restaurant'. A few little tables, chairs, and a little kitchen in the corner. Although everything was very spartan, I felt good in that bunker.

Suddenly I had access to those glorified higher military circles. A world that is so convinced of itself that the reality, the horror of war, seems to be a long way away, and passes it by leaving barely a trace. For the first time I had influence, I felt a sense of power, I was one of the people who dictate. One of those who dictate mercilessly while at the same time being very careful never to cross the invisible boundaries. Never to make a mistake, never to antagonise the people who really have the final say in Iraq: the members of Saddam's clan. No little jokes, no thoughtless remarks about the President, not a word about his family and their lackeys and lickspittles.

As I have said, I couldn't explain why they had drawn me

so quickly into their circle, why they gave me the feeling of being something special. That was until it slipped out of Mohammed Ghaleb, while making small-talk over a glass of tea. Ghaleb drew me paternally to him, took my right hand, raised his glass to me with a smile and said, almost in a whisper: 'You have good connections with influential circles in Baghdad. You're part of them, after all . . .'

I said nothing, smiled back, took another sip, wiped my moustache dry with the back of my hand and nodded. At that moment I understood what was going on here: all that time they had believed that I was a relative of Saddam Hussein, that I was the spitting image of his son Uday. Of course none of the men knew what Uday really looked like. They only knew him from newspapers and television, and those pictures weren't terribly good. But none of them had direct access to the President's family, and so none of them was able to check. It was my great resemblance to Uday and my well-cared-for appearance that had led them to their false conclusion. Ghaleb was so convinced that I was a member of the clan that he even suggested that I become the political leader of the unit. A special distinction for a young officer, but one which I had to turn down as I didn't belong to the Ba'ath Party, whose members are higher up in the hierarchy than mere military men. That job then went to a young second lieutenant sent to us by the Party in Baghdad.

I didn't care, particularly as I had no time to get annoyed. On 20 September 1987 there was sudden uproar among the officers in my unit. A secret despatch had arrived from the President's office. That was a very unusual event. And the despatch concerned me, Latif Yahia, the lieutenant who was the spitting image of Uday Saddam Hussein. Ghaleb called me to him and asked me excitedly: 'Yahia, have you done something, have you broken the law?'

I was surprised. 'No, never, why?'

Ghaleb smiled superciliously and then said, with a warm, fatherly expression, 'Yahia, you're to go to Baghdad as fast as possible. It's an important secret mission.'

I wanted to ask Ghaleb something, but he dismissed me with an elegant and pompous gesture of his hand. 'No questions, Yahia, my friend, off you go,' he said with a broad grin, as though he knew what it was about. In fact he had no idea, but I didn't know that yet.

Twenty-four hours later I was in headquarters in Baghdad. It was six o'clock in the evening, and I was still wearing my uniform from the front, sweaty and dust-covered. At reception in headquarters I met Party member Kaiser Harb Al-Tikritti. He seemed to be waiting for me and told me to come and sit down, because my car would soon arrive. We stood there in silence for ten minutes, and only once did he ask me how things were at the front, and I said, 'Fine, fascinating, I'm proud to have the opportunity to be there.' I lied because lying is a necessary form of self-protection in Iraq, both because everyone lies, and because lies have become a part of our society.

After ten more minutes the black Mercedes with the chauffeur was outside the door. I got in, and we set off towards the palace grounds, which were only a few streets away. Even before I got in I had noticed the second Mercedes limousine that had stopped behind my car. When we set off I turned around for a moment and saw it following us. Three men were sitting in that car, their faces grave, and I knew that something important was going on here because ordinary arrests are carried out quite differently in Iraq.

So what have I done wrong? We've been gliding along for

five minutes now, an endless time. I ask the chauffeur for a cigarette, but he hasn't got any. My whole period of military service passes before my eyes as though in a film. Question after question: Have I vilified the war in any way? Who have I talked to about the President? Surely I couldn't have said anything wrong to my father, when I had told him about my problems on my home leave? No, no, it couldn't be that. Not my father, no, certainly not. It couldn't have been a member of my family. At least not intentionally. But the eyes and ears of the clan are everywhere. And anyway: why did Commander Ghaleb keep going on about the President's family to me? Had they just been testing me, checking my loyalty? And were the references to my resemblance to Uday just a trick to throw me? Were they trying to test my dependability?

I can't come up with an answer, and I'm about to ask my chauffeur if he has any idea where things are going, but he stares with concentration at the wide asphalted street. I'm sitting diagonally behind him on the back seat, I press myself up against the door on the right and stare at him. He shows no reaction, just strokes his thick moustache once and looks in the rear-view mirror. Our eyes meet, and I'm about to frame a question, but then keep it to myself. 'Perhaps it's all a mistake,' I say to reassure myself. If it wasn't, the chauffeur would have given a hint of it. He must know the thousands of rumours and accusations that circulate here. Everone in Baghdad knows about these stories, so he must know them too. It's not a secret, I rage inwardly, that innocent people are regularly accused and executed for the errors and cruelties of the President's family. Only recently, a few weeks ago, slavering onlookers had poured into Rasheed Street, Baghdad's big shopping and strolling street.

Four men were on display, their hands and feet bound

with chains, flanked by heavily armed soldiers, and handed over to the public fury. For a good hour hysterical women screamed at them, pulled them by the hair, spat into their distorted faces. Then the unfortunate men were led away – straight to the scaffold. The offenders were Baghdad businessmen who had been condemned to death on the orders of Saddam Hussein. At the time Saddam had said on television, which we were also able to receive at the front, that 'these low creatures had damaged the people through simple greed, and sold goods at outrageous prices', and everyone knew it was a lie. Saddam's clan just wanted to get rid of its opponents, who disturbed its social circles and had allowed something to slip out, voiced the opinion that the clan had the whole country in a grip of steel.

These executions reveal only too clearly how frightened Saddam is of his own people. But the people are also afraid of Saddam. We're all afraid of each other, and like an idiot I had thought I had learned to live with it.

I haven't. Now, all of a sudden, everything has changed. All of a sudden I'm in the middle of this spiral that drags everything down. I'm a protagonist in a bloody drama called Iraq, my homeland.

'They must be getting me mixed up with somebody else,' I say to give myself courage, and catch myself moving my lips. Beads of sweat stand on my forehead, my short hair is wet, my shirt sticks to my skin. 'So now I have to pay for someone else's crime. Is that how my life is to end?'

It's the beginning.

My Mercedes stops outside Nissr-Baghdad Palace, the official building of Uday Saddam Hussein, Saddam's notorious son. I know the building, although no one from my family has ever been here before. I've seen it hundreds of times on television and in the newspapers. Yes, that's Uday's palace. It must be something to do with him. What could Uday want from me?

My chauffeur gets out and opens my door. Once again he doesn't say a word and avoids my eye, his face blank. Two uniformed men collect me and bring me in. I have to wait for five or six minutes, standing in a kind of vestibule. On the wall there's a big mirror, and next to it white leather furniture decorated with gold. Suddenly the door opens and he's standing in front of me. Grinning, with a thick Havana between his index and his middle fingers. Uday Saddam Hussein. The first thing I think is: 'He's hardly changed, we could still be twins.'

TWO

Paradise

I've known Uday for years. We were in the same class at Baghdad High School for Boys. Uday, whose father was vice president of Iraq at the time, is only four days younger than I am. He was born on 18 June 1964, and I was born on the 14th. In my childhood I didn't pay much attention to the politician's son. I had an excellent home in my parents' house. We lived in a large, imposing house in the Al-Aadamiya district, one of the best residential areas of Baghdad. My parents were affluent. My father, Yahia Al-Salihi, was a factory owner with three successful shops in Baghdad, selling electrical goods and cookers. He also dealt in marble and other natural stones. We were upper-class, but I wasn't as aware of the fact when I was at grammar school as I was later on. I only knew I was the eldest son, the pride and joy of my mother, Bahar Al-Midjadi, and a good Moslem. I could have anything I wanted. Just like my brothers Jotie, Robie and Omeed, and my sisters Gallalha and Juan. We wanted for nothing.

We lived as though in paradise, and Baghdad was still paradise in those days. I liked going to school, and my father worked with me and on me; he taught me, supported me, encouraged my talents. I think my father loved me best of all his children, but that might have been a subjective impression: I'm the eldest son. In the summer holidays he took me to his shops and showed me how to negotiate and sell things. He always said, 'You must become like me, a good businessman,' and I didn't disappoint him. My six years of primary school were very successful. I was best in the class, and my teacher, Madame Fawzya, told my father, 'Your son is very gifted, he will make a mark.'

At the time my greatest passion lay in watching electrical goods being dismantled, repaired and put back together again in my father's shops: tape recorders, televisions, video recorders. I was quite desperate to learn something. I wanted to know everything. Every single thing. And I also had a gift for painting. I painted big, kitschily realistic pictures with strong, bright colours. Mosques, houses, trees. The Tigris, my teacher, my brothers and sisters. I can't say why, but I found it easy to draw scenes from memory.

Baghdad College High School for Boys was the absolute elite school in Iraq, and remains so today. No children from ordinary families were allowed to go to this school. It was only for the children from wealthy and elegant families, the sons of politicians, military men, influential people. This was Iraq's elite, and anyone who wasn't from a wealthy family was only allowed in if he had excellent marks and recommendations from primary school teachers, or was able to demonstrate talents that were worthy of encouragement. This was where the urbane young men were to be educated, the ones who would be giving the leading nation within the Arab camp an even more prominent place in the world.

The school consisted of one main building and two side buildings, and extended over an area of about a square kilometre. Beneath the school there was an ingenious system of bunkers. The Americans had built it to withstand nuclear attack. There were atom bomb-resistant rooms, endless

passages with bowling alleys, table-tennis tables and shelters
with food stores. The school was at once an elite centre and
a military installation.

Just as select as the pupils who were allowed to attend
Baghdad High School were the professors who taught there.
Saddam personally ensured that only the best teachers were
able to come to the school. We were Iraq's poster boys, the
young tip of a system in which the privileged enjoyed every
imaginable advantage, and those who were socially not so
well off basically had no chance of rising to the top. A
complete inversion of socialism, education on the capitalist
model.

We were screened off, nurtured, protected. The simple
folk, the plebs, were to have no opportunity to distract us
from the high aims of education. Thus the school was more
or less constantly under the protection of the secret service
Jehaaz Al-Amen Al-Khass, because all the children of the
most important men in Iraq attended this school. The Jehaaz
Al-Amen Al-Khass is practically sacred, the highest of Iraq's
four secret services. Gardeners, school janitors, domestic
staff, they were all members of the secret service. Around
the school in the district of Al-Aadamiya, only a few hundred
yards away from my home, they had erected control posts in
which a guard always sat observing, checking. It was
impossible for outsiders even to walk on to the school
grounds. We lived as though in an educational glass box.

If anyone tried to get around this strict regulation and
enter the school grounds, he was arrested. The same
happened to anyone who tried to bring along people who
weren't from the institution. The hapless companion would
be arrested, and the one who had tried to smuggle him in
was immediately expelled from the school. We were
constantly guarded, checked, prisoners of a school system

that had only two goals: to give young men the best education and at the same time to bring them up from earliest childhood to be perfect Party soldiers. We weren't asked to have a will of our own, what was important was that the rules of the game were adhered to 'one thousand percent'.

A specially organised teachers' commission had to ensure that the professors were ideologically pure, and held leading positions in the Ba'ath Party. The commission was run by our headmaster Fasaa, a massive man who looked cruel and frightening. Fasaa must have weighed 16 stone, was about 45 years old, and what struck everybody immediately was his big head and his muscular body. Fasaa had been a boxer, and had even made it to national champion. Everyone suffered under him. He was brutal, an animal, but powerful, so we and the teachers had to endure this evil man. He was probably a good Party soldier, and had received this job as a result.

The professors passed the pressure that Fasaa exerted on them directly to the pupils: from the age of 12 each of us had to become a Party member. There was no getting around this regulation. The first stage of Party membership was called Majeed.

The first class was hard for me because everything was new, but I studied hard and wanted to be the best. The Party was more important than anything else. How is the hierarchy constructed, what are its basic features, what are its goals, its programmes, its structures? The Party is the highest thing of all, and without the Party you are nothing. The most important book was thus the Party's programme, 'The Central Report of the Ninth National Conference of the Ba'ath Party', the history of the Party from its foundation to the present day. Everyone in Iraq had to know this book by heart, every line, every word. The Party programme was even more important than the Koran.

I thought that completely normal at the time, I was 12 years old and I didn't know anything else. Because everybody had to do it, I didn't see it as harassment when we were drilled for two hours a week at Party meetings. Our teachers ensured that we fulfilled our Party duties 100 percent. We were tested on it at school, and anyone who didn't join in was given extra homework. If he didn't do it then, he would be expelled from school, immediately. So we devoted ourselves to the programmes, as though they were the holiest of holies, and basically that was the case.

The first step of the Party hierarchy is that of sympathiser. From ordinary sympathiser you become an active sympathiser, then a pioneer and finally an active member. If you are then an active member, you can rise to become company leader, division leader and finally leading member on communal and trans-regional level. I didn't feel Party work to be particularly troublesome, because we were all in the same boat.

As far as I was concerned, it was much more important for me to meet other important young boys in the high school: Ali Mohammed Saleh, for example, whose father was a Party leader, an important man in Iraq. Or Wamied Al-Saadoun: his father was an officer in Al-Khass. Oussama Kahtan was from the family of the head of the Iraqi Central Bank. And above all Siad Meeshel Aflak. His father was the man who introduced the Arab-socialist Ba'ath Party to Iraq, spreading it and making it successful. He was a pioneer, and Saddam's most important political adviser.

Siad was a pleasant boy who had had a perfect upbringing. He was something special, and that was immediately apparent: in his straight, elegant walk, his manners, his way

of speaking and behaving. At the age of 14 he was like other
people at 30. An almost perfect personality.

I thought it particularly important to win his friendship,
and worked determinedly to do so. Slowly, cautiously,
because I didn't want to rush things, and didn't want anyone
to notice that I was desperate to be his friend.

At break-time I tried to make conversation with him, I
sometimes smiled at him in class, and, in November 1978 –
it was a Monday and we had just done some very hard school
work – he suddenly came over to me and suggested that we
meet outside school, in the Al-Alwia Club.

The Al-Alwia Club – a dream, a world that could have
been on another planet as far as I was concerned.

The Al-Alwia Club was right behind the Sheraton Hotel, and
reflected the other Baghdad. Exclusive, wealthy, elegant
Baghdad. Iraq was at the time still the darling of the West.
People invested, traded, billions of dollars were transferred.
There was hardly a large Western concern that didn't have
branches in Iraq; international hotels were sprouting up all
over the place: Sheraton, Hilton, all those names. Baghdad
was the centre, and everything flowed to it. Businessmen
and arms traders, chancers and pleasure-seekers from our
Arab brother countries, because Baghdad was Western, and
you could find anything there: night-clubs, bars, alcohol and
women. Beautiful women were to be had for little money.
Oil traders and arms dealers of every nation and every colour
lived there and threw money around as though it was just
coloured paper.

I didn't dare ask Siad what membership of the club cost,
because the sums I had heard were so gigantic that I thought
it was impossible for anyone to pay it: 2000 to 3000 dollars,
it was said, per month.

Siad collected me, one Friday morning, in a Mercedes that he drove himself although he was, like myself, only 14. But in Iraq there were no prohibitions and no rules. Children from wealthy and powerful houses had complete freedom, because no one, no single policeman, would dare to check members of this class, or even stop them and ask to see their driving licence. This absurd system was organised so feudally that the people at the top were able to do whatever they wanted.

I had put on my finest suit. Siad wore a pale Armani linen suit, an Yves Saint Laurent tie and Gucci shoes. And he smelled of a heavy, sweet, expensive perfume.

Even the entrance to the club was impressive: a big gate with two bodyguards checking everyone who drove in. Siad had a sticker on his windscreen which indicated that he was a member. Immediately after the entrance came the car park, with its armada of cars, not a single one cheaper than a Mercedes. Everything gleamed here, the polished chrome of the bumpers flashed like silver in the brilliant sun.

Then security again after the car park. Siad casually showed his membership card, a plastic thing with his name and address, and a laminated photograph.

I was nervous when security asked us for our membership cards. But Siad solved my problem in an elegant way that was all his own. He just clutched my arm, told the guards that I was his friend, and that was enough.

Then the club itself, a paradise the like of which barely exists anywhere in the West, at least not in this form: restaurants, huge halls full of computer games, videos, billiard tables. Everything. Party rooms as big as St Peter's Square in Rome or St Stephen's Square in Vienna. These party rooms can be hired. For noisy celebrations with opulent decoration, for weddings and birthday parties. For such occasions less wealthy people would rent one of the party rooms in the Hotel Al-Rashid, the Sheraton or the Al-Mansur. But anyone who really wanted to be someone in Baghdad society came here.

There were elegant terraced swimming pools built into this system of gaming rooms and restaurants, and there was also a polo pitch, a cricket pitch and two basketball fields. Siad knew almost all the young men in the club. On that day I stayed in the background, seeking shelter behind Siad's perfect manners. I listened with interest as he talked to friends of his father's, as they talked about the latest cars, and the conversation turned to the absolute non-plus-ultra of Iraqi society: the Al-Said Club.

The Al-Said Club is a step more elegant, more worldly and perfect than the Al-Alwia, however impossible that may seem. There, only members of Saddam Hussein's family, the families of the advisers and friends of the President, as well as the families of the ministers have access. The Club is in the district of Al-Mansour.

Siad got terribly excited as he talked about the first time he went to the Al-Said Club with his father: 'It's paradise, it's really paradise,' he said, and we stood nearby and listened to him as though he were a prophet.

'Al-Said isn't Sunset Boulevard or Ocean Drive in Miami Beach, it's more than that,' he chattered, casually holding his glass of gin and tonic, ice and lemon. 'The lawn is green. Not a normal green,' he went on, and our mouths gaped open. 'That lawn would make you think about the best golf courses in England, you'd feel like bursting into tears. Dark, thick, juicy grass. Life, the sun, the stars, the universe. Al-Said is all of that.'

Siad's gestures were like those of Bing Crosby when he

seeks the favours of Grace Kelly in *High Society*.

'And then the swimming pools. There are winter pools, summer pools. The pools are decorated with mosaics, and the water is sapphire-blue – really great.'

The conversation turned into a monologue, and finally Siad was speaking almost without interruption. 'Only ministers go there, security know every identity card, every name, every detail.'

And then he launched out on a story that sounded totally incredible: 'Once a Mercedes 500 SEL drove up there. At first I couldn't recognise a driver, but there must have been someone sitting at the wheel, because a Mercedes doesn't drive on its own, after all. Then the driver got out.'

None of us dared to interrupt Siad, and we waited excitedly to hear how the story continued. 'He was a twelve-year-old boy in a white smoking-jacket. He had a gun at his hip, and the child was accompanied by four bodyguards. He was a minister's son.'

I could have listened to Siad for ever, and indeed he went on for ever. 'If you cause the smallest problem in this club, they throw you out immediately. Regardless of who your father is, regardless of what influence your family has. If you cause the slightest problem, your father will never see your face again, because they'll finish you off. They'll really finish you off.'

One of us interrupted Siad, to ask a logical but ludicrous question: 'What about girls?'

Siad got furious, took a deep breath, clutched his head dramatically and let rip: 'What sort of an idiot are you? They're absolutely taboo. If they want to meet you and smile at you, look away. Look at the ground, at the side, at the sky. Do something, anything. Walk faster, whistle, whatever, but for God's sake don't talk to them. The girls are untouchable, unattainable, from another world. Even to me.'

He took a deep breath, pressed his lips together for a moment and said instructively, like a survival trainer, 'Enjoy yourself, play billiards or basketball, but hands off those girls. They're under constant surveillance, and if you see them and talk to them, you'll be under surveillance as well, and that means you'll be in the mills of the secret services, and those wheels will crush you sooner or later. You'll lose your future, your hopes, your life. You'll lose everything. The evil spirits will never let you go, particularly if one of those girls is Uday's girlfriend.'

At the end of that day I was profoundly impressed, confused and excited at the same time. The club, the stories, the lunch with Siad, this elegant young gentleman. I felt big, and was completely sure that you could only achieve something in the country if you were a member. When Siad wanted to drop me off at home with his Mercedes, I asked him to stop in a side street and let me out. I didn't want him to park right in front of our house, because although our house was big and imposing, I suddenly felt inferior and small.

When I got out he called to me, 'Latif, I'd be happy if you could become a member as well.' Two days later I was a proud member of the Al-Alwia Club. Siad had organised the card for me. Free. I never asked him how he did that, but no doubt his father had something to do with it. Siad accepted me as his friend, and from then on we spent every free moment in the club. Once – it was a Friday afternoon and we were playing basketball, five-a-side – we suddenly heard the sound of gunfire. Salvoes from a machine-gun. The shots came from the terrace swimming pool. We ran over there and saw several boys wearing dark brown djellabas, traditional costume.

One of them was standing right by the cash desk with a

machine-gun in one hand and a till receipt in the other. Beside him were a number of older boys. They too were wearing brown djellabas. The men negotiated, argued, the boy with the machine-gun shouted and fired another few salvoes into the air.

I asked one of the waiters who the guy at the cash-desk was, and he hissed at me, 'Pssst, that's Uday Saddam.'

So that's the notorious son of Saddam Hussein, I said to myself, and although I could only see him from the side, I was struck by the fact that we looked deceptively similar. His eyes, his nose, his hair. He looked like me.

I repressed the event, and didn't mention it to my father or my brothers. Neither did I try to find out why Uday had fired his gun. I thought of Siad's words on our first day in the club: 'If you notice something, look away, ignore everything, look uninterested. Never try to come into contact with them or find out anything about them, because they're stronger and more powerful than you and your parents. They are Iraq.'

It was a year later, 1979, more or less in the middle of the school year, when our teacher announced the arrival of a new pupil: 'The young gentleman,' he said, 'comes from Al-Mansur High School, and is going to be your new class-mate.'

It was Uday Saddam Hussein. Uday's father had chosen our class for him because we were the best and most active of our year. None of us had bad marks, and there were never any problems with our political training.

His first appearance in the school was like a scene from a bad film: the door flew open, Uday, who was 15 years old like the rest of us, walked in with his head held high. No greeting. Two powerful-looking bodyguards assumed positions beside the door, two at the other end of the classroom, and a fifth sat down beside Uday and carried his school books for him.

There was great excitement, none of us could concentrate, and it was too much for the teacher as well. This spectacle was repeated every day from then on. First came the bodyguards, then Uday, generally in jeans and a shirt, like a cowboy. Uday wore his hair longer than we did, and had a mop of tousled hair like Jimi Hendrix.

After a few weeks we had become used to Uday's daily appearance. There was nothing friendly about him, nothing normal, nothing ordinary, and from the first day I found him repulsive. He had no respect for any of the teachers, or anyone who wanted to tell him anything or give him orders. He didn't care about the exams or his school work. He didn't care about anything. There were 24 boys in the class, and while everyone else tried to be successful, Uday wasn't interested in anything. If a teacher dared to bring him to the blackboard, he threw chalk at him, ordered him to change the subject or simply leave him in peace. Uday came whenever he wanted, went whenever he wanted, did whatever he wanted. And he never brought any books with him. None the less, at the end of school, he was the first, the best in the class.

Uday didn't obey any rules. He drove his Porsche into the playground, and even broke the strictest taboo of the High School: girls.

One day he brought his girlfriend into class. Salwa Ahmad Al-Sabty had thick black hair, light skin, green eyes. She looked wonderful in her suit. None of us said anything, and there was an embarrassed silence. He sat down in his place, Salwa sat next to him. She looked uneasy, as though Uday had forced her to come. When our professor came in you could have heard a pin drop. We waited tensely for his reaction. For an explosion, a shouting match, but he just went up to Uday, bowed and said in a half-whisper, 'Mr Uday, this won't do . . .'

We sensed how humiliating this play-acting must be for our professor, how he was seething inwardly, and desperately trying not to lose control. Uday enjoyed his impotence, interrupted the man and hissed at him, without the slightest respect, in a commanding tone: 'You do your job, I'll do mine. Get on with the class.'

Then there was brief eye contact between him and the professor. Uday lounged in his chair, played with a gold fountain pen, laughed, grinned, held the hand of his girlfriend, who sat silent and cowering beside him. Uday knew the professor had no power to do anything, and the professor knew it as well. He began his lecture as though nothing had happened.

After a little more than half an hour Uday jumped up, took his uneasily smiling girl by the arm and disappeared from the classroom without a word of goodbye. He just got up and went. We could hardly believe it, but that was what happened, and for the first time we experienced how much power Uday really had. He was the son of Saddam Hussein, who was by now the President of the Republic of Iraq.

The professor who had dared to talk to Uday about his girlfriend had vanished by the next day. None of us ever saw him again or found out what happened to him.

There was a room in the school reserved for drawing lessons. We worked there two hours a week, and they were the finest classes for me, because drawing was my passion. My first pictures were drawings from nature, I drew scenes from Kurdistan. In the summer holidays I had gone to Kurdistan with my father in his white Volvo, to Sersensk and

Shaklawa. My grandparents came from this beautiful region in the north of Iraq. My grandfather had left Kurdistan before my father was born, and set up a shop in Baghdad. But we still had numerous relations in Northern Iraq, and I enjoyed those summer holidays. And that supplied the atmosphere of my large, colourful pictures.

My drawing teacher was so enthusiastic about our drawings that he made a special room available to exhibit them. The opening was a complete success, my pictures were the most striking of all, and I even received a prize for the best picture. It was my picture of Kurdistan.

All my friends congratulated me, even Uday. After the exhibition he came over to me and put his arms around me, clapped me on the shoulders and said, 'I want you to paint a picture for me. A portrait of my father, the President. I want to give it to him.'

This was in 1980. Saddam Hussein had formally assumed the office of head of state and government on 16 May 1979. At the same time he also became General Secretary of the Ba'ath Party and General Commander of the Armed Forces. He followed President Ahmed Hassan Al-Bakr, who had died of a heart attack. At least, that was the official version. Privately, however, everyone said that Saddam had had him killed, with poison. Al-Bakr's wife and his eldest child are also supposed to have been liquidated: they had died shortly before, in a car accident. A truck had rammed their car.

Saddam had for a long time planned to assume Al-Bakr's role, and had basically been the secret president of Iraq for many years. He constantly appeared on television, and people in Iraq saw him as the saviour, the direct descendant of the prophet, the god who could make Iraq great and strong and powerful, a new Babylon. Iraq was a modern descendant of the New Babylonian Empire of antiquity, Saddam drilled into us.

Admittedly the new president had lots of people executed, 'putschists' as my father always said. But we barely noticed that. What was more important was that Saddam declared war on illiteracy in my country, and gave women all the rights of which Islam deprives them in other countries. He also forced up petroleum production, and the profits of the oil economy benefited us, the people.

When Uday talked to me and asked whether I could paint his father, I was filled with pride, because I thought of the day when Saddam had come to power: the whole of Baghdad, the whole of Iraq had been on its feet. I ran through the streets of Baghdad, like my friends, shouting, 'Saddam, Saddam.' And millions shouted along with me. People embraced each other, they were happy, and even my father, otherwise a rather level-headed man, was utterly over the moon: 'Now everything will be better, and Iraq will be the leading Arab nation.'

We were all mistaken, but none of us realised that at the time.

I only knew that the son of this great man was asking me to paint his father. A great honour. At the time Saddam had dozens of resident painters. Every artist in Iraq was desperate to have a piece of his bizarre and unbounded personality cult. Everywhere in Iraq, on every street corner, on every barracks, on every public building, huge, kitsch pictures of Saddam Hussein could be seen. Saddam as a soldier, Saddam as a peasant, as the president, as a strong and powerful man. Saddam, everywhere.

I was surprised that Uday wanted to bestow this honour

on me, but played the whole business down somewhat. 'Okay,' I said, 'I'll do it.'

From his car, which he had parked, as always, in the playground, Uday brought me some portrait photographs of his father. 'I'll need four days,' I said, and Uday just nodded.

I was finished three days later, and the portrait was really quite good. I took the picture into school, gave it to Uday after class, and he heaped me with compliments. 'Thimply perfect, thimply perfect,' he lisped, because he had slightly protruding teeth and thus a slight speech defect, although no one ever mentioned it.

I was rewarded for my work some days later. Uday had contacted Saleh Al-Juburi, a Party boss, and ordered him to promote me to the next stage of the Party hierarchy. At the time I was on the Majeed stage. Now I reached the Nassir stage.

But that wasn't all: Uday suddenly sought my company, spoke to me every day, wanted to meet me, even promised that he would give me everything I wanted, he would sort it all out.

But instinctively I kept him at a distance. First of all my external resemblance to him was so unpleasant to me that I reacted aggressively every time any of my classmates mentioned it to me. 'Look, here comes Uday,' they mocked, and their words expressed mostly envy, because they hoped to get something from him. Secondly, my parents advised me to keep my distance from him because his escapades were gradually becoming a topic of conversation in Baghdad society. 'Be friendly,' my father warned me, 'but keep your distance.'

After our final exams, I wrote first to the Technical University, because I had always wanted to be an engineer. When Uday also opted for technology, I withdrew, and started my legal studies. After that I lost sight of Uday, and only heard from him every now and again. I successfully completed my studies in 1986.

THREE

The Serf

So here I am standing in front of him again, and he seems to be hardly any different from the time when he asked me for that picture for his father: his big brown eyes, his pronounced eyebrows, straight nose, two-day stubble. Only his hair is shorter. Not the Jimi Hendrix tangle he had as an adolescent, but a short crop with pomade, glistening but not greasy.

Uday, with his thick Havana in his right hand, laughs showily, and offers me a seat on a green patterned couch. He himself sits down in a white, throne-like leather armchair. Above him is a huge, gold-rimmed mirror.

Uday is friendly, he asks me chattily how I am, and my nerves gradually subside, although I still can't make out what's going on here, why I'm sitting here, why they've dragged me away from the front in such mysterious circumstances.

'How do you like it at the front?' he asks, apparently interested, and then, 'I've heard that you've become a good soldier!'

I give a brief answer, careful not to say a word out of place, a thoughtless remark, because I can remember Uday's attacks of rage from our schooldays. I know he's a powerful man, he could crush me, destroy me, and nothing and no one could stop him. 'What I'm doing is okay,' I reply modestly. 'Another two or three years, and then I'm going to go back to my father's company. Import, export. Yes, my father imports machines that make gas cookers, from Europe. That's a good business.'

Not a word about the fact that I doubt the meaning of this war, in which more than half a million men have fallen so far, not a syllable about the dead and the wounded that I've seen. Iraq is great, Saddam is great and so is his family.

As regards my career plans, I feel, particularly since the mood for these first few minutes is friendly and pleasant, that complete openness is the best thing. Why shouldn't I tell him the truth, why should I lie that I'm interested in a career in the army?

Uday accepts that, he even seems to like it. 'Fine, great, I'm a businessman too, as you probably aren't aware, as you probably couldn't be aware. I admire independent entrepreneurs.'

He leans back and draws pleasurably on his Havana. He doesn't inhale, but blows the blue smoke straight back out, looks me deep in the eyes and suddenly says with a superiority that allows no doubt about the distribution of roles between us, 'Don't try to prettify anything, touch anything up, I know everything about you anyway. Everything.'

He says that in a razor-sharp voice, and it makes me think of Mohammed Ghaleb, my squadron leader in the artillery unit where I had been until very recently. And the elegant officers Nassir Baker and Saad Ahmad, the two perfect Party soldiers. They were always going on about my resemblance to Uday, they were always wanting to know *whether I came from the family*. They were Uday's henchmen, secret service operatives in the service of the bosses of Baghdad.

'Do you want some orange juice?' says Uday, hauling me out of my thoughts.

'Yes, yes, please,' I reply, and what happens next is curious. Uday doesn't say a word, he doesn't ring a bell, make a phone call, nothing, and even so a door suddenly opens and a servant in black trousers, white jacket and white gloves brings in orange juice. Freshly pressed, unsweetened orange juice. He doesn't say a word, puts down the glass of juice and disappears again. Completely silent, his head bowed humbly. And once again I'm struck that none of Uday's employees dare to look the boss or his guest in the eye. If their eyes happen to meet, they quickly dart away.

The meeting room where we are sitting has magnificent pastel-coloured wallpaper. No brightly coloured kitsch, nothing showy or excessive. The carpets are thick and costly, the furniture from Europe, the flowers refined and chosen with reticent taste.

I take a sip of the orange juice and hold the glass in my hand. Uday still isn't saying anything. I look at him, and he looks back at me. I have the feeling that at that moment he's thinking the same thing as I am: we both have that slightly curly, strong black hair, expressive brown eyes with long lashes and thick, dark crescent-shaped eyebrows that rise far into our foreheads. Then there's the straight shape of our heads: slightly oval, no marked cheek-bones, no striking features.

Uday draws on the Havana again. His upper lip is barely visible, because like myself he has the thick, wide moustache that all Moslems grow after the age of 16. The beard is the symbol of our dignity, a second self. Normally I would tend to wear a beard. Not a bushy beard, but well tended and trimmed, which is forbidden in the army because if you have a beard it's impossible to put on a gas mask so that it closes properly – and gas warfare is imaginable at any time, because our arsenals and those of the Iranians are full of mustard gas and other chemical weapons.

During our schooldays, Uday's slightly protruding teeth were more striking. With his moustache and the Havana in his mouth they're barely noticeable. He's a little taller than I am, I think to myself. I'd noticed that the minute he came into the room and greeted me. Did he shake my hand? I wonder. I can't remember.

I'd really like to ask him how his architectural studies at the Technical University went. After we left school I lost sight of him. I only saw him every now and again when he drove his Ferraris, Porsches, Maseratis or Lamborghinis ostentatiously up and down in front of the university, keeping an eye out for girls. If he liked one, he would have one of his bodyguards talk to her and pick her up. Any girls who refused were simply abducted. His reputation at university was even worse than it was at school. But that didn't bother me, because I had broken away from him, even if that was hard for me because there was always someone talking to me about my 'divine blessing', my resemblance to him.

I decide not to ask. The mood is friendly on this late September day in that screened-off room, but I still feel uncomfortable.

'Latif,' Uday begins, and his mouth spreads into a grin once again. 'I'm a direct person, and I don't want to beat around the bush.'

He jumps to his feet, walks around for a moment, and then leans his left hand on the arm of the chair: 'I want you to work with me.'

'Work with you?' I reply. I'm irritated and alarmed, but I stay calm and collected, and say, 'I'm not talking to the

President's son, am I? I'm talking to a school friend, the man who was so keen on that picture of mine. You remember?'

My attempt at evasion bothers him; he hisses, 'Yes, yes', and asks me again, 'Do you want to work with me?'

'We can speak openly,' I say, and make a short break to get to the point. 'What do you want from me?'

'I want you to be my fiday.'

'Fiday?'

The word is like a hammer-blow. I brood about it all day and reflect. I have the oppressive feeling that something bad is heading towards me from the horizon. And everything I saw, heard and felt made me uneasy: the man in Party headquarters, the Mercedes, the silent chauffeur, the elegance of the palace grounds, the quiet hum of the engine. I wanted to run, to swim, to watch the drifting shadows of the clouds, sweat out my insecurity until I couldn't feel the wet sweat on my sticky uniform shirt.

And now this: *fiday* – the word roars in my head.

A fiday is more than a mere double. A fiday is everything. In Arab culture fiday means a disciple, a fighter and partisan. A serf, who must always be prepared to give up his life for his master.

Saddam Hussein has two doubles, two *fidays*, everyone in Iraq knows that, and presumably the Western secret services know it as well. But there's nothing sensational about that, because it's an ancient fact that dictators have doubles.

But in his paranoia, Saddam has built up and developed a system of fidays to perfection. Whenever assassination attempts are threatened, he brings on his doubles. One Saddam double died promptly in one such attack, in 1984. Now he has only one, Faoaz Al-Emari, as they say in Iraq, where everybody knows about the role of the fidays, even if the public appearances, planned with military precision, can't always be seen through. I remember that my commander had once mentioned Faoaz Al-Emari to me. 'Do you know Faoaz?' he had asked me. I shook my head and thought Ghaleb was a madman, because I couldn't work out what his question meant.

I hesitate briefly when Uday asks me if I want to be his fiday. I try to gain time so that I can finally have a clear idea; but I don't manage it, and I find my whole body shaking: 'I don't understand your question. Am I supposed to protect you, or what do you mean?'

Uday raises his head, inhales deeply through his nose, puts his Havana in the ashtray and spreads his arms theatrically wide, like an actor who can't give his voice sufficient drama and therefore constantly gesticulates wildly with his arms. 'It must be an honour for you to be the President's son on my instructions,' he says dramatically. He takes his Havana out of the ashtray and draws once again on the ragged, wet, badly cut end.

'But we're all the President's sons,' I reply, using a cliché from my political training.

'That won't get you anywhere. We've had you under observation for a long time now, we know everything about you. I know where you're going, who you're talking to, what your parents do. I know about the bank accounts of your father and your mother, and also your own account. Everything, you understand, everything. I want you, because you're the right one.'

'I could protect you, I'm . . .' I say. But he cuts in.

'. . . you don't need to protect me, I want you to *be* me. Everywhere, always.'

When I hesitate once again, Uday's features change in a

flash. He has trouble controlling himself, and yells at me: 'What, don't you want to be Saddam Hussein's son?'

The question is a threat, it goes right to my heart. Hitherto, only members of the President's family have been used as doubles. Usually a relation whose resemblance has been passed on by the blood-line is given the job. Saddam Hussein's second, younger son, Qusay, employs a distant cousin as a fiday. But for Uday they clearly haven't found anyone suitable, and for that reason the choice fell on his schoolmate, me. On Latif Yahia, the eldest son of a respected Baghdad family.

I am *the chosen one*. For Uday this is a distinction, an honour that has been made to me. Because everyone in Iraq wants to be a member of the Issaba, the clan, the group that surrounds the President.

But I feel that I'm a victim, because I know that I have no chance, and that my fate is sealed on this 23 September 1987. There's no point resisting, because Uday won't tolerate contradiction, his wishes are the wishes of Allah, and even that thought hurts me, because I am a religious person.

I struggle for words, and feel like a cornered animal. Uday is the executor, the lord of being and non-being, the prophet: 'Do you expect me to extinguish my name and my personality in order to be Uday Saddam Hussein?'

Uday's reply sounds like a croupier's *Rien ne va plus*: 'Exactly!' he says, and juts his chin towards me.

That's it. My fate seems to have been decided, and none the less I try to contradict the son of the great President and appeal to the school friend in him: 'I'm honoured that you want to work with me, but I can't be anyone but myself.'

'Take your time,' he replies generously, 'you don't have to decide immediately.'

For two or three seconds Uday doesn't say anything, then he goes on: 'I'll leave you on your own to think about it. When I come back I want a clear yes or no.'

Although Uday's demand was direct enough, my anxiety subsides. It's like one of those mornings when you wake up completely changed. Uday's words, the whole situation, his suggestion have gone through me like an earthquake. On the one hand it's clear to me that his suggestion is unacceptable to me. On the other hand that initial, oppressive feeling has fled me so completely that I'm suddenly interested to know what would happen if I refused. How would he deal with that?

Things work out for Uday. He managed to get through school despite the fact that he could barely write, he could only draw letters that looked as though he was paralysed down one side. He can't read literary Arabic, he can't write a sentence without making mistakes and he's probably never opened a book, let alone read one all the way through.

'What happens if I refuse?' I ask.

He barely reacts, says, 'I'll tell you later,' disappears into a side room and leaves me there in complete confusion.

For a very long ten minutes nothing at all happens. I sit there on the patterned couch, almost paralysed, staring into space, running my hand over my moustache a few times and thinking about Uday's face. He looks quite nice. But appearances can be deceptive. I've already seen terrible things done to other people, things that left them broken. I think about Sattar and the cockroaches. How we piled them into his mouth until he threw up, and we didn't stop because we'd been ordered to do it, and because no one can resist an order. Or can they?

Sometimes behind a human face there lurks a brain that

is worse than anything that a pathologist could imagine. I need an extra layer of skin, a carapace for my soul.

I can't sit there calmly any more, I cross my legs, then cross them the other way. I'd like to smoke a cigarette, but hold back from doing so out of manners, although the room already smells strongly enough of the smoke from the thick Havana.

I stand up, rub my hands and am about to take a few steps. Almost immediately the door through which Uday disappeared opens. A servant appears in the door and asks me what I would like.

'A glass of water, please,' I say.

The servant brings it to me immediately, I drain the glass, put it down and pace across the room, measuring it as I go. One, two, three ... I walk back and forth, fold my arms, stretch in front of the mirror, yawn, look at my bad skin and think that I should do something about my complexion. Uday has smooth skin. I look in the mirror again, but it never occurs to me that someone might be standing behind it.

Although Uday has said he'll be back in ten minutes, an hour passes and there's no sign of him. Waiting is presumably part of the system. After a while, people waiting lose their self-respect, particularly if they know that they have to wait because they have no other chance.

Making people wait is a sign of power.

After another half hour Uday suddenly comes back. Grinning, with big, resolute footsteps: 'Why are you so unsettled, my friend?' Now, for the first time, I realise that he must have been watching me walking back and forth, running hither and thither. Through a camera, through the mirror or however.

'What if I say yes?'

'Then you're my brother, and you'll get whatever you want.

I'll give you that in writing. You'll have the finest life on earth, your every desire will be fulfilled, everything that belongs to me will belong to you, too. You understand, you will be my brother.'

'Well, sir, that's all very nice, but I can't do it. I'm an army officer, and I will be serving the army for months and years to come. But then I want to become a businessman, I can't take on this task, it's too big for me. Please understand, sir, please understand . . . I can't do it.'

When I refuse, Uday storms to the door, pulls it open, turns around and hisses with a hard, resolute face: 'That isn't a problem, we'll stay friends anyway.'

He slams the door shut. After only a few moments, two bodyguards come in, Azzam Al-Tikritti and Salam Al-Aoussi.

They march straight up to me, grab me by the arms and tear my two-star epaulettes off, bind my eyes, lead me outside and push me into a car. I don't know what kind of car, probably the Mercedes I came in. The inside of the car smells just as it did before, the leather seats are soft and smooth.

The chauffeur starts the engine, and my door only falls dully into the lock with the jolt with which we set off. That soft thud – that could only be a Mercedes door.

We drive for a long time, for perhaps half an hour or 45 minutes, but I never get rid of the feeling that we're driving around in a circle. We can't hear any other cars, or even the sounds you hear when you pass a block of flats at high speed. And we don't stop once, which we would have had to do at one of the gates if we'd left the palace grounds, because Saddam's centre of power is surrounded by a wall with an electrically charged barbed-wire fence.

The palace is in the district of Karrade Mariam, near

Al-Karch, on the banks of the Tigris River. The palace
grounds cover several square kilometres. To the east and the
south the Tigris forms the natural border between the palace
and the city.

So we can't be there, because otherwise I would hear the
sound of running water. Sometimes the sounds of the tyres
bounce at rapid intervals. Now we're gliding past the big
houses of the President's family, I conclude.

The architecture of these buildings is very fine, I noticed
that on the way in. While millions of us were fighting against
the Khomeinis at the front, Saddam was having his castle
renovated from the ground up by a French firm, refurnished
and equipped with every imaginable security precaution,
because occasional Iranian rockets reached Baghdad, and
Khomeini's chief goal was the murder of our godless
President.

The palace has four main entrances. The first of them is on
the western side, near the suspension bridge. They call it the
'Family Gate', because it's the private gate for Saddam and
his family, his ministers and their families. I was brought in
through that entrance.

The second entrance is by the Republican Bridge to the
north of the palace. The 'Baghdad Gate' is only for the
members of the Revolutionary Leadership Committee and
the National Committee.

A third gate connecting the east and the north wings is
reserved for the inhabitants of the President's palace, and
the fourth entrance, the 'Lion Gate', is for the head of the
Secret Service and the members of the secret service
branches Jehaaz Al-Amen Al-Khass and Jehaaz Al-
Mukhabarat Al-Amen.

These gates are about a mile away from Saddam's castle,

and so armed that they couldn't be easily penetrated even by a tank. Nine hundred metres beyond those entrances metal rails are laid in the asphalt. They are about 30 centimetres wide. If you drive your car over them, you feel a slight bump and hear a short *tack, tack*. Presumably these metal rails contain strips of nails that shoot upwards the minute a guard presses a button. So there's no chance for a suicide bomber to get anywhere near the palace. (The same nail chains are used by our pioneers at the front.) We haven't passed those security positions either; I would have heard and felt them.

So we're a long way away from the main entrances at which the third, fifth, seventh and ninth units of the Republican Guards alternately stand watch.

But the first two main entrances don't yet represent the start of the actual palace grounds; they are about three kilometres away from the road that serves ordinary vehicular and pedestrian traffic.

Between the road and the palace there's a buffer zone, a kind of no-man's-land. All the buildings near the palace have been taken over by the secret services. There used to be foreign embassies here, but they were moved when Saddam Hussein came to power. They even took over the hospital of Ibn Sina. Previously it had been a private hospital of moderate quality, which Saddam Hussein had European and American firms renovate and bring to the latest state of technology. All the doctors and nurses who had worked there were dismissed and replaced by ideologically trained staff. Since then the hospital has served as Saddam's private clinic.

After about half an hour in the car I have completely lost my bearings. Suddenly my driver stops abruptly. I don't know where we are. Azzam Al-Tikritti and Salam Al-Aoussi, the bodyguards who bound my eyes, order me to get out, grab me by the arms and lead me first up a flight of steps, and then through various rooms and doors, and finally down some steps and through two doors.

When they take off my blindfold, I find myself in a little room hardly any bigger than a shower cabin that can't be more than one metre by one-and-a-half metres. No window, no bed, no latrine. There isn't even a basin. Everything in the room is red: red walls, a gleaming lamp giving off bright red light, a red concrete floor, and on the floor and deep red woollen blanket. The room has an incredibly high ceiling.

Without a word the two bodyguards close the red iron door behind them.

One hour, two hours. 'They want to make me colour-blind, that's right, colour-blind.' I close my inflamed eyes. I open them again, wider than ever before, and that hurts even more. I pull the blanket over my head, but feel that the blanket is red and so is the floor. Red, red, red. Everything is red.

I press my balled fists into my closed eyes for a long, long time. I see stars, flashes, coarse and fine grids of light. When I take my hands away, at first I see nothing but black, and then everything is that terrible red again.

There's nothing to tell me what time it is, I'm alone in the timeless room. Where am I? I don't know whether it's day or still night. There's no toilet and no water, nothing, just that red.

I don't know how long I've been crouching there. Half a day, longer? I don't know, I've lost all sense of time. I think of my comrades at the front, I think about my parents. But what good will that do? They don't know where I am, what I'm doing, what's going on.

Suddenly I hear footsteps, then voices, and then the rattle

of keys. Hell, get away from the door frame! I cower in the corner, my heart pounding. If I had a revolver now, my finger would be on the trigger. The gun would be cocked and levelled, and I would be staring down my gun barrel as I was taught to do.

The door is opened. I can just make out Azzam in the red light. He is holding a tray, and hands it to me and says only, 'Eat something.'

Then he turns around again and closes the door. I squat down and stuff the food into my mouth.

It goes on like that for days. I can't stretch out and lie down. My legs hurt. I crouch in the corner and ponder to myself, constantly thinking. At some point I start talking to myself. Not in the form of proper sentences, but only in a mumble. Like a child, a baby. I move my lips, emit sounds, until the guards bring me food and water again. Then I know whether it's afternoon or evening.

At lunchtime there is white bread and water. In the evening, warm, sticky rice and water. During the first 48 hours I try to control myself, and only urinate once, for a short time. When I see the urine flowing over my blanket, I pull myself together.

I hold back my stools until my intestines are almost bursting. I shout, rage, hammer my fists against the walls and beg and plead not to be humiliated like this. But no one reacts, and at some point I cease to care about my honour, myself, my upbringing.

I defecate in a corner, so that I won't end up lying in my own excrement. The stench is so revolting that my eyes sting. I find encrusted blood on the walls, it can't be mine, because things aren't as bad as that yet. The bloodstains must be from someone else. It's probably just a matter of time before people start mutilating themselves, I say to myself. But I swear on Allah and my father's name that Uday will never bring me to that.

I always keep half a glass of water so that I can maintain at least a trace of hygiene. Finally I just crouch in my corner. In the other is my shit, over which I have placed my blanket; it was already drenched in my urine, so I couldn't wrap it around me. At least it meant that I didn't have to look at my faeces.

Seven times they have brought me bread, seven times they have brought me rice. That's how I know that I've been in this cell for a week when Uday himself appears in the doorway. I can't see him, I just hear his mocking 'Hello, Latif, how do you like it here?' His bodyguards bind my eyes, then we go down several flights of steps, through two doors, through a number of rooms and then down the steps into the open air.

I can feel the September sun, I feel grass beneath my feet. With a jolt they tear the blindfold off me. It's as though a great flash had exploded into my eyes. I can't see anything, I hold my hands in front of my face and press the balls of my hands into my closed eyes, as I did in the cell. I stand there like that for 10 or 20 seconds, then I carefully take my hands away, blink, try to open my eyes for a moment. Everything is red. The grass, the trees, the whole garden. Even Uday, who is standing in front of me, is red. His shirt, his trousers, his face, his protruding teeth are red.

'Have you thought about my suggestion?' he asks. I can see vaguely that he is unshaven, like myself. He has allowed a beard to grow – to look more like me?

'You've changed your mind, haven't you?' He knows what I've been through. I'm sure he knows this cell; they've probably finished off hundreds of people there, and derived sadistic amusement from the fact that they could break people's pride. That proud men could fall so far as to lie in their own shit, that they would even roll about in it, because they had no choice, because the cell was too small.

I still can't see properly, my eyes are watering. But my fury exceeds my reason: 'Officers of the Iraqi army cannot be held captive without the knowledge of the Ministry of Defence. That is the law. I haven't murdered anyone, I haven't pulled your family through the shit . . . the ministry must . . .'

'Must what? A thousand officers like you aren't even worth the soles of my shoes.'

A ridiculous son of a bitch, I think, and don't reply. My vision gradually returns, I blink, vaguely make out the trees and the lawn. I put my uniform on. I'm covered with shit, covered with crusted, dried-on shit. I must look pathetic.

'I'll set my dogs on you and your sisters if you say no again,' Uday shouts at me. At that moment it is clear to me that further resistance is pointless. Uday is a person who is capable of anything. It wouldn't be the first time that he had set his killer dogs on someone. I remember an event from my student days: one day Nahle Sabet, a pretty girl who studied architecture like Uday, disappeared. Uday had abducted her from the university grounds and had her brought to his property to the north of Baghdad. It was disguised as a farm, but in fact it served as a training ground for Uday's fighting dogs. Bullish rottweilers, powerful mastiffs, slim and muscular dobermanns, all toughened up with blows and raw meat.

For weeks Nahle Sabet was held prisoner, beaten, abused, raped, deprived of her will. When Uday had had his fun with her, he locked her in a cell with his starving dogs.

FOUR

Training

Our car journey lasts only 15 minutes. My eyes gradually get used to the sunlight again. When we leave the palace through the Family Gate, our four-car convoy isn't stopped by the guards. The drivers have only briefly slowed down when we bumped over the *tack-tack* security rails, and when the guards with their Kalashnikovs recognise that these are Uday's cars, they wave us through. Then we turn left, down an avenue, and after about a kilometre we turn off towards 'Project Number 7', one of Uday's many private residences. With me in the car are my two guards and the chauffeur who collected me from headquarters a week ago.

I feel empty and burned-out, betrayed and sold. I'm still wearing my dirty uniform, everything still seems like a bad dream, like a film I've ended up in by chance. I can't rationally understand what's really happening here. But I know that I've agreed to be Uday's *Fiday*, and that I've thus sold myself and my soul to a person whom I find weird and repellent. Uday gave a filthy, supercilious grin when I gave in before, and said generously, 'You see, from now on you're not just my friend, you're my brother.'

His brother, what does that mean? Couldn't I have continued to resist? No, no. I repress the question. It's pointless, because if I'd said no, Uday could have had me and my whole family killed. The Saddam clan has already had thousands of people killed. They disappeared from one day to the next. No one in Iraq knows where they ended up, but it's clear that they were liquidated.

My car stops outside the entrance to Project Number 7. Outside the building are several car parks which cannot be seen from the road. Next to them is a well-tended patch of green with a short, juicy lawn and behind it a heavy wooden gate with massive double wing doors, on which a larger-than-life green, black and white Iraqi eagle stands, our emblem. Above the eagle are three black stars, inlaid in ceramic mosaics. On either side of the door are automatic cameras, which I hear whirring; so we're expected, we're being observed.

There is no name-plate on the door, only an intercom in a niche in the wall, screened off by panes of mirrored glass.

The double door opens automatically and silently, and my two guards bring me inside the two-storey building, which doesn't look like anything very much from outside. There are thousands of such buildings in Baghdad, because Baghdad is rich, and the upper class lives in feudal opulence and likes to put its wealth on display.

But external impressions are deceptive. A wide, imposing oval internal courtyard is dominated by an imposing swimming pool. Six wide, curving steps lead to the pool, which is edged with black marble. To the right of the pool is a walled, sickle-shaped bar, also made in that gleaming black marble with its faint white veins, probably imported from Italy – Carrara marble. Next to the bar are loungers made of stout white bamboo, with white cushions whose edges are hemmed with gold. The side rooms lead off the swimming pool in a star shape.

First they bring me into the room to the right of the pool,

to Uday's study. And once again I'm impressed by his taste: the room is generously designed, without an excess of oriental kitsch. No plush white velvet, no gold, no fanciful decorations, no column capitals, no curved and tacky stucco. The room is straight-lined, clear, bright. In one corner stands a heavy desk with a dark, shining work surface, and beside it two armchairs upholstered in a light-coloured fabric.

Behind the desk is a bookshelf full of Arabic literature. Pure decoration, I think, amused at his pomposity. Uday will never have touched all those books. On his desk are a few files, a Cartier fountain pen, a Dupont lighter and a black electric cable. The cable is thick and round, about two feet long.

The most striking thing about this room with the pastel-coloured wallpaper is a pale yellow set of couches that must seat twenty people. In front of it is a low table with a black, veined marble plate. Everywhere there are silver bowls of peanuts, sweets, cigarettes and flower arrangements.

Waiting for me are three men who are clearly fully informed, and who have helped to plan the whole operation. The first is Munem Hammed Al-Tikritti, the head of the Al-Khass security service. Munem Hammed looks refined and reticent. He is slim, a little taller than I am, grey at the temples. He gives me a very friendly greeting. This is the first time I see him.

The second man I know from hearsay, like everyone else in Iraq: Captain Siad Hassan Hashem Al-Nassiri, a friend of Saddam Hussein and the brother-in-law of Rokan, the President's personal bodyguard. Siad Hassan Hashem Al-Nassiri is one of the worst criminals in Iraq, a mass-murderer, a powerful, dangerous man with grey eyes, a sharp, striking face and an extremely hooked eagle's nose. Ice-cold, sadistic, an animal. He supervises all the executions and all the crimes that Saddam Hussein orders to be carried out.

When I shake his hand his face remains motionless, his dead face stays cold.

The third man is Captain Saadi Daham Hasaa Al-Nassiri, a cousin of Saddam, small, bullish, unpleasant.

Azzam, Uday's bodyguard, introduces me to the three officers. Munem Hammed Al-Tikritti begins the conversation with sympathetic words: 'Sit down, relax, Uday has already told us about you, and said that you are a brave and resolute fighter. I'm glad that you've come to us of your own free will.'

Free will? What nonsense! But there's something calming in his voice. Munem Hammed talks to me as though I were not his 'serf', but an accepted partner on a complicated mission.

I don't know why, but at that moment I think, this man is the first Iraqi officer I've come across who isn't completely crazy and opinionated and contemptuous of his fellow man.

Munem Hammed seems to notice the fact that I like him. He speaks quietly, but in good Arabic, clear and distinct. His friendly voice doesn't slip into that contemptuous, cutting commanding voice, not on one single word.

'You'll have to get used to it, Latif,' he says, putting his arm around my shoulder: 'Let's take a look at the house for the time being, and afterwards you can go and freshen up.' The others nod in agreement.

Like a consultant making his rounds, Munem Hammed leaves the room, and we follow him. 'That was Uday's study, incidentally,' he explains, and then asks, 'You know each other from your student days, don't you?'

I nod, 'Yes, yes, from my student days,' and he points to the turquoise pool with the black marble edge, and says I can use it whenever I feel like it.

'The changing rooms and the towels,' he says, pointing to a side room, 'are in there.'

In an open room directly behind the bar I see several changing rooms with baskets full of fresh, thick towels, a shower, a toilet, washbasins and mirrors.

I don't dare to ask if I can finally go and wash, because Munem Hammed is already going into the next room. They can all be reached from the pool.

'That's the guest bedroom,' my guide explains. In the ample room I see a French double bed with a beige knitted counterpane and matching curtains. Next to the bed are a wardrobe, a desk, a little couch and a television. Sony brand.

Right next to the guest bedroom are the stairs leading to the first floor.

But first we look at Uday's bedroom. In fact it looks like the guest room, but with a larger bed. In place of the desk there are a round table with a black table-top and several chairs. Just in front of the bed is an unusually large television, connected to a video recorder.

'From now on,' laughs Munem,' this room belongs to you. That's how Uday wants it. You're his brother, so he'd like you to live in his room.'

Next to the table stands a telephone, and at first glance I can't see any hidden video cameras.

After that they show me the drawing room, a hall-like room with four different sets of furniture, as well as the party room on the first floor of the building, which looks like a discotheque: a dominant stage with a sound system, and in front of it several groups of bright red chairs.

That red again. Always that red.

Munem Hammed ends the first guided tour with the words, 'So, Latif, I'm sure you want to rest, and I'm absolutely sure you want a shower.'

Everyone laughs. So do I.

They bring me to Uday's bedroom, which is now my bedroom, and leave the door to the pool open. A cool breeze stirs the white curtains.

I sit down on the bed, shake my head, laugh and shake my head again: 'What's going on?'

I stand up, walk over to the door, pull the curtains aside. There's no one to be seen at the pool. But I sense that they're there. I'm sure they're everywhere, and Uday is probably sitting somewhere watching me through a video camera, just as he did when I was sitting in his office.

The phone. I see the big, rectangular telephone, an American make. I know it would be ridiculous to pick up the receiver and just dial the number of my family in Baghdad. That would never work, I tell myself, it would be extremely incautious of them, if the telephone really worked. When I pick it up anyway, I hear the engaged tone. I press a few buttons, zero, zero, double zero – still the engaged tone.

It makes sense that it doesn't work.

Then the mirror catches my eye. When I was in the car I had tried to look in the rear-view mirror to see myself with a full beard. I stand up, walk in front of the mirror and say to myself, 'So that's Latif Yahia, the officer of the proud Iraqi army?'

I take a long, hot shower. The bathroom, which is also lined with black marble, has everything you could possibly want, like a bathroom in a five-star hotel: disposable razor, bath gel, shaving foam, shampoo, toothpaste, toothbrush, hair-cream, hair-brush. Everything – a dressing gown, big, thick towels, body lotion. I scrub off the filth of the past few weeks and realise I'm getting tired.

I sleep deeply and soundly that night.

*

The next morning I wake up early. It is early October 1987, and Baghdad is still sultry and hot. My filthy uniform, which I threw over a stool the previous evening, has gone. So are my shoes and my underwear. Instead there are fresh clothes on the chair by the wardrobe. A pale suit, a white shirt, underwear. Next to them are fresh towels and a new dressing gown. There's breakfast on the table. Tea, sweets, fresh fruit. I just take a sip from the thermos and eat an orange. How come I didn't notice when these things were brought into my room, and by whom?

I shower, get dressed and wait. It's just after nine, and the officers from the day before come and collect me. They bring me back to Uday's study. There Munem Hammed hands me a two-page text: 'Read that closely, and then sign it,' he tells me, and offers me a seat on the yellow couch.

It's a contract. A contract between me and the Republic of Iraq.

I, Latif Yahia, 1st Lieutenant, swear to pass on nothing from the life of Uday Saddam to the public. Everything I hear, see and experience with him during our collaboration is bound by a duty of secrecy.

I am forbidden to pass on files, photographs, videos or any other notes to third parties.

Any contravention of this contract will be punishable by death by hanging.

Latif Yahia, Baghdad, 2. 10. 1987.

I sign it. For the next ten days absolutely nothing happens. Munem Hammed had reminded me, 'Now you are Uday Saddam Hussein, the President's son. Don't speak to any of the domestic staff, and don't try to make contact with them.'

The domestic staff – a cook, four chambermaids and a kind of butler – have in turn been strictly forbidden to exchange so much as a word with me. They are to treat me as though I were Uday Saddam, and they stick rigidly to that rule. They avoid my eye, every day they bring me fresh linen and the best food that has ever been served to me. Every day there is meat, prepared in the European style, with fresh vegetables and a lot of fruit. I'm even allowed to serve myself from the bar by the pool. There's no one there to tell me what to do. I'm living in paradise, but my paradise is a gilded cage. I'm well aware of that, but what really oppresses me is the fact that I'm not allowed to tell anyone, and certainly not my parents, where and how I am.

My parents have heard nothing from me for three weeks. Fine, that often happens; there's a war on, and they think I'm at the front. Often in the past I haven't got in touch with them for weeks at a time.

But curiously it isn't just my concerns about my new job that I want to communicate to my parents. Above all I'd like them to know about the heavenly conditions I'm living in, tell them where I'm living, how I'm living, what's happening to me here.

I make an excellent recovery. I spend my days lounging by the pool, in the evening I watch the television news and prepare myself for bed with a few gin and tonics. Admittedly I'm sometimes troubled by thoughts about the future, but somehow I'm starting to feel closer to Uday from within, too. There is a certain satisfaction in having devoted staff at your disposal, reacting to every wave of your hand. I lie by the pool in the autumn sun, raise my hand – and there's immediately somebody there to whom I can give an order: 'A sandwich.' I notice that I'm getting used to not saying 'please' and 'thank you', and that I'm gradually assuming that sense of superiority that I've always accused other people of having. 'Not so much ice,' I yell at the girl, 'I've told you that a hundred times.'

And she apologises politely and brings me a fresh glass with less ice. She treats me as though I were the son of the President. No one there ever contradicts me, it's as though I were packed in cotton wool. No corners, no sharp edges, no problems, just luxury, even if that luxury is restricted to the area around the villa.

I wander through all the rooms, have my towels changed daily and even use expensive, heavy, sweet perfume, although there's no one there for me to impress with it. I do it because I can, and because there isn't anyone to stop me being licentious.

Am I Uday?

It's 12 October, late afternoon. I'm lying on my bed, and suddenly the phone rings. 'Come to the office,' says a male voice. I get dressed and walk the short distance past the pool to Uday's office.

Uday is standing there with Munem Hammed and two men who don't seem at all like Arabs. One of them is a little taller than me, brown-haired, with a round face. He is pale. The second is shorter, stocky, but not fat. Uday greets me effusively, kisses me on the cheeks like a brother and introduces me to the men, who shake hands but don't say a word: 'They're doctors, specialists who are going to examine you.'

I'm surprised, because I'm in good health, but I don't want to ask any more questions. 'Fine, where do they want to examine me, here? Immediately?'

Uday says yes, the men nod, and Munem Hammed says, 'It's a routine examination, nothing special, you can be completely relaxed.'

Then one of the doctors says something to Munem Hammed, in a language that I don't understand. But it isn't English, French, Italian or German, it sounds more like Russian or Polish. Probably a Slavic language. Hammed translates: 'Please undress.'

I have to strip right down. I don't like it, but it has to be done.

I am weighed and measured. They look in my mouth, in my ears, they shine a light into my eyes. They palpate me, test to see whether I have a rupture, peer into my anus, listen to my heart, measure my blood pressure, take a blood sample and a urine sample.

The questionnaire that they go through point by point is several pages long. The examination lasts almost two hours.

After that they study my skin with a specialist instrument. I have to do speech exercises. Howl like a dog, declaim like an orator, laugh hysterically. Everything is captured on tape, everything is noted down. Several times, the two doctors talk to one another in that language that sounds almost like a code.

Uday doesn't seem terribly interested in any of it, and goes after ten minutes. 'I'll look at the results when they're ready, gentlemen,' he says and disappears.

Uday gets the report on the tests the following day. He calls me in, beams, looks enthusiastic.

Hammed reads out the report: my skin colour is 99 percent identical with Uday's. Shape of face, hair, ears, nose and physique are almost identical. I'm just three centimetres shorter than Uday, and two kilograms lighter. Uday weighs 83 kilos, and I weigh 81. 'Weight,' Hammed argues, 'isn't a problem, and neither is height. We can easily compensate for that with special shoes with platform soles.'

Our voices are also almost 100 percent identical. Uday only has problems with pronunciation of the letter R, because of his slightly protruding teeth, the cause of his speech defect, his lisp, which Munem Hammed is careful not to mention.

'Can the teeth be corrected?' asks Uday. Hammed nods.

We have different eyes, too. Mine are a little larger than Uday's, but that could be easily sorted out with make-up, Munem Hammed explains.

'But your teeth,' says Hammed almost apologetically, 'will have to be surgically altered. Do you agree to that?'

What a question, I think to myself, I have no other choice. None the less I feel that my internal resistance has been almost entirely erased. I slowly start enjoying this game in paradise: 'Of course I agree,' I say.

Twenty-four hours later I am collected and brought to the Ibn-Sina Hospital in the palace grounds. We go into the office of Dr Ahmed Al-Samrai. He is the private dentist of the family of Saddam Hussein, and has studied in the USA. He already knows what he has to do.

I am made to lie down on the white dentist's chair, which is actually a hydraulically operated bed. Ahmed Al-Samrai shines a light into my mouth and examines my teeth one by one. Then he sends me to the x-ray room and finally tells them to bring me back the following day.

On my second examination he presses a pink mass into my mouth that slowly swells. It stays in my mouth for ten minutes, then he pulls it out and blows away the residues of my saliva with pressurised air. But he isn't happy with the result, and repeats the procedure.

Plaster models are made from this second impression, but I don't learn that until later on. Then my plaster model is compared with Uday's, and on that basis Dr Ahmed decides what dental corrections he's going to undertake on me.

The operation takes place four days later. Under local anaesthetic my incisors and the two teeth next to them are filed down to the roots. Then another cast is taken. The only unpleasant thing about it is the cold air that the dentist blows into my mouth before this is done.

It is two days before my crowns are ready. During that period I can hardly eat anything, because my temporary dentures don't fit very well, and it hurts if I drink anything too cold.

The implantation of the four new teeth lasts only a few minutes. While this is going on, Dr Ahmed is closely observed by his foreign colleagues, but the two men don't talk to one another.

The operation appears to have been successful. At least that's what Dr Ahmed claims when he takes a good look at my teeth once again, and tells me to bite them together a number of times. He files my incisors down a little more, and then I'm ready. I touch my new, curiously smooth, crooked teeth. They ask me to say something. A completely new feeling: I lisp. Not strongly, but I push differently with my tongue.

My reflection looks strange, too: all of a sudden my full upper lip looks even bigger than it did. When I bite my teeth together, I don't bite on my incisors, but on my molars. It's as though the positions of all my teeth has changed, and my jaw will have to get used to them. I bite my teeth together several times, speak a few sentences and can't help saying, 'It's unfamiliar, but it's sensational!'

I'm pleased, although I have had to sacrifice my healthy teeth, and Uday is very pleased with the result of the operation. He's very enthusiastic. Now we really do look like two peas in a pod.

'Now we must start the training,' urges Uday, and all of a sudden I pay very close attention to the way he speaks. He says: 'Wi musst sstat the twaining.'

The following day they come with a barber who painstakingly adapts my hairstyle to Uday's. Hair for hair, so to speak. Then my beard: he shapes that, too, into the one that I see on Uday's face. My treatment by the barber takes almost as long as my examination by the doctors.

It's now that my actual training gets under way. They collect me, bring me to secret service headquarters and up to the second floor. They show me the room where I'm to be trained, a large office with two desks and a wall of shelves. The shelves don't hold boxes of files or books, but television sets: Panasonic. They are larger than normal, about three feet wide and two feet tall. Next to them stand video recorders; on a table in front of them are dozens of video cassettes, all with writing on them. In front of the video wall there are three microphone stands, without microphones. And in front of those, as in a private cinema, rows and rows of seats. The windows are fitted with heavy, long, plastic-coated curtains, and in the corners loudspeakers are arranged into towers. The big round loudspeakers for the bass tones at the bottom, the smaller ones for high tones at the top. In between is a mixing desk with hundreds of red, yellow and white buttons and dials that can be moved up and down.

'A sound studio,' I think to myself. I can't work any of it out. I don't know what's supposed to happen here. Munem Hammed takes me by the arm, points to the video wall and says, 'We're going to be spending the next few weeks here in this room.'

Nothing happens for ten minutes. Munem Hammed talks

to his own officers, but I can't make out what they say. Then they all leave the room together. I sit down on a chair, pick up a cassette and read the inscription: '26 May 1987, Mr Uday Saddam Hussein at the general meeting of the Iraqi Sports Association. Close-ups, hands, face, walk.'

Munem Hammed comes back with the officers and introduces me to one of them. I don't catch his name, because Munem Hammed speaks quickly and indistinctly. And I'm not very interested in his name; over the past few weeks I've met too many people who all seem to be important. The tall officer has dark skin, a thick moustache, expressive brown eyes, the left one apparently larger than the right. He seems friendly, and offers me his hand, although his handshake is slack and doesn't suit such a powerful-looking man.

He asks me to follow him: 'We're going to another room.' We climb the main stairs to the first storey. Munem Hammed stays behind. I'm surprised. So far he's been my shadow, my father, my mother, my protector – my everything. Through a cushioned double door we walk into a room that resembles the one on the second floor, although it's smaller and the video wall here consists only of three televisions: no mixing desks and no cinema-style rows of seats. The officer invites me to take a seat, and explains that what I'm about to see is a small selection from Saddam's 'Special Treatment Department'.

Now it's clear to me. I'm in the chamber of horrors, the Black Museum. In the centre of complete contempt for one's fellow man.

The officer puts in a video cassette. It's silent. There are flickering black dots on the screen, the run-up that lasts a few seconds, and then the first picture.

*

I see a man of about thirty, his head shorn, his face clean-shaven, his body wracked, tortured, bent. They have tied him to a chair. A big, heavy wooden chair fastened to the floor with screws. The man is seen to groan, his cheeks are hollow, his eyes closed; they are deep in their sockets. Only now am I struck by the fact that they have even shaved off his eyebrows.

I want to ask the officer what's happening to the man, but he just grins at me and nods towards the television. That probably means that I'm supposed to look at what's on the screen, and concentrate on it.

The man claws his hands into the arms of the chair. The veins on the backs of his hands and his forearms look as though they're about to burst. His torso is naked, I can see his ribs, his sternum, his collarbones, which stand out as though they didn't belong to him.

The man barely weighs more than seven stone. And he must be quite tall, but I can't tell exactly, because he's hanging from the chair in such a twisted posture.

Crocodile clips hang from his nipples, which are as long as a woman's. The jagged clips are made of shining steel, about two centimetres long, and cut deep into the dark flesh of his nipples.

More such crocodile clips are fastened to the man's eyelids, ears and genitals.

On the handles of the clips there are bright-blue, semi-circular plastic isolating devices, with cables fastened to them. On the left-hand side a red cable, about three millimetres thick, and on the right a black one that is equally thick. The cables lead to an enormous battery.

The device is guided from a monitor that has been set up right beside the chair. Behind this desk sits a man in uniform. You can only see his hands, big, coarse, hairy hands. I see these hands pressing a button. Then the camera swings to the haggard man on the chair. His body starts to twitch, his whole body shakes like an aggressive terrier, his face twists into a grimace, his head shakes and vibrates, the corners of his mouth twist convulsively downwards, the veins on his forehead stand out, his lips have turned white and are pressed tight together. The camera zooms in closer on his face, his sunken eyes are still closed, and it looks as though they might pop out at any moment like glass balls. The man tries to control himself, he fights against pain and unconsciousness, he doesn't want to bend, he wants to show that he's strong, but he doesn't manage. The shocks are stronger than his will, and foamy saliva flows from between his clamped lips; he opens them slightly, and I can see his clenched teeth, dark brown at the edges, presumably from chewing tobacco.

He shakes his head as though his brain is about to burst, for several seconds – half an eternity. Suddenly he tears his mouth open and shouts. I can't hear the shout, because there is no soundtrack, but I hear him anyway, feel him, sense him, feel his pain just as he does.

The torture is played several times. But I don't find out whether the man survives it. Because all of a sudden all that can be seen is that flickering, and my officer looks at me as though inquiring how I liked this introduction. I control myself, hold my feelings back, because it would be sheer suicide to convey my thoughts and feelings to the people with the power.

The officer explains to me that they've taken most of their methods of torture from the Soviet secret service. Some of them also came from East Germany. There were currently more than ten thousand Soviet military experts in Iraq. They worked on the computer stations in the missile bases, waited for the MIG fighter plane fleet, controlled the country's whole military technology, 60 percent of which came from the Soviet Union.

They were supported by experts from the East German state security service, which sold their knowledge to Iraq in return for convertible currency.

No one knows exactly how many there are in Baghdad, but it's no secret that the men of the state security service are absolute specialists above all in the field of information technology, the listening service and the construction of autonomously controlled security devices.

Other expert staff helping to support Saddam's regime of terror come from Angola and Cuba.

The next tape begins. On the screen, once again, is a man with his hair shorn off. He's younger, his body isn't gaunt but very fit, his muscles are round and smooth, his torso is also naked. He wears green army trousers, faded but not in rags. His hands are bound, his shoulders dangling, his eyes lowered, he clearly doesn't want to look into the camera. All of a sudden he jerks his head up and stares into the camera with his eyes wide open: he must have been ordered to do so. The man stares into the camera for five or six minutes; his eyes are empty, the young man seems to be broken.

'He was a policeman,' my officer explains threateningly, 'who refused to obey orders.' He doesn't say what orders he refused to carry out, he says nothing more on the subject, and he probably doesn't know the man's history. People's destinies aren't important in Iraq. There's violence everywhere, the individual counts for nothing. Thousands die for Saddam, and because they are executed in such large numbers, their death has become normality, routine.

The man turns around slowly and shows his back to the

camera. His broad back is a battlefield. Deep, long wounds. Dozens of blue strips, skin that has been burst by massive blows. The wounds are ragged at the edge, brown and red. Crusted blood, yellowish in some places. There is pus.

A man walks up behind the pitifully injured policeman, clutching a black electrical cable, about two feet long.

There was a cable just like that on . . . I think to myself. But I can't remember where I've seen it before. The man takes a step back, and brings his cable crashing down on the policeman's back. He twitches, his muscles convulse. I close my eyes. I don't want to see the mass of sepsis spraying away. I just hear that imaginary hissing when the cable cuts through the air and lands with a crash on the man's back. There was a cable just like that on Uday's desk. The man doing the beating in the video couldn't be Uday, could it? No, it's not him, it's someone else, clearly they all use these black cables as torture instruments.

They haven't beaten me so far. Psychological violence was enough for me. The red room, the red walls, the red blanket, the week in the cabin-like cell, where many others before me have mutilated themselves, where I saw crusted blood on the wall. They have actually treated me with kid gloves. I'm valuable. They need me. My resemblance to Uday is a piece of capital that I can use, that I can put on the plus side of my account. I just need to play. Do what they say, put my personality in the drawer, but what will the end be like? When can it stop? It can never stop. I repress my thoughts, accentuate the positive. The house, life with Uday. Access to the clan. I'm part of it, I'm at the top and at the same time I'm a prisoner. But I'm alive, and I'm better off than I was at the front.

The next video begins. This time there are two men.

They're wearing handcuffs, and are also bound around the legs with thick chains. The chains are connected to each other, and the men can only take small steps. They are in the courtyard of a barracks-like building; I can't work out exactly where it is, but I assume it's Al-Rashid camp, the big extermination camp on the edge of Baghdad. The men are being led to execution. Death by hanging. The hangman puts them on a wooden platform, lays the rope around their neck, pulls the noose tight, and with a jolt trapdoors open up under the offenders' legs. Their bodies stay bolt upright, fall a few inches, the nooses pull tight, and their heads tip loosely to the right – a broken neck.

These videos are only the prelude. They show me another whole series of revolting teaching examples of the way opponents are dealt with in Saddam's regime.

Video 4: A naked man stands legs apart over a dark green wine-bottle with a long neck. The prisoner is bound by the arms, and is forced to sit down on the bottle until it disappears into his anus. The man screams, begs for help, but the torturers laugh and grin and make jokes: 'Don't you like it?'

Saddam Hussein is proud of his torturers, he calls them 'the sharp swords of the government'.

The bottle in his anus must have given the man very severe internal injuries. I see blood, the man topples over, unconscious.

Video 5: The spectacle is called 'sitting on the gas ring'. The criminal is tied naked to a gas ring. It is turned on, and the bluish flames burn the prisoner's skin.

Video 6: They fasten the prisoner by the legs to a fixture that looks like a fan, which is screwed to the wall. The prisoner's head points down. The fan is switched on, and the man's body rotates as though he is pirouetting. The torturers beat the spinning man's head with wooden truncheons. The ravaged man hangs from the fan for more than an hour – it looks as though he has very little chance of survival.

Video 7: Burning of the beard, moustache, eyebrows and hair. This method is only used on Islamic fundamentalists like the members of the Al-Daawa party.

Video 8: Burning of hands, tying of the prisoner's arms to an electric heater. The heater is switched on, and the glowing wires eat their way into the skin.

Video 9: The iron. A skewer is heated up until it is red hot and then pressed on the prisoner's hands, legs and back. Like the branding of an animal.

Video 10: Drilling of the hands and feet with an electric drill.

Video 11: The nose is broken with a heavy iron hammer.

Video 12: Tearing the mouth apart until the jaw breaks. A method of torture applied to those who vilify Saddam Hussein.

Video 13: The prisoner is seated on a metal chair, strapped tightly to it, and the torturers pull out his fingernails with pliers.

Video 14: Removal of the arms and legs with an electric saw. Sometimes this is simply done with an axe.

Video 15: Introduction of an air-pump into the anus. Air is pumped in until the tissue tears.

Video 16: The prisoner is tied to a carpenter's bench with his hands behind his back. His shoulders are broken by being moved up and down.

Video 17: The water method. The prisoner is tied directly under a water-tap. The water-tap is turned on, for hours. It usually doesn't take more than half an hour before the prisoner loses control of his bodily functions.

Video 18: The well. It is filled to a depth of about a foot and a half with brackish water, and the prisoner is held fast in it for days.

Video 19: Blows with a stick on the head and between the legs.

Video 20: Psychological terror. The prisoner is pushed blindfolded into an empty room. As soon as he tries to go to sleep, a system of loudspeakers make high-pitched noises.

Video 21: The prisoner stands by a wall, with his head wedged between two wooden wedges. His ears are nailed to it with iron rods. Once the criminal can no longer stand, he pulls his own ears off.

Video 22: The prisoners are bound and kept for weeks in an airless room. At the height of summer, the temperature in these cells rises to more than 50 degrees Celsius.

Video 23: Drilling or pulling out of teeth.

Video 24: Needles are pushed under the fingernails.

Video 25: Spraying of acid on to the body.

Video 26: Murdered bodies are thrown into the cells of other prisoners.

Video 27: Fighting dogs are let into the prisoner's cell.

Video 28: The prisoner's nose is blocked so that he can only breathe through his mouth.

Video 29: Penetration of the tongue with needles.

Video 30: Feet and hands in boiling oil.

Video 31: Insect spray in the eyes.

The next videos show women and children being tortured:

Video 32: Hands tied, the women are suspended by their hair. Their husbands and children are forced to watch.

Video 33: Women are raped in front of their husbands.

Video 34: A menstruating woman is hung by her feet, and has to stay like that for the duration of her period.

Video 35: Children are imprisoned in a room with a beehive. Their parents are forced to watch as they scurry naked around the room, sustaining hundreds of stings.

The horror show is endless. I have more than enough. I know what they are trying to tell me by showing it to me, but I'm not very impressed.

These methods of torture are nothing new for me. I know the system, I'm an officer in the Iraqi army, I'm a lieutenant. They've given me that rank for my courage in the face of the enemy. We have run through these cruelties in our minds hundreds of times at the front. But I couldn't have imagined that people were really capable of putting them into action, that people were capable of carrying out such orders. But the scenes in the videos were real. No show, no illusion, these people were really dying, and they were dying with the camera running.

The officer gives me a supercilious grin; I feel nothing but repulsion for him. An animal, a desk-bound perpetrator who derives amusement from this madness. What was Uday thinking about when he ordered him to show me these videos?

I can't bring myself to think about it any further.

He shows me the next video. In it they're working on a man with a chainsaw, cutting off his genitals. Blood spurts, it's hideous, but it doesn't affect me. They throw two more men, hands bound, into a lake; another has his arms broken with iron bars, his head crushed between the steel plates of a vice, which are slowly pressed together. Suddenly, with a jolt, his skull collapses and his brain protrudes.

They take me back to the video room. Munem Hammed asks

if I'm okay. I nod and lie, 'Yes, why not? I'm fine. What interests me more than those videos, though, is what happens next.'

Munem Hammed explains in his quiet, supercilious and elegant manner how we're going to proceed next. The fascinating thing about Munem Hammed is that he never waves his hands about as he makes his explanations, that he isn't long-winded, that he's very direct and immediately gets to the point. There's nothing flowery, flabby or extravagant about him. There's nothing oriental about Hammed. He's more British, like a relic from the time when Iraq was still a British crown colony.

'Here you're going to see videos about Uday Saddam Hussein,' he tells me, pointing to the cassettes that stand neatly side by side on a table in front of the wall of videos. 'Take a good look, note every detail, and copy Uday as though you were a monkey.'

Munem Hammed puts in the first video. It's the one from 26 May 1987, showing Uday at a meeting of the football section of the sports association. Uday is sitting at a negotiating table with half a dozen elegant gentlemen. They are representatives of the Iraqi Football Association, of which Uday is president. Who knows why Uday of all people should be president of the association, he isn't at all athletic.

The presidential office is an honorary one, a function given to Uday because Saddam fills all important offices with family members, and the Saddam clan needs such functions so that the family can present a complacent face to the ordinary people. Contact between the President's family, the clan, and the masses, needs to be nurtured. Functions such as president of the Football Association are very well suited to this. First of all, the president always sits in the director's box, and is thus sufficiently far removed from the mob. Secondly, football games regularly take place. That ensures his regular, inconspicuous presence.

Drinks and ashtrays stand on the long, podium-like table covered with a white table-cloth. Uday sits in the middle, or rather he is draped casually in his chair. Uday is by some way the youngest person there.

He doesn't say a word. One of the gentlemen delivers a monologue about the financing of a football club. Uday wears a light cotton suit, a white button-down shirt, a brightly coloured tie and matching handkerchief. Between the index and middle fingers of his left hand he holds his obligatory cigar, a Havana, Montecristo No. 6, imported directly from Cuba.

I can't see his legs, but they're probably crossed. Munem Hammed orders me to slump in my chair like Uday does. It's easy for me because Uday used to sit like that at school, and we often copied him.

I sit down on a chair and let my right arm dangle: my left shoulder is significantly lower than my right. I bend my left arm and arrange my fingers as though I were holding a cigar.

Munem Hammed laughs and says, 'Latif, we're idiots, we forgot the cigar,' and yells, 'Bring us the cigars.' They bring a box of Montecristo No. 6. Munem Hammed gives me one, and I take it, but don't light it.

Once again, the same business from the top: slump in the chair, right arm draped casually over the arm of the chair, left shoulder lowered, left arm slightly bent and fat cigar between index and middle fingers. I hold my fingers too stiffly, too straight. 'Bend them slightly,' says Munem Hammed, showing me. 'Hold the cigar like this.' I hold the cigar as Munem Hammed shows me. I look alternately at him and the video, and within less than ten minutes I've learned the hand posture. I laugh and strike my thigh with my right hand. Munem Hammed laughs just as loudly.

Then comes the next sequence: the video shows Uday pleasurably putting the cigar to his mouth and taking a long drag on it. He doesn't inhale the smoke, but just keeps the smoke in his mouth for a few seconds. As he does so he throws his head back in a theatrical gesture, tips it over to the right in a bored way, presses his lips together.

It looks funny. Uday's protruding teeth, his fleshy, pursed lips – it all reminds me of something from the animal world. Somehow people look like animals in certain situations. That's it, Uday sticks out his lower lip, just as chimpanzees do when they're chewing on something.

I chuckle to myself, and fail to notice that it's myself I'm chuckling at. The operation gave me similarly protruding teeth, an overbite. I've completely forgotten that, because I don't feel the pain any more, and my four porcelain teeth already feel as though they were my own.

I take the cigar, put it to my mouth and bump the tip of the cigar against my artificial teeth. It reminds me of the operation and shows me that I'm still Latif Yahia and not Uday Saddam Hussein. The sequences of motion are still mine, not his. My bodily movements are still being guided by Latif Yahia, not Uday Saddam Hussein. I'm thinking about how he, Uday, would move, and that's bad.

The fragments of seconds that my brain takes to pass on the commands to my limbs make my movements artificial. 'You'll only be able to behave completely synchronically,' Munem Hammed explains, and his words suggest that he has done this often in the past, 'when you don't need to concentrate on it. It's just like speaking foreign languages. You'll only be able to speak English perfectly when you can think in English. As long as you're thinking in your mother tongue and concentrating on vocabulary and intonation, you'll never be able to speak English without an accent.'

I spend another four hours in the video room, watching films of Uday. I don't copy him, I just concentrate. On his movements, his facial expressions, his gestures. He walks upright, his chest jutting forwards, trying to keep his shoulders straight. He actually strides. He strides with a spring in his step.

And he doesn't sit, either. He *hangs* in his chair. His legs are never side by side, always crossed. He always throws his left leg over his right, stays like that for a few minutes, sometimes wiggles his foot back and forth, and after that he throws his right leg over his left.

When he laughs, his laugh isn't loud, deep and rumbling. He has a staccato giggle: heeheeheehee ... Then he stops for a second, then he goes on giggling again: Meeheeheeheee. His whole torso shakes and pulls his body slightly forwards and the corners of his mouth downwards: Heeheeheeheehee.

For three days I do nothing but study these videos. From nine o'clock in the morning until Moslem evening prayer. Although no one in Uday's immediate circle regularly prays, I try to pray five times a day, and they accept that, although it makes me smile. For them, the fundamental rules of the Moslem faith are a relic: they are modern Moslems, and modern Moslems are Western. Faith is scorned, faith diminishes man, particularly if he lives it out as the Koran decrees.

Iraq under Saddam Hussein is very different from states with fundamentalist governments like Saudi Arabia, Kuwait or even Iran. With the Ba'ath Party and Saddam Hussein, Iraq was governed by Arabs with Western, socialist ideas for whom religion is of secondary importance. What counts is socialism as a form of society, not the Koran. Our prophet is not Mohammed, but Saddam Hussein with his faith in the heroic goals of the party. Our women have complete equality. They don't have to wear the chador if they don't want to, or if their husbands don't expressly require them to do so, and they don't need to hide their faces. Mosques have been degraded to tourist destinations, there is alcohol and there are drunks, prostitution and night-clubs. Baghdad is Babylon.

After the third day I think I know Uday so well that I know how he feels, thinks and acts. I have incorporated his movements to such an extent that I can stand like him, sit like him, act like him.

We start with language training, and that's the most complicated thing of all. His overbite, which was much more extreme when he was at school than it is now, gives him problems saying the letter R. Since my operation I have the same problem, but not in such a pronounced form, because I still try to speak clearly. It makes me open my mouth wider, and twist the corners of my mouth in a more extreme way than Uday. Munem Hammed is constantly criticising me, ceaselessly repeating, 'Be a parrot, Latif. A parrot.'

Hundreds of times we run through how Uday would open a conference, how he is around his friends, how he watches a parade. Munem Hammed dins into me that as a rule Uday doesn't look anyone in the eyes or shake anyone by the hand, he's always surrounded by bodyguards. Uday receives everyone with his nose in the air, without the ghost of a smile, without saying much. He is the President's son, he is authority, power. So everything he does must be patriotic, or at least look that way. He must also be utterly detached in his treatment of his bodyguards: they aren't soldiers like myself, they are my subordinates, they must carry out my orders, without question. There are no claps on the shoulder, no friendly smiles, hugs or fraternal kisses. There's just dictatorial detachment.

Uday generally wears dark glasses, Ray-Bans, and he is constantly looking past the person talking to him so as to make the distance between him and the rest of the world even clearer.

In equally great detail we practise how Uday would leave a room and walk into the open. This moment is seen as one of the most dangerous, because it's the moment when potential assassins have the greatest degree of success. When he walks between a closed room and the waiting line of cars he is at his most vulnerable.

When a conference is over, Uday stands up and says goodbye with a nod to the other participants. His body-guards crowd around him, and he leaves the room walking at a quick pace. He charges into the open and runs to his car, which is waiting with its door open. The path from the building to the car must be covered as quickly as possible so as not to give snipers a chance.

Uday never uses a chauffeur; like his father, he drives his own car. We practise driving as well. Sitting casually at the wheel, never holding it with both hands, the left hand always leaning on the door, elbow bent. He sits casually and crookedly, and drives his cars roaring through Baghdad at about 120 miles an hour. Always at top speed, constantly double-clutching. Uday is in radio contact with his bodyguards, who drive in cars ahead of and behind his own. There is usually a convoy of four cars. They travel closely in single file, and on Uday's command they constantly overtake one another. He orders: 'Three overtake two, one fall back.

Take number three position.' This constant overtaking and falling back is supposed to distract potential assassins. They're never supposed to know who is in which car. If the sequence of the column were constant, assassins would be able to concentrate on one vehicle. As things stand, the whole convoy would have to be blown up, and that would be rather difficult.

I learn in a metallic Mercedes and a pale blue Porsche. Uday has more than 100 cars in his garages: Ferraris, Maseratis, Porsches, Jaguars; I haven't seen any of these cars yet, I've just been told that the colours are very important for Uday. They have to go with his suit. If he's wearing grey, his car has to be grey as well.

This story seems wildly unlikely to me, but it's actually true.

But for the time being I don't concentrate on it any further, and try to carry out my training – which isn't unlike the training of a horse or a dog – to the best of my ability.

All the training sequences are edited together on tape and shown to Uday every day. But throughout this time I never get to see Uday face to face, and he doesn't live in Project Number 7.

On 15 October 1987 Munem Hammed calls me into Uday's office. He informs me that he is reasonably pleased with my progress. I'm disappointed. I think I'm doing well, I've mastered the speech defect and I'm moving almost exactly as Uday does. They should be enthusiastic, so I find myself thinking it's just a distracting manoeuvre.

Munem Hammed has a letter on the table in front of him, with the Iraqi eagle as a letterhead. An official communication. Munem Hammed says, 'We shall now inform the President. Lieutenant General Al-Nassiri has written it and given it to me for counter-signature.'

That comes as a blow: 'You haven't told him? The kidnapping, the psychological terror in the cell, all that training – you've done all that without his knowledge?'

It's an independent initiative on the part of Uday and his officers. The attempt of a domesticated mummy's boy to emancipate himself. He probably wants to impress his father and prove that he's capable of organising his own protection for himself. He's been the first to find a fiday who isn't a family member, and who is good and convincing none the less.

Munem Hammed shows me the letter that they're going to send to the President that day.

Iraqi Republic
Head of the Chancellery of the Republic
Secret Service Organisation

In the name of merciful God

Honourable President of the Iraqi Republic, may God preserve and protect your rule . . .

Mr President, I should like to inform your Lordship that our Secret Service Organisation, Security Department, under the leadership of the following officers:

1) *Major Munem Shabib Munem Hammed Al-Tikritti*
2) *Captain Siad Hassan Hashem Al-Nassiri*
3) *Captain Saadi Daham Hasaa Al-Nassiri*

Has successfully recruited Lieutenant Latif Yahia Latif Al-Salihi, who bears a very strong resemblance to Mr

Uday Saddam Hussein, to our organisation.

After making inquiries and investigations into him and his family we have been able to establish the following:

1) His name is Latif Yahia Latif Al-Salihi, Kurd, born 14 June 1964 in Baghdad, Moslem, Sunni.
2) Studied government and law, graduating in 1986.
3) He began his career and his military service as a second lieutenant with the special commando unit. After six months he was promoted to lieutenant for his commitment and courage.
4) He has never been noted for political or other errors.
5) He owns an import-export office, 'Achawain-Import-Export' on Diali Street in the Mansoor district.

He owns two Mercedes cars, and has an account with the Iraqi Central bank.

After we had discovered these details, and because of his resemblance to Mr Uday Saddam Hussein, we decided, with the written agreement of Mr Uday Saddam Hussein, to use him as a serf and fiday for Mr Uday Saddam Hussein in difficult, important and dangerous operations and tasks.

We have begun his training and established that he is an intelligent man, and willing to serve his fatherland, Iraq.

Everything else is left up to you, and you, sir, have the final word.

May the Iraqi flag under your rule fly long in our dear Iraq.

Signed
Lieutenant General
Fanaz Zibn Al-Nassiri
Director of the Secret Service Organisation
15 October 1987

I shudder as I read the letter. It slowly becomes clear to me that I have been a mere plaything so far, a plaything for Uday and his officers. They have sought me out, started my training and noticed that I am talented and ideologically secure. That I'm interested in Uday's life, that I'm fascinated by the idea of living in paradise.

But what have I got from it? Nothing. It was all just a prelude. The decision lies with the President, and if he says no . . . what then?

'Munem Hammed, sir, what happens if his lordship Saddam Hussein rejects me as a fiday for his son? What will you do with me?' I ask.

Munem Hammed avoids my eye, says nothing, gets up and leaves the room.

I know what that means. I'm a dead man, I'll disappear as though I had never existed if the President doesn't accept me. Once again I think of the bloodstains in the torture chamber, and I think of the video in the office of the civilian police and the men in the Al-Rashid camp being led to the gallows with their hands bound and chains around the ankles.

The trapdoor opens beneath their feet without a sound, a brief jolt, the noose tightens, their heads tip to one side. A broken neck. Perhaps they'll only shoot me . . .

FIVE

Saddam Hussein

Munem Hammed Al-Tikritti is excited. I've never seen him like this over the past few weeks. He had always been detached, reticent, superior, balanced. An elegant man whom I admire, although the feeling that he sees me as an object is getting stronger and stronger in me.

It is 23 October 1987, shortly after eight o'clock in the morning, and it's hot in Baghdad. 'So far so good,' says Munem Hammed, and I know what he means. Yesterday the reply came from the palace: the President would like to see me. Now he wants to meet me personally, I say to myself, and feel proud, although I haven't really got anything to be proud about. I'm a dead man if his lordship refuses me, if Saddam Hussein doesn't want me. It's possible that Munem Hammed's own fate hangs on this as well.

None the less, I don't feel nervous or frightened as I did when they came and got me from the front. I know what's going on, and I understand that it now depends on me as well. I can preserve myself, and I want to preserve myself. They fetched me, and I'm good, and I know that.

'Our meeting has been set for four o'clock in the afternoon, so prepare yourself,' Munem Hammed says to me in a peremptory tone that I haven't heard before.

The wounds from the operation on my teeth have healed, and the training was so intensive that I don't just imitate Uday's speech defect; I do it intuitively, automatically, without thinking about it. 'You mustn't concentrate on it,' they kept telling me a thousand times, 'it must flow from you.' I move like Uday, I hold my hand like he does, I have his grin, his wink, his hysterical laugh.

Saddam sends me his own car with the officers Abed Hamid, Arshad Al-Yassin and Fehan Al-Tikritti. Saddam Hussein always surrounds himself with a whole staff of personal confidants, all of whom I will meet over time:

- Colonel Arshad Yassin is responsible for the safety of Saddam Hussein, and directs a whole staff of guards
- Colonel Abed Hamid Al-Tikritti is an old friend of the President who has known Saddam since his school days
- Major Rokan Al-Tikritti has served alongside Saddam for decades. He is responsible for gun training of all the bodyguards and sentries in the presidential palace
- Saddam Kamel is Saddam Hussein's oldest friend, and officer of the information office in the conference palace
- Captain Jamal Saad Dahham, Saddam's second escort, is responsible for the information office in the conference palace
- Lieutenant Addi Omar, bodyguard
- Lieutenant Mohammed Fadel, bodyguard, later imprisoned for murdering two dancers who withheld their favours at a private party of Saddam Hussein's
- Lieutenant Rafed Al-Abed, bodyguard and nephew of Colonel Abed Hamid Al-Tikritti

- Lieutenant Hakim Kamel, bodyguard, brother of Hussein Kamel, the husband of Saddam's youngest daughter Hala
- Second Lieutenant Nazem Ahmad Al-Tikritti, bodyguard
- Second Lieutenant Mohammed Kamal Douri, bodyguard
- Second Lieutenant Saadi Nahi Al-Tikritti, bodyguard
- Second Lieutenant Rafed Al-Tikritti, bodyguard
- Second Lieutenant Riad Mohammed Al-Tikritti, bodyguard

These men form the President's closest circle.

They come and collect me at three o'clock on the dot. We hurry through the foyer into the open, run to the Mercedes. A man opens the door, I jump into the back seat, and the column drives off with its doors open. The doors fly shut: two Mercedes in front of us, two behind. We travel the short journey from Project Number 7 to the Family Gate near the palace entrance at more than 60 miles an hour.

Near the entrance we slow down a little, the sentries wave us through, we pass the tank barriers, the hospital and the ministerial apartments, and 20 minutes later we stop by the information building, the east wing of Saddam's palace.

My bodyguards jump out of the car, secure my car, and only when they are in position do I get out. Everything has to look right, the way it did in my training – make sure nothing goes wrong now. I jump out of the car, Saddam's men beside me, and we run towards the wide, inviting steps leading up to the information building. Four officers are waiting for us there, one of them is Rokan.

We hurry into the foyer, Rokan disappears into a side room, everything is ready for my visit. For ten minutes nothing happens. We stand in the foyer and wait. No one speaks, no one smokes.

Then a high-ranking officer comes in. An athletic man with broad shoulders, a bullish neck, powerful hands: his green uniform jacket stretches over his chest, everything about him seems too big, too weighty, too powerful. The officer knows me even though he's never seen me before: 'So you're Latif. Do you know the rules?'

'I know them.'

I know about Saddam's phobia concerning poison, his obsession, his fascination. During my training they told me the story of Minister of the Interior Ezzat Ibrahim. Ibrahim, for whom nothing was sacred, who used everything that could be used for the purposes of killing, was summoned to see the President. Before Saddam received him they undressed Ibrahim, threw him into the pool and then rubbed his body with Dettol. Saddam suspected Ibrahim of carrying mysterious microbes or a deadly poison that can be passed on by a handshake

Everyone, not just me, has to undergo a very detailed examination before being allowed into an audience with the President.

First the officer begins with a close physical examination. He goes through everything. My pockets, the folds in my uniform jacket; he reaches under my armpits, runs his hands over my bottom, my crotch and my legs and orders me to take off my shoes and socks. Saddam hates his subordinates facing him with socks that have been worn, even if they're wearing shoes. He can't bear socks that have been worn.

So the officer gives me fresh socks. Cotton, white, size nine. I put the socks on, and the officer calls the doctor.

Like both the doctors who examined me weeks ago, this one doesn't seem to be an Arab. He doesn't say a word, puts his brown leather medical case on the table and opens it. The doctor has red hair, his sharp-edged face is scattered with freckles and his eyes are unusually close together. The man looks mysterious, sly.

Then he starts his examination, which seems ludicrously exaggerated, as I wouldn't have had a chance to hide anything on my person. I'm constantly under surveillance, I'm a prisoner, Uday's doctors have examined me several times. Or does Saddam Hussein even suspect his own son, I wonder, and the question amuses me.

The doctor runs his hands over my skin, wipes my face, my ears, my neck with a wad of cotton wool that he has already dipped in a tincture. He changes the cotton wool a number of times, dips the used pieces in a blue solution. The indicator solution doesn't change colour. It probably would have done if I had some kind of special poison on my body.

He inspects my eyes, pulls the lids down, checks my mucous membranes. Tears come to my eyes, but that seems to be normal because the doctor doesn't react to it. The officer orders me to open my mouth wide. The doctor swabs my tongue, inspects my jaw with a little chrome lamp, examines my teeth and finally runs his index finger over my gums. Top and bottom, inside and outside.

A ludicrous ceremony, a ritual, a paranoid schizophrenic spectacle. I'm not sure whether this examination could really have achieved anything, or stopped anything from happening.

Although I'm not a doctor, the last point of this examination seems the most sensible: the doctor gives me a little plastic bottle of Dettol and tells me to rub it into my hands. I spray the solution on the palms of my hands and rub them carefully until my hands are dry again.

That brings the examination to an end, the doctor packs

his things away and disappears. And he says to me in a paternal voice, 'Latif, remember not to kiss Saddam.'

So now I'm ready for the big moment. I'm prepared like a Moslem on the holy Hajj in Mecca, before he kisses the Kaaba. The crucial difference; the Hajj is the highest fulfilment, the absolute duty of a Moslem. Every Moslem must have visited Mecca at least once, according to the Koran.

But my journey to see President Saddam Hussein is a life-and-death moment. If he rejects me, my fate is sealed.

I'm surprised to be so calm, so relaxed. Saddam is the prophet, the incarnation of power, the one who decides good and evil. Millions of people in Iraq would give everything for this moment; they would even give themselves. But I'm no more nervous than I would be if I drove to the Tigris with my father in his white Volvo to go fishing. I'm not afraid of dying.

The door opens. The officer steps forward and asks me to follow him. I'm standing in the President's office.

The room looks like a copy of Uday's office in Project Number 7, and I'm sure that Uday has designed his office on the model of his father's. The same pastel-coloured wallpaper, the dominant pale yellow couch, the weighty English desk. The shelves full of Arabic literature.

Saddam is sitting behind his desk, talking on the telephone and pointedly ignoring me. Another parallel with Uday. Uday would never immediately greet anyone. It's his mania to keep people waiting, because making people wait means exercising power. Uday has clearly learned that from his father.

Saddam, the President, wears a dark double-breasted suit, and a brightly coloured floral tie without a tiepin. He

holds the receiver (Siemens brand) in his left hand, and his
right hand lies on the desk. He taps rhythmically with his
middle finger on the desk. He laughs at brief intervals. His
voice sounds soft and warm, almost tearful. There's no
strength, no violence in his voice, it doesn't sound like the
voice of a leader. He speaks without punctuation, without
peaks, without any particular emphasis. Nothing striking
or dominant, no word you might linger over; Saddam is
talking to an advisor about a speech that he is about to
deliver. On the back of his right hand I can see the remains
of a tattoo that he had done years ago. At first I think they
are the kind of patches of pigment that you often see in old
people. But they are the remains of a tattoo that was badly
removed.

His fingernails are carefully manicured and lacquered.
His haircut is perfect, and so is his moustache. When he
laughs, you can see his immaculate teeth.

His eyes are brown and expressive, and the only thing to
suggest that this man is over 50 years old are the bags that
are beginning to form under his eyes, which you can just see
if you look very carefully, and the deep wrinkles between
nose and mouth. He looks like a mixture of the young Jean
Gabin and Sultan Saladin. Saddam is a handsome, tall, slim,
well-presented, imposing man.

He puts down the receiver, springs to his feet, walks out
from behind his desk and laughs loudly, a deep, throaty
laugh, when he sees me.

His laugh isn't fake, it's genuine and powerful. Saddam
takes two steps towards me, and starts making insignificant
small-talk. He asks me about my time at the front, about my
parents, about my brothers and sisters. He doesn't give me
time to answer, but supplies the answers himself, and I
always nod in agreement. Saddam looks me up and down,

studies my hands, my lips, my eyes, my facial expressions and hand gestures. He doesn't say, but I think I know what he's thinking: 'He really does look very like my son. We're doing very good work here.'

It takes me completely by surprise when he suddenly spreads his arms and says, 'Yes, it's you. Allah gave me two sons, and now I have three.'

I'm confused. The whole ceremonial before, the examinations, the clear suspicion, the physical and psychological pressure that's being exerted on me, this alternation of ice-cold force and calculating gratitude for what I have achieved seems to have gone. I'm alive, I've survived and passed the first and most important test. Saddam's statement pleases and frightens me to equal degrees. He has accepted me as a fiday, as a double of his son. So now I'm a member of the clan, I'm part of it – and yet I don't accept it. I'm no longer anything but an instrument, a useful object. A toy that you throw away when you no longer need it. When will I stop being Uday's fiday? Will there ever be an end? Can it be a positive end?

But more than my self-doubt I'm touched by the nature of Saddam Hussein, whom I imagined quite differently: more lordly, colder, more arrogant, more brutal, crueller.

He must be different from the way he appears, I think, he has hundreds of thousands of people on his conscience. But does he have a conscience? Probably not. Presumably cruelty becomes anonymous if it occurs 'in the public interest'. Killing one person is a crime; if I kill thousands, it's an act of state. That must be how Saddam thinks and feels.

Nothing about the President seems cruel, cold or repulsive. He's very charismatic, he has a captivating manner.

So this is the man who has a whole country by the throat,

who transforms the crowd into a fanatical and euphoric mass which unconditionally sacrifices itself for him.

Saddam Hussein has emerged from a culture to which Western values are just as alien as the humanitarian values of Islam are to the West.

He was born on 28 April 1937 in Al-Ouja near Tikrit – the birthplace of the legendary Sultan Saladin – a child of peasant farmers. His place of birth is a little provincial village eighty miles north of Baghdad. They called him Hussein Saddam Al-Tikritti. He was given the name Saddam, the steadfast one, because his mother didn't manage to 'lose' him. Subha Tulfah had fallen pregnant with Saddam out of wedlock. She tried to abort her unwanted child with extremely hard physical labour. Saddam's father died before his son was born.

Subha Tulfah then married Ibrahim Al-Hassan. But he didn't want to have anything to do with a stranger's child. Saddam was passed on to his uncle, Khairallah Tulfah. He was an officer in an Iraqi unit which took part in an uprising against the Hashemite King Faisal II. As a result he spent several years in jail.

Between 1936 and 1941, Iraq underwent six such attempted uprisings, so young Saddam grew up in a revolutionary period. After the head of the family was released from imprisonment, his uncle's clan supported itself with trade, but also with street robbery and frauds involving the water supply.

The village community knew about Saddam's illegitimacy and rejected him.

He was as tough as old boots, he skipped school, and his headmistress in Tikrit despaired of him: at the age of ten he was already showing signs of the violence that would later catapult him to the head of a totalitarian system. He was never parted from the iron truncheon with which he kept his schoolmates and the stray dogs in the village at a distance. At school he hid it behind his djellaba, sometimes heating it red-hot in the fire and, surrounded by his classmates, inserting it in the anuses of captured cats and dogs. The truncheon was his fetish, his father, his power, his only friend and his protection in the face of a hard society that rejected him because his father was dead and his mother had married someone else and no one knew where she lived. Presumably he hated society because society hated him, and the only thing he could cling to was his red-hot iron truncheon, which he used to torture to death those things to which he considered himself superior: animals.

In 1955 his uncle moved to Baghdad, and Saddam was sent to the El-Karkh school. He grew up in the district of Tekarte. Many members of the Tikrit clan earned their livelihood with street robbery, and ruled over the people of Baghdad like a mafia. The Tikrit clan gradually acquired more and more influence. Family feuds had bloody resolutions.

It was here that Saddam committed his first murder. At the age of nineteen, on his uncle's orders, he shot a rival bandit, his distant uncle Saadi, and thus underlined his close connection with the Tikrit clan. The first step towards earning his own livelihood with unbridled violence.

Despite these brutal inclinations, Saddam developed a personality of his own and an incredible compulsion to acquire knowledge. He graduated successfully from his grammar school in Baghdad.

Hussein's political enthusiasms as a schoolboy were for the nationalist, revolutionary goals of the Iraqi Ba'ath Party, the Party of Arab renewal, which was still operating in the underground at the time.

In 1957 he became a member of this banned Ba'ath
Party, and thus an active opponent of the Iraqi dictator
General Kassem. On 17 October 1959 he was chosen to
take part in an attempt on the dictator's life. Small wonder,
because the Party had taken on borrowed European
ideologies like nationalism and socialism, and wanted to
enforce them with violence, in accordance with the rules of
the region. General Kassem also came out with the obligatory watchwords, but he made the mistake of not being one
of the Tikritis, and not being a member of the Ba'ath. He
wasn't a member of the clan, and this made him an enemy
who had to be eliminated. The Ba'ath had wide support
among the Iraqi population, because Kassem brutally
suppressed and exploited people.

The attempt on his life was a failure, and Hussein was
slightly injured in the leg.

Saddam had to flee. He cut the bullet out of his leg,
escaped to Syria and stayed there for six months; the lawyer
Michel Aflaq, founder of the Ba'ath Party, became his
political mentor. In 1962 he went to Egypt, where he started
to study law. He also became a leading member of the Ba'ath
office in Cairo. Although he had played a subordinate role in
the attempt on General Kassem's life, his participation in
the attempted putsch became a cornerstone of that heroic
myth which was later to grow up around him.

While Saddam was studying in Cairo, Kassem was toppled
and publicly executed in Baghdad under the leadership of
Hassan Al-Bakr Al-Tikritti. Hussein returned home and
asked his uncle for the hand of his cousin Sajida.

This marriage had been arranged when they were both
very young, in line with the rules of the Al-Tikritti clan.
Where possible, you don't marry outside of your own
extended family.

But the young couple found no peace: a few months later Hassan Al-Bakr was driven out of office by Marshal Aref and his men, embittered opponents of the Ba'ath. As a member of the Party leadership, Hussein found himself being persecuted once again, and was put in jail. Still under arrest, he was elected deputy party leader at the eighth Ba'ath National Congress. A short time later he managed to escape.

It wasn't until 1968, after several years of conflicts reminiscent of a civil war, that the Ba'ath managed to regain power and depose Marshal Aref. Hassan Al-Bakr was head of state, and the second, strongest man in the regime was Saddam Hussein Al-Tikritti.

Saddam assumed the leadership of the 'investigation committee', based in the notorious prison of Kasr Nihaja.

Kasr Al-Nihaja means 'Palace of No Return'. Within a few weeks hundreds of political opponents were tortured and killed.

Saddam also had more than 100 men hanged as 'agents of Israel and the USA' before fanatical onlookers in Republic Square in Baghdad.

As Deputy General Secretary, Hussein carried out his own party work, and proved to be a capable planner and organiser. In 1972 he nationalised the hitherto Western-oriented oil industry, and signed a friendship treaty with the USSR. The co-operation treaty led to the military armament of Iraq. President Al-Bakr had resisted this friendship treaty for a long time. He only agreed to change his mind when Saddam pulled out a gun in his office and shot him in the forearm.

Despite the treaty with the USSR, Saddam killed huge numbers of communists and opponents of all colours. President Al-Bakr increasingly declined into a symbolic figure. On 16 May 1979 he died of heart failure. That's the official version: he was really poisoned. Saddam Hussein was only 42 when he assumed power.

He was now the most important man in Iraq, and mercilessly exploited his position: he had high-ranking officials executed, including the mayor of Baghdad.

The President imposed the death penalty for criticism of himself, and developed a personality cult not unlike that of Nicolai Ceausescu.

Saddam, like Ceausescu, transferred the most important and influential posts to relations. With Saddam the whole Al-Tikritti clan came to power. They made Iraq into something like their own private club, as the rules of the oriental clan society decree. Just as Arabia became Saudi Arabia, Iraq became – albeit less visibly – Tikriti Iraq. Officially, the country was governed by a 15-man 'revolutionary commandership', with Saddam Hussein at its head. Next to it, however, there was a 'special office', which was nothing but a family council controlling the whole country. And there is one other clear point of comparison between Ceausescu and Saddam Hussein: both had sons who turned out badly. Nicu Ceausescu, whom Uday Saddam Hussein knows personally, made headlines with wild drinking-sprees and rapes. On one occasion, drunk at the wheel, he knocked down two pedestrians and fatally injured them. The secret service hushed up the event, just as the Iraqi secret service would veil Uday's crimes.

And now I, Latif Yahia, am also part of it; not as a full member of the clan, but as a fiday I am at the heart of power, being familiarised with structures of command and details that are hidden from millions of others. I am able to take part in their lives. I am Uday, and the 'third son of Saddam Hussein', as the President has just said.

For the first time I feel nervous, but I don't show it. The President says: 'What I require from you is to do your work well.'

'Yes, sir,' I interrupt him, and Saddam goes on: 'If you do your work well, I will be pleased with you. If you do fulfil your duties one hundred percent, I will always be there for you, for all your problems . . .'

He pauses briefly, breathes through his nose for a moment, and says, '. . . and for any problems you might have with Uday. Just make sure that I have no reason to be angry with you.'

I wait for a few seconds, and then reply formally, 'I hope I will do everything correctly and well, sir.'

Saddam Hussein says nothing more; he turns around and walks over to his desk without having shaken my hand. He picks up the phone, presses a red button, and shortly afterwards I am fetched by the officers and taken out of the room. In the foyer they clap me on the shoulder, and one of them asks me how I feel. I just nod briefly and say, almost in passing, 'I'm okay.'

SIX

My First Public Appearance

I'm stretching out on my wide bed in Uday's bedroom in Project Number 7, inhaling the clean autumn air. It's late October, and Baghdad isn't as hot as it has been recently. Since my visit to the President they've intensified my training. They're forever picking me up, taking me to the video room, forcing me to watch the films of Uday, almost all of which I now know off by heart. The rhythm barely changes; two days of video study, then two days of parrot practice: copying the voice, copying the movements, dialogue training. Munem Hammed is almost the only person I talk to. He plays his parts to perfection, even if he's bothered that 'Bulldog' Siad Hassan Hashem Al-Nassiri, the mass murderer, Saddam's executioner-in-chief, is always breathing down his neck. The 'Bulldog' drives us onwards, and even Uday has a spark of respect for the 'Bulldog', particularly since he seems to have a direct line to Saddam Hussein.

One day we're practising the role 'Uday as President of a sports club', the next he's the President's son inspecting a special unit. Munem Hammed teaches me to salute as sloppily as Uday, always to ensure that my clothes are perfect, and to master the business with the glasses to perfection: slowly taking the gold-armed Ray-Bans out of their case, casually flipping them open and then looking past the people with his nose in the air.

My eyes slowly become accustomed to the glasses, and like Uday I wear them all the time, even in closed rooms. The glasses spare me my daily make-up; my eyes are bigger than Uday's, after all.

During all those weeks of training there is not actually a single day when I have time to be Latif Yahia. Even in my golden prison, Project Number 7, I'm constantly playing Uday, and the staff have to treat me as the President's son, without asking any questions. Any contraventions receive special treatment from the 'Bulldog', and everyone in this house knows what that means. So they all keep to the absurd rules of the game.

Only in one single point has my life changed crucially since my visit to the President: before, Uday had barely stayed at Project Number 7. Now he's here all the time, personally overseeing my training and not just limiting himself to the study of the videos that they make of me. He wants to be near me, but is at pains to avoid any kind of friendship with me.

It's rather the reverse: the longer my training lasts, the more extreme are his outbreaks of rage. I make an effort, I'm entirely committed, but he ignores me more and more, as though I were his worst enemy in the world.

It's now early November 1987, and Uday's father appoints him President of the Iraqi Olympic Committee. I have no idea whether an Iraqi sportsman has ever won a medal, or come anywhere close to winning one. So the chairman's job is another pretext for Saddam's boy.

This greatly changes my job, in that I'm now no longer just

a double for the head of the national sports associations, but also a fiday for the chairman of the national Olympic committee, and that means that I will have to receive international guests as Uday Saddam Hussein.

Uday's appointment takes place on a Tuesday, and is broadcast on Iraqi television the same day, on the main news. The Iraqi newspapers also carry long reports on the subject, and even the *Baghdad Observer*, the only English-language newspaper in Iraq, considers my boss's appointment worthy of a long article.

The next day we're sitting back in our video theatre, and Munem Hammed is acting out the scene with me: 'The chairman of the Iraqi Olympic Committee welcoming an Olympic delegation at the airport.'

That day Uday is in the video room for the first time. He sits on a chair at the back of the room, observing everything very closely. I'm standing in front of a podium with microphones, my bodyguards next to me, all wearing dark glasses.

Red carpet, flower arrangements. The video room has been furnished, as fast as possible, exactly the same as the reception room in Saddam Hussein's private airport.

We visited this airport in the morning so that I can precisely imagine all the locations. It's about seven miles from the palace, and consists of two runways built so that jumbo jets can land on them.

The journey from the palace to the airport is connected by a well-built road constantly monitored by policemen. They belong to the secret service, wear police uniforms only as a disguise, and are changed over every four hours. In Baghdad these officers, who stand like trees at the side of the road, are called 'Ba Murur'.

But their actual task isn't to monitor the airport road,

because Saddam Hussein doesn't often leave Iraq. Instead, he uses the road every day to reach another private home, his castle in Al A'mriya. It's to the west of the airport road, and halfway along the road branches off to this private home, which Saddam calls 'Muyamaa Al-Riasi', the headquarters.

Even as schoolchildren we knew that the use of the road was forbidden to ordinary mortals, on pain of punishment. Anyone who accidentally comes along this road in his car is arrested and locked up, and possibly even executed, because the officers are all-powerful, and can do as they like.

The actual airport building isn't very big, it's more like the administrative wing of a middle-sized business. In front of the airport there is a large car park, so that the presidential convoy can comfortably drive up. The main room in the airport is a large reception lounge with chairs lined up in units and separated by potted plants.

The room is dominated by a huge portrait of Saddam Hussein, with the Iraqi eagle and the red, white and black flag with the three green stars underneath.

Beneath the picture of Saddam is a podium with microphones, standing on a kind of stage. There are thick carpets everywhere. On state visits, this is where the first addresses are delivered, and polite small-talk exchanged.

In the hangars with hydraulically operated gates, there are always two Boeing long-distance aeroplanes, five helicopters and two MIG fighters. These planes always have full tanks, are always ready to fly. The crews have to be prepared to work for the President day and night.

One of the pilots is a friend of mine, Captain Mazhar Al-Tikritti. He's a helicopter pilot, and flies most of the President's missions. Saddam Hussein affectionately calls his aeroplane crews 'The eagles of the Iraqi airspace'.

I don't learn the locations off by heart, that would be too

much, but I concentrate on the way Uday would behave when meeting the foreign delegation.

Back in the video room, I have to stand on the red carpet by the podium. 'The delegation has just landed, and you will cordially welcome the leaders of the delegation to walk along the guard of honour immediately afterwards.'

I try to keep a straight face, walk up to the imaginary head of the delegation and shake his hand. Suddenly it all strikes me as terribly funny. I can't walk along the imaginary formation of honour as seriously as I should. I feel as though I'm in a comic strip, and burst out laughing. I immediately apologise, but it's too late: Uday leaps to his feet and charges over to me. In his right hand he holds his electrical cable; his face is stony, I can't see his eyes as he has his Ray-Bans on.

He shouts at me to turn around. I obey, and know what's going to happen. Uday starts laying into me with his electrical cable. He goes berserk, and brings the cable crashing down on my back, again and again. It is as though he is in a trance; he groans, forcing his breath out through his nostrils with each blow. None of the officers dares to hold him back. I feel the stinging pain, but I endure this 'education' without a word. The humiliation is more painful than the pain. Uday had hardly any reason to lash into me. What had I done? I'd laughed during my training.

That was enough to make him lose his temper.

I count each blow. Thirty-three, then he stops. He is breathing hard, his hairline is drenched in sweat, and he suddenly laughs hysterically, that staccato heeheehee. He seems satisfied, liberated, as though his spontaneous outbreak of violence had given him a sexual satisfaction. Is Uday a sadist, can he only get rid of his sexual and intellectual inhibitions by living out bestial violence? Immature, incomplete personalities hate without reason, they have a tendency to aggression which they deflect on to defenceless objects in order to work them off. Only immature people are sadists.

In his youth Saddam Hussein also vented his aggression on animals with his red-hot iron rod. What has Uday inherited from his father? Might he even be worse than Saddam? This senseless outbreak of violence is nothing but an excuse to himself, a legitimation – in all likelihood Uday hates himself.

'Go on,' Uday orders, when he has regained his composure, and leaves the room breathing heavily. We continue the exercise as though nothing had happened. Concentrated, painstakingly precise, perfected to the last detail.

Until 27 December we practise in front of the video wall. In the evening we go through the videos, analysing the mistakes in order to eradicate them the following day.

During these weeks I get to know Uday better. I study him, I pay attention to his every word, I try to remember every aspect of his behaviour. I'd like to note everything down, but at first I don't dare, because I'm worried about the consequences of one of the bodyguards discovering such a document.

And in any case my training isn't over yet. We're going to be spending the next few weeks on training in hand-to-hand combat and shooting. It's interesting additional training in itself, but it's old hat as far as I'm concerned – I've learned all that in the army. So this training is almost identical to my officer's course.

They teach me how Uday, who always carried a magnum as a child, draws and uses his gun. How he cocks a machine-gun, just for fun, and lets it rip, just as an expression of childish delight.

I am drilled to play with the revolver the way Uday does. Like a western hero. Completely unmotivated, he sometimes takes his revolver out of its holster in the middle of a conversation, plays with it, aims at the person he is talking to, puts his index finger on the trigger, laughs, takes the revolver in his other hand and spins it like a cowboy in a film.

A curious exercise, but I have to train to do it. Uday loves playing with his gun like that, he's fascinated with the idea of cocking his revolver, aiming it at someone and acting as though he's going to fire.

I've stopped thinking about whether my training is doing me any good or not. The longer I spend in the service of the Dictator's son, the further removed I am from reality. My whole life by Uday's side is so over the top and unreal that discussions or reflections about deeper issues are quite pointless. He's a person who has completely lost his equilibrium. The system he lives in is, in turn, so absurd that such extravagances are nothing special, and just represent normality.

For Uday I am a double, a lookalike, a brother and an object on which he can work off his aggressions. I'm the one he can *educate*. On 29 February 1988 my training as a fiday finally comes to an end. The following day, 1 March 1988, Munem Hammed Al-Tikritti dictates a short letter to the head of the secret service.

Iraqi Republic
Director of the Chancellery of the Republic
Secret Service Organisation
Secret Persecution Department.

In the name of God the merciful

Secret and strictly confidential

To the honourable Director of the Secret Service
   I should like to make your lordship aware that I and my group of officers, who were responsible for the special training of Lieutenant Latif Yahia Latif Al-Salihi, have concluded this secret training. Lieutenant Latif Yahia Latif Al-Salihi has studied the use of all kinds of weapons in order to serve as a representative of Mr Uday Saddam Hussein. He has successfully survived the practice period.
   Everything else is within your hands, sir.

Major Munem Shabib Hammed Al-Tikritti
Head of the Secret Persecution Department
1 March 1988

The letter is a pure formality. My training is over, I am accepted by Uday, and presumably also by his father. At least there has not so far been any reaction from the palace, which means that everything must be all right.

After Munem Hammed has sent the letter, I receive dozens of uniforms: a bodyguard's uniform, a pilot's uniform, a black uniform bearing the name of Uday.

I am also given new papers with a false name. Sometimes I'm Captain Ahib Al-Hadisi, a secret service officer from Al-Khass, then Mohammed Sami Ahmed from the Social Affairs Ministry, or Muteb Al-Kemali, a clerk in the Ministry of the Economy. If anything were to go wrong and I were to be assassinated, there would be no shortage of arguments: the man shot would not be Uday Saddam Hussein or Latif Yahia, who has officially ceased to exist, but Captain Ahib Al-Hadisi, a secret service man.

Everyone congratulates me on this day, and even Uday is

friendly, and drinks a brandy with me. Hennessy, no ice, served in crystal goblets.

Nothing happens for five days. Uday orders me to relax. No videos, no language exercises, switch off. I hang around the swimming pool, lie in the spring sun, allow the staff to spoil me. I go through the wardrobes with all those hundreds of suits, the silk underwear, the socks from Paris and the handmade shoes from Rome. I'm living in a world of illusion, I feel exclusive, and the food they bring me is the very best. Every day I get meat, fresh vegetables, fresh salad, prepared in the European style, because Uday isn't very fond of Arab cuisine.

This siesta lasts four days, and during that time I don't really think about anything. I don't want to be forever tormenting myself with self-doubts, I accept my fate for what it is, and that inner attachment does me good. Constant reflection and consideration is pointless, as there's no hope of changing the situation anyway.

On the evening of 4 March 1988 Uday comes to my room with the 'Bulldog'. At first I don't even notice the two of them, because the door to my room is open, and I'm watching a video. Japanese hand-to-hand combat techniques, Samurai using their sword, Kung Fu fighters shadow-boxing. Uday loves these videos, and I like them too; they have no real plot, yet there's always something going on. It's actually a reflection of my life at the moment.

Uday sits down on a chair, the 'Bulldog' stays where he is and says in his hectic, hysterical style, 'Latif, it's the perfect opportunity. We're going to test you.'

'When?'

'The day after tomorrow, late afternoon, in the people's

stadium.' There's going to be a football match between two Iraqi teams. A social event with more than 50,000 spectators expected. The President's family has its own box in the people's stadium. It's a long way away from the common people; ordinary spectators would only be able to see me from a long distance, so possible mistakes on my part wouldn't be of all that much importance. 'Latif, it's your first big appearance, concentrate on it: everything that happens on this day will be crucial for future events.'

If I fail, presumably I'm a dead man. If everything goes like a dream, my life as a fiday can really get going.

Uday leaves after he says this, and I don't see him again until 6 March. I'm completely at ease, just as relaxed as I was when they brought me to his lordship Saddam Hussein.

Yassem Al-Helou, Uday's personal adviser in matters of clothing, brings me a light-coloured suit. Yassem has been part of the clan for years. He comes from a poor family in Baghdad, trained as a tailor and is probably homosexual. At least I've never seen him with a woman. His movements could practically be called feminine, his voice is gentle and his words well-chosen, and he always smells beautifully of those deep, heavy, oriental perfumes.

Uday has never had good taste where clothes are concerned. 'He used to run about the place like a vulgar little peasant boy,' rages Yassem. 'He was constantly choosing colours that didn't match.' I'm amused about Yassem, particularly over the way he holds his hand. Every time he talks about Uday's clothes problems, in his slightly feminine, screeching way, he darts on mincing little steps to the wardrobe, opens it up, stares in horror at the dozens of suits and hisses, 'What am I supposed to make the young gentleman wear this time?'

Yassem decides, and Uday obeys. All that Uday has in the

way of taste and style he got from Yassem. The tailor flies with him when Uday goes to London, Paris, Rome or Milan to spend an enjoyable weekend. Yassem is always there, and supplies Uday's every desire. Shoes, underwear, shirts, suits.

Normally Uday changes his suits four times a day. For conferences or conversations in the club he brings Yassem into the office as his personal dresser.

Yassem hands me the light-coloured suit, a striped shirt and a burgundy tie and asks me excitedly why Ismail isn't here. Ismail Al-Azami is Uday's personal hairdresser. He's a factotum like Yassem, and cuts Uday's hair every ten days. Uday has given him three hairdressing salons for his loyal service. He is seen as *the* hairdresser of the Iraqi capital. Ismail was also the one who trimmed my hair and beard before I went to see the President.

I dress carefully. Yassem straightens my tie. I put on my glasses, they're dirty, so I wipe them with a towel that's lying on the bed.

I feel like an actor who has learned his role *ad nauseam* – but I have no stage-fright, no butterflies in my stomach. The tension only rises when Azzam and the other bodyguards come and fetch me.

Our convoy consists of more than ten cars; this time I'm driving my Mercedes myself. We pelt through Baghdad to the stadium on Palestine Street, one of Baghdad's great boulevards. Very straight, two lanes in both directions, with grandstands on either side.

This is where the Party's tribute presentations are held.

The traffic regulations don't apply to us; ordinary drivers have to dive off to the side of the road and wait there patiently until we've passed. A convoy from the President's palace always has precedence. Munem Hammed sits next to me. He asks me several times how I'm feeling, and the closer we get to the stadium, the stronger that barely describable feeling in my belly becomes, a kind of tickling feeling, butterflies. 'So you're nervous, Latif,' Munem Hammed calls across to me as we drive into the car park and up to the entrance to the VIP box.

'Nothing's going to happen,' he says reassuringly. I open the door, and Munem Hammed reminds me: 'Uday, the cigars,' and grins. I grin back, take the silver case with the Montecristo No. 6, put it in the inside pocket of my jacket and get out of the car. While my bodyguards are making the walk to the stairs safe, I straighten my jacket and tie, and put on my dark Ray Bans. We dash towards the stairs. There are hardly any people in the car park, and the game isn't going to start for a few minutes, but my heart is starting to race. I feel it pounding, I feel it in every fibre of my body. My pulse must be higher than 130, but I try not to give a sign of my excitement.

My bodyguards hurry me to the VIP box. It's in sector A of the long side of the stadium. Upholstered chairs, artificial grass on the floors, Iraqi flags and the obligatory enormous picture of the President. I take my place in the first row, with my bodyguards sitting beside me. The 50,000 people in the stadium acknowledge my appearance with applause. No euphoric outbreaks of sympathy – they're applauding because applause is a duty when a member of the President's family enters the VIP box.

The game begins, I light my first Montecristo and smoke the way I was taught to do in my training. I pay attention to every little detail, I move my hand like Uday Hussein, and have even cut the end off my cigar with my silver cigar-cutter the way he always does. A waste of time, in fact, because the plebs are too far away to make out such details. For the people in the stadium I'm Uday Saddam Hussein, the son of the President.

I'm concentrating so hard on the task at hand that I completely miss the game. There are no climaxes, and at half-time the score stands at 0–0. The Iraqi television camera which is recording the match swings across the VIP box a number of times. I'm never captured in such a way that I appear in close up either face-on or in profile. Uday's media experts have instructed the cameramen accordingly, and Uday pointed out a number of times that there would be no close-ups, and that I was not to worry on that account.

The pilots' club team secures a clear victory. The goals are scored in the second half, but I'd be lying if I claimed to know who scored them. After the game Munem Hammed presses eleven little burgundy velvet cases into my hand. 'Give your best, Latif, think of God's help,' he says encouragingly. I am to hand the cases to the victorious players of the pilots' club. I rise to my feet like a good patriot, and wave twice to the spectators. My bodyguards bring me on to the playing field to greet the winning team. The escort of bodyguards is so dense that I barely know what is going on around me.

I'm too excited to pay attention to any details. As far as I'm concerned there's only one: handing over the cases, shaking hands, nods of acknowledgement. Not a word, not a syllable, just as I've been instructed. A bodyguard hands me the boxes, I take them and give them to the players. Strong handshake, then on to the next one. None of the players dares to ask me a question, and I'm careful not to look any of the players in the eye, although that's pointless too because I've got my sunglasses on and they can't see my eyes anyway.

It's an eternity before I've walked along the line of players. After that I briefly turn around again and wave to the rest of the spectators still in the stadium. Then we hurry back to the cars, and race back to Project Number 7.

Munem Hammed says I was very, very good, and that

relaxes me a little. I have no idea whether I really was convincing. I feel uncertain, and have no idea of the quality of my performance. It's like an encounter with a woman. You look at her, she returns your glance, and you don't know whether her glance was only friendly, or whether it was more meaningful than that.

Uncertainty. I have to overcome this uncertainty, I say to myself. It doesn't matter in the slightest whether my bodyguards think I'm good or not. What I've got to get myself is this supercilious, dictatorial arrogance. I've got to be convincingly arrogant, and then I'll have got it right. Everything else is secondary; what's important is that I keep my eye focussed on the final goal. The final goal is: I am Uday Saddam Hussein.

Uday is already waiting for me at the swimming pool. He has two brandy glasses in his hand, flies up to me and kisses me on the mouth. 'I saw you on television,' he gushes, 'you were absolutely outstanding. It was perfect. No one noticed a thing, everyone thought you were me. Everyone, including the players.'

He takes me by the arm, puts a brandy glass in my hand and says, 'Have a drink, we'll go through the video recordings tomorrow.'

The next day they wake me at eight. I just have a black coffee. Then Munem Hammed calls me into Uday's office. For the first time we don't go to the video room, but look at the previous day's recordings. And true enough, everything looks immaculate. Me in the VIP box, me waving, me handing over the presents. Uday must repeat the word *perfect* 30 times. He's proud of me, and I feel liberated, relieved. The months of training, the permanent self-doubt and Uday's constant rages – it's as though it's all suddenly been wiped away, and only one thought remains:

Latif Yahia no longer exists.

I can't help thinking about my parents. They haven't heard from me for more than six months, they don't know where I am, what I'm doing, how I am. They don't even know if I'm still alive. I could have died in the war or been imprisoned by the Iranians. They don't know. Before, I used to write my parents at least a short letter every week, or phoned them up from headquarters if I had the chance. But now? No letter, no phone-call, nothing.

I wonder how my mother is, and become quite pre-occupied with the question. I may be 24 and an officer in the Iraqi army, but my parents have always been something sacred to me, my mother a goddess. She loves me and I love her, she has a right to know what her eldest is doing, how he is.

I'm going to talk to Uday about it, but not yet, it's too early for that. On the other hand this would be an excellent moment, because Uday is really euphoric about my performance in the stadium.

But I decide it makes more sense not to make any demands for the time being; I want to enjoy my first victory and not annoy him.

Uday is devoted to pleasure. Normally he sleeps until half past ten in the morning. His bodyguards have to stay up all night guarding him.

They generally sit by the pool next to the bar, cleaning their guns, talking trivia. I gradually get to know all of them

Their boss is Azzam Al-Tikritti. Azzam is only two years' older than Uday. I remember him from school, he was always a bad pupil.

Once – after my appearance in the People's Stadium – we are sitting by the pool, drinking. After a few glasses he confides in me that he faked his documents at school. When the headmaster found out, he reported Azzam to the teachers' commission. They showed no mercy, and threw the 16-year-old in prison for 6 months. He left without graduating.

He came to Uday via Dabi Al-Masihi. Dabi was a real social animal. Whenever he showed up at the Al-Alwia Club, he always provided the atmosphere. He had a persuasive, winning manner; he was cultured, sensitive and funny, and a handsome young man with a fascinating, immaculate face. Dabi had the purest, palest skin that I have ever seen in a man.

He was Uday's friend, and also knew Azzam. He introduced the two, and Uday spontaneously declared Azzam to be his best friend and escort.

A few months later Dabi vanished without a trace, after trying to talk to one of Uday's girlfriends at a party. Uday ensured that he was excluded from the Al-Alwia Club and from now on would be ostracised from Baghdad society.

As we sit by the pool, I ask Azzam what ever became of Dabi. He lowers his head, avoids my eye and just says, 'I saw Dabi recently, he looks terrible. I don't know what they did to him.'

Uday's second confidant among his bodyguards is Ahmad Souleiman, a sinewy man of medium height. He has a degree, is a trained karate teacher and can turn on incredible charm when dealing with other people, particularly girls.

He has absolutely no inhibitions about speaking to anyone. If Uday wants to make contact with a girl, he sends Ahmad. Ahmad isn't just Uday's bodyguard, he is also his girl-finder-in-chief, a constant parasitical presence. He uses his position mercilessly, and is a brutal rapist and murderer, although I'm not to discover that until later.

The 'spy' is Salam Al-Aoussi, a walking notepad. He spies on Uday's friends and reports back on their activities. One wrong word, one thoughtless remark, and you're in Salam's notebook. And being in Salam's notebook amounts to an indictment. Salam is a slimy character, although you wouldn't immediately spot it.

The 'animal' is Muajed Fadel. He has a university degree, but is completely unscrupulous, and enjoys carrying out rapes on Uday's orders.

The 'torture specialist' is Saadoun Al-Tikritti. He has a college qualification too. The only question is what faculty it's from. Saadoun is a cold fish, willing to commit any crime.

Namir Al-Tikritti is responsible for the organisation of parties. He is closely related to Uday, and an expert in his field, which turns every party into an orgy; a master of ceremonies with a good feeling for decorations and music.

Maksud Al-Tikritti looks after Uday's phone-book, organises the master's appointments and decides which girl receives Uday's secret phone numbers and which doesn't.

Mohammed Al-Duri is the chauffeur. He collects Uday's girlfriends, is considered very discreet and is a kind of 'porter'.

But the list of Uday's friends is much longer than that; it reads like an extract from a list of Baghdad's *demi-monde*. Uday loves these murky characters. He is deeply attracted by this subterranean world, of which every shade is present in Baghdad. Worse, more extreme, more perverse – that's his motto, and after the first few months by his side I'm quite sure that he wouldn't be capable of leading any kind of normal life if he didn't think he was constantly at risk of falling victim to an assassin.

And that is a constant threat, because he has huge numbers of enemies.

In fact it gradually becomes clear to me why they recruited me now of all times. Why they were keen to find and train a double for Uday as quickly as possible, and above all before spring 1988.

The clan knew months in advance that in the spring of 1988 a crime would take place of a kind that had only been seen once in human history, and that was in the Second World War. Back then it was the gassing of the Jews. Saddam planned something similar: the use of mustard gas, against his own people.

SEVEN

Fear of Assassination

Ali Hassan Al-Majid looks like a carbon copy of Saddam Hussein. He is about the same height, he has the same stature, although with the beginnings of a belly, and the same moustache and haircut as Saddam Hussein. The only crucial difference is that he only ever appears in uniform.

Al-Majid is also from the district of Tikrit, and is Saddam Hussein's cousin. In the seventies he was a deputy officer in President Ahmad Hassan Al-Bakr's army. One particular characteristic of this NCO is his barely describable brutality. This butcher is particularly ruthless in his treatment of the Kurds.

The Kurdish liberation struggle has already been going on for decades. It isn't just restricted to Iraq, because the Kurdish people are distributed across five countries: Turkey, Iran, Syria, the states of the former Soviet Union and Iraq.

Even under President Ahmad Hassan Al-Bakr, the Kurdish Peshmergas were engaged in a furious struggle against the regime in Baghdad. They are excellent fighters. 'Peshmerga' means 'those who look death in the face'.

The Peshmerga battalions hid in the caves of the Makok mountains in Northern Iraq. It was from there that they launched their attacks on oil fields in Iraq, Iran, Syria and Turkey.

The units came largely out of Iran, and their guns came almost exclusively from the arsenals of the Iranian army.

The government in Baghdad used everything it could think of to fight the rebels: even with MIG fighters, helicopters and several divisions of ground forces they were barely a match for the Peshmergas.

In the seventies, Ali Hassan Al-Majid took part in this war. In an advance by Iraqi ground troops he was taken prisoner by the Peshmergas. He should actually have been executed, but the Kurdish leadership hesitated for too long. He bribed one of his guards, promising him the career of his dreams in Baghdad. Al-Majid boasted about his connections with Saddam Hussein.

The corrupt warder freed Al-Majid and brought him to Baghdad. But instead of carrying out his promise, he killed the warder.

The flight and the murder made headlines in Iraq. Ali Hassan Al-Majid was promoted to officer and rose quite far through the Party hierarchy. Saddam Hussein supported his cousin's speedy rise through the ranks, and held his ruthlessness in high regard.

That was in 1972, when the struggle for power between President Al-Bakr and the rising popular hero Saddam Hussein was first becoming apparent. In the end Al-Bakr was only a symbol. Saddam Hussein made the treaties. Thus, in 1975, he signed a treaty with the Persian Shah Rewza Pahlevi, who was temporarily controlling the disputed shipping rights in the Shatt Al-Arab. Baghdad withdrew its claims to the Left Bank, and in return the ruler of Tehran promised no longer to support Kurdish separatists fighting to free their region from Baghdad.

The deal gave Saddam the freedom to strike at the Kurds, who represent about 20 percent of the population of Iraq.

This was Al-Majid's moment: his troops killed thousands of Kurds, and hundreds of thousands were resettled. But Saddam Hussein could not bring peace to Kurdistan, and the conflict smouldered on.

After this first wave of killings in Northern Iraq was over, Saddam Hussein sent his bloodhound Al-Majid to the South. Saddam later made one further concession to the Shah of Persia: from 1987, Iraq would cease to grant political asylum to members of the Iranian opposition.

These Iranians lived in the South of Iraq, where the population is predominantly Shi'ite. The Shi'ites had repeatedly protested against the godless society of the Ba'ath Party in Baghdad. This protest movement was led by Ayatollah Bakr-el-Sadr.

One of his guests was Ayatollah Khomeini. He was banished from Iran under Shah Pahlevi, and went into exile in Iraq. For 14 years he had been living in the holy city of Najaf, under constant surveillance by the secret service and forbidden to spread his fundamentalist theories.

In 1978, when Shi'ite unrest increased, Saddam signed his second treaty with the Shah and banished all Iranians, including Ayatollah Khomeini, from Iraq from one day to the next. The Ayatollah was effectively beaten out of Iraq. This humiliation formed the basis for the furious hatred with which Khomeini pursued Saddam Hussein henceforward.

Khomeini went to Paris, where he began to prepare the fall of the Shah's regime.

In Najaf, Al-Majid raged on behalf of Saddam Hussein (Saddam is a Sunni Moslem): he threw the leader of the Shi'ite organisation Daawa, Bakr-el-Sadr, into jail, and did the same to his two sisters. In prison Al-Majid had the Ayatollah strangled, and the women were hanged. The official charge against Bakr-el-Sadr was incitement and an attempt on Saddam Hussein's life.

The Daawa Party was forbidden, and even its sympathisers were threatened with the death penalty. Al-Majid had large numbers of Shi'ites executed. Twenty thousand Shi'ites fled to Iran.

In 1979 Ayatollah Khomeini returned to Iran, toppled Saddam's ally the Shah and transformed Iran into a religious dictatorship.

In parallel with this, Saddam Hussein launched a political and psychological offensive with a view to inciting the Arab world against Iran. At every summit meeting he attended he warned that the Sunnis, of whom he was one, could be overrun by fanatical Shi'ites. 'Iran under Ayatollah Khomeini is a hostage of humanity,' Saddam repeated, and many Western statesmen believed and supported him.

On 22 September 1980 Saddam Hussein declared war on his mortal enemy, Khomeini. Six Iraqi divisions numbering 400,000 men invaded Iran. It was supposed to be a Blitzkrieg; it wasn't.

The war had now been going on for eight years, and although Saddam Hussein gave repeated assurances that Iraq would win, no one in the country believed it, particularly since fighting was continually flaring up in the North of the country. Iraqi Kurds who had gone into hiding in Iran started launching regular attacks against Iraq from there.

On 16 March 1988, or just two weeks after my first appearance as a double, Saddam Hussein sent Al-Majid to Kurdistan with a fiendish plan. Al-Majid was now Iraqi Home Affairs Minister and a powerful, influential man.

In order to bring the Kurdish uprising to an end at a stroke, Al-Majid had suggested that Saddam use poison gas.

And Al-Majid outdid himself in cruelty: he had mustard gas sprayed out of helicopters flying at an altitude of barely 30 feet. In the village of Halabja alone, 5,000 people died in this attack.

Women, children, old people – no one had a chance. In a radius of several kilometres everything died: trees, plants, animals, people. It was as a result of this initiative that Al-Majid earned the sobriquet of 'Chemical Ali'.

In Project Number 7 the poison gas attack was not discussed, although everyone in Iraq knew about it because pictures of its terrible effects were shown several times in the main news. I too had to keep my mouth shut, because my grandparents are from Kurdistan. Uday knows that. He hates the Peshmergas: 'A wild, murdering mountain people incited by Israel and Iran. They are sheer murderers.' That is his standard argument: 'They should all be exterminated.'

But I was accepted by Uday, despite my grandparents. I was born in Baghdad, like a hundred thousand other Kurds. We Baghdad Kurds are fully integrated Iraqis, and we are loyal to the government of Saddam Hussein. There are even some Kurds in the government.

The whole world was furious about the deployment of poison gas, and even in the President's inner circle there were some who called him a criminal.

The most violent criticisms of these criminal actions came from the chief of police, Faisal Barat. He publicly complained about Home Affairs Minister Al-Majid. The chief of police was liquidated, as were 28 of his colleagues.

Saddam Hussein personally executed another of his critics: Health Minister Rijad Ibrahim, who condemned the use of poison gas against the Kurds just as he criticised its use in the Iraq–Iran war. Ibrahim even demanded Saddam's resignation in parliament. Saddam reacted in his own way: he drew his gun, pulled Ibrahim's head back by the hair and shot him in the mouth.

And that brought an end to the ministerial session – and the discussion of Saddam as well.

Nonetheless a resistance movement formed across the whole of the country. Both the Kurds in the North and the underground fighters of the Shi'ite Daawa declared war on the regime. Dozens of assassination attempts followed, but Saddam escaped them all. In public no one heard anything about any of this.

There was one striking thing: previously Saddam Hussein had liked to be close to the people. He travelled to the smallest villages, visiting ordinary family homes, giving everyone encouragement. Admittedly Saddam always came with several hundred bodyguards, who closed off whole parts of town before his arrival, stopping the traffic. But he did show himself to the people. Such spontaneous encounters with the people then became increasingly rare, and finally came to a complete stop.

Over the past few years Saddam had always sent his fidays. This was a justified precaution: shortly before I was recruited as a fiday for Uday, Saddam's first fiday was killed in an attack by Daawa terrorists.

So the use of a fiday is anything but a private whim of Uday's. It's a question of survival for the son of the President, because an attack could happen anywhere and at any time.

Uday knows that, and it's become clearer to me since the poison attack on Halabja. Previously I had been swept away by the playboy life, but all of a sudden the events of the past few days have appeared in a different, darker light.

I don't have long to think. The Saddam family needs public appearances. Saddam's second double, Faoaz Al-Emari, is appearing time and again. I see him being used on television, and Munem Hammed always sniggers when he sees Faoaz; he looks deceptively like the President, but those in the know recognise him immediately.

My next appearance is already being prepared. It's supposed to happen on 28 April. A far more difficult task than that of visiting a football match.

Munem Hammed and Uday are sending me to the front, to the South, to the 4th Division.

Twenty-eighth April is Saddam's birthday, and festivities will be held throughout the whole country.

The 4th Division is to the south of Basra, the centre of the Daawa movement. The plan is that I will be flown there with my bodyguards in a helicopter, that I will land at headquarters, get out, shake hands with the commanders and officers and hold a brief conversation about the situation with the commander.

Yassem, the house tailor, brings me Uday's black officer's uniform, a gun, a belt. We are scheduled to set off at ten o'clock in the morning, and everything goes exactly according to plan. The helicopter flight from Saddam's private airport to the headquarters of the 4th Division takes two hours.

We land on the parade ground. Several companies have lined up, rank and file, with their commander and some of his officers. First Munem Hammed, Captain Siad Hassan Hashem Al-Nassiri and Captain Saadi Daham Hasaa Al-Nassiri climb out of the helicopter. Then my bodyguards, and finally myself.

I hurry towards the commander, Munem Hammed

introduces me and we walk respectfully along the line-up. Then the photographers come. The cameraman whose task it is to record the scene for television is a member of Munem Hammed's crew.

We are photographed for more than ten minutes, and the conversation between the commander and myself is utterly trivial: I ask how things are at the front, the commander rattles off the state of play and assures us how delighted he is that I am here and that he is thus able to congratulate the great leader Saddam Hussein on his birthday.

I am sure that the commander has never seen either Saddam Hussein or Uday in person ever before.

I concentrate on avoiding making any promises; political questions and matters of military strategy are dealt with by Saadi Daham Hasaa Al-Nassiri.

We stay on the military base for two hours, drink to the good fortune of our leader, and at 14.30 the helicopter takes off again.

We fly back to Baghdad. Uday's reaction is just as euphoric as it was after the first time: 'Fantastic.' He heaps me with words of thanks after he has looked at the video of my appearance.

'One hundred percent, once again,' he says, delighted.

After this public appearance events come pell-mell; delegations from different Arab states are announced for 7 May. They are representatives of various different sports associations, who plan to stay in Baghdad for a number of days. But Uday plans a trip to Europe which he wants under no circumstances to postpone.

His plan is a risky one: I'm to collect the delegation from the airport, greet them and take them to the hotel where the conference is due to take place.

Uday himself will open the conference. He will take part

in the discussions for two days. And then it will be my duty, once again, to say goodbye to the delegation.

Seventh of May, morning. I am sitting with my bodyguards in the reception room of the airport, waiting for the plane carrying the delegation to land, nobody but the heads of sports associations from Saudi Arabia, Kuwait, Bahrain. As I greet them, none of them notices anything, although the Kuwaiti representative puts me in an embarrassing situation. After I have shaken his hand and greeted him, he passes on greetings from my friend Fahd, and asks if he should return my greetings to him.

I have no idea who Fahd is, and I don't know that Uday has a close friend in Kuwait. Not until we're back in the car does Munem Hammed tell me about Fahd: 'Uday has known him for a long time,' says Munem, 'Fahd Al-Ahmed Al-Sabah is the brother of the Kuwaiti Emir.' Apart from that, Fahd is vice president of the international football association FIFA, chairman of the Kuwait Olympic Committee and thus a colleague of Uday, as well as president of the Kuwaiti Football Association.

After the reception at the airport I bring the group to the Olympic Club, where they will be staying. There I disappear through a back door, and Uday takes my place. No one notices a thing.

After lunch Uday disappears again, I meet him in a side room for a few moments, he tells me that 'the people bore him', and I take the group to the conference centre, the Ashtar Sheraton Hotel in Baghdad.

In the evening Uday looks after the group again, but the next morning, 8 May, he wants to fly to Europe, earlier than planned.

This creates a terrible atmosphere. Munem Hammed tries

to persuade him that it's madness, but Uday has made his mind up, and his commentary is clear enough: 'Latif is to do it, and if anything goes wrong I'll throw him to the dogs.'

In addition to the conference, another major event is planned with Uday taking part. On 9 May the Iraqi national football team is playing a friendly against a European club team. They are arriving in Baghdad on the afternoon of 8 May. It is complete chaos. The only people who don't lose their composure are my officers.

Uday is excused participation in the conference for reasons that aren't disclosed to me. I have to go to the airport again to receive the Europeans – a home game for me, because of course the sportsmen haven't the faintest idea what Uday Saddam Hussein looks like.

They are also staying in the Sheraton. At first everything's very hectic and stressful, but it all seems to be going to plan.

No one notices anything, the journalists write excellent articles about Uday and his appearances. The most detailed articles appear in *Al-Baas-Al-Rijadi* and *Babel*.

These newspapers belong to Uday; he's in charge of them. His father gave them to him, and they are the only media that are not the immediate responsibility of the Minister of Information. The director of the newspapers is Abbas Al-Janabi, who was wangled the job by Uday: as compensation after Uday raped his niece.

The friendly is being held on 9 May at four o'clock in the afternoon in the People's Stadium. The conference participants are also sitting in my box. In the stadium the spectators are frenetically cheering on our team. But the Iraqi team loses. A scandal! How can that happen? Iraqi teams must never lose.

None the less I hand out my gifts to the players once again, and invite the members of both teams to dinner in the Sheraton. I do just what I've been instructed to do.

The dinner is formal. My entourage and I only stay for a short time. Nothing special – nothing specially dreadful – happens that my escorts could have recorded in their minutes. The foreign players and the delegations stay until the following day, I say goodbye to the teams at the airport, and actually feel quite good. I think that Uday will be pleased with me when he gets back from his holiday.

Uday is in Switzerland; Geneva, his favourite place. He flies there regularly, like the Dictator's whole family. Only Saddam Hussein avoids these social excursions, which would also be much too complicated for him. He's known in Europe, while his family are unknown to the wider public.

In Geneva, Uday always stays with his uncle, Barzan Al-Tikritti. Barzan Al-Tikritti is a half-brother of Saddam Hussein's, and has had a dream career. He started as an officer, became head of the secret service and invited the PLO terrorist Abu Nidal to Iraq several times, and appeared with him in public.

But his true task lies in administering the Saddam clan's incredible wealth. For that reason he is known in Iraq as the 'secret finance minister'.

After his dismissal as head of the secret service, Barzan Al-Tikritti went to Geneva as permanent Iraqi representative of the UN. But his actual task is different; the transfer of Saddam's money from Iraq to Switzerland, as well as the acquisition of all of the country's weapon systems. Barzan is the key figure in the purchase of nuclear equipment. 'International concerns are practically knocking his doors down,' Uday stressed several times before he flew off.

Uday comes back from Geneva on 18 May. He's in a bad

mood. Milad comes with him to Project Number 7. Milad is a stewardess.

It isn't long before I learn from his bodyguards why Uday is so furious. He lost in the casino. As there are no casinos in Switzerland he took a trip to a neighbouring country.

With him were his bodyguards and his friends Muajed, Said Kammuneh, Ahmad Kola and Dureid Ghannaoui, as well as the pilot, the co-pilot, the aviation technician of his private jet and the stewardesses who work under Milad.

Uday has slept with Milad several times, and since then he has taken her along with him as head stewardess on all his European trips. Milad is tall, has long, brown hair, a big mouth with big lips and skin so pale and tender that you can even see her veins glimmering through.

Uncle Barzan Al-Tikritti was also on the casino trip.

Uday's pockets were full of dollars, certainly more than a million, because he loves gambling. 'You can only win big money if you play big stakes,' he always reasons. Sometimes he wins, too, but not this time.

Whatever combination of numbers he bet on, other numbers came up.

Uday had the croupiers switched around time and again, and even reserved a whole table for himself. Even the rule concerning the highest stakes was removed for him, which meant that Uday was able to bet more money than the other players. The higher the sums involved, the more trance-like Uday's gambling.

I've seen him like this before. He gets red patches on his face, his expression becomes rigid, the slightest thing makes him furious, raging. He simply can't bear it when something doesn't go his way.

He can't bear it if anyone contradicts him, if his will is not the supreme law.

Roulette wheels aren't impressed by that kind of thinking, and neither are croupiers with their automatic smiles. They elegantly pulled the tokens from his table, and finally Uday started writing out cheques.

Barzan Al-Tikritti tried to stop him, but Uday wouldn't listen, because he was convinced that he would win back the money he had lost. It was as though he was intoxicated, he downed one cognac after another, and finally he had lost more than four million dollars. I couldn't believe that, but everyone there assured me it was the case. Uncle Barzan wouldn't give him any more cheques and left the casino early, which made Uday even more furious.

Another gambler, also from Iraq, suggested a deal. The man had a safe in the casino. He suggested, 'I'll lend you another million, and Milad is mine for the night.'

Uday just looked at Milad for a moment and nodded, and Milad knew what she had to do. That was the first time that Uday acted as a pimp. The son of the President and President of the Iraqi Olympic Committee sold a woman so that his friend would lend him money for gambling. A scandal.

He lost this million, too.

When he comes back from his European trip, he is dragging Milad along behind him. He takes her into his office. The door stays open so that everyone can here him screaming hysterically at Milad: 'What did my friend do to you? Tell me, what?'

Milad says nothing. Uday hits her. We can hear the slaps as far away as the pool.

'What, tell me, what?'

Milad is crying. Uday hits her again, and she yells at him, 'He said you were presumptuous and arrogant. He bought me to teach you a lesson. Yes, that's what he said. I was to pass that on to you.'

Uday has Milad taken away, and we all know we will never see her again.

Then Uday comes to see me. He is ranting, he's completely incensed, and when he learns on top of everything else that the Iraqi team lost, he completely loses his temper. He hits me, ignoring my observation that there are always winners and losers. He doesn't want to listen to me, and orders Azzam to lead me away. They take me to a cell in head-quarters, and I spend almost two weeks there. It's bigger than the horrific cell where they put me before my training as a Fiday. The food is normal, and the guards treat me well.

On the 15th day they collect me again, but they bring me not to Project Number 7, but to the palace grounds of the Al-Hayat, a modern building nine storeys high. It's admini-stered by the secret service, and I get a kind of office-cum-flat there: a sitting-room with a desk, a side room with a toilet, a bathroom. My bed is in the sitting-room as well.

Uday visits me in the Al-Hayat. He's as friendly, calm and superior as ever. He comes very close to me so that I can feel his hot breath. He takes off his glasses, stares at me and hisses, 'Don't interfere in my affairs ever again. Your job is to obey me, not to talk to me.'

EIGHT

Excess

Eighteenth June 1988, a Monday. Uday has called me in the late morning, and told me he'll have me picked up in the evening. I'm to shave off my beard, just leave my moustache and put on a normal bodyguard's uniform. Although rather abrupt, his voice still sounds friendly enough.

Our differences of opinion are forgotten, and Uday has even got me a new flat: the apartment is in the palace grounds, in the Mujamaa Al-Kadesija, a house that is also used by the secret service. The flat is imposing, with a large sitting room, an office, a reception room and various side rooms. I have staff, too.

Four days previously, on 14 June, it was my 24th birthday. I didn't celebrate that birthday. What was there to celebrate? I was alone in my apartment, the staff was gone, and I strode around the flat, wondering how my parents were coping, given that my birthday was always a day of celebration for them.

This 24th birthday could have been a great party, I thought, imagining what we could have done: hire a hall in a hotel, with music, singers, dancing-girls. It would have been perfect.

Fourteenth June 1988 was a Thursday, and that's a special day in Iraq. On Thursdays most hotels and cabarets stay open all night, because Friday is a day off, the Islamic Sunday.

In all the hotels there are bars and nightclubs with singers, dancers, dancing-girls.

My friends would all have come, I said to myself, continuing my soliloquy. But at the same moment, my self-doubts returned, I couldn't help questioning my current situation. Would they really have come? They haven't heard from me for months, do they even think about me?

I drowned this growing self-pity in whisky, and that freed my thoughts again: of course they were thinking of me, and they've been phoning my parents and asking if they've heard from me. Everyone must already know that I'm lost.

So now Uday has invited me after all, and I'm pleased about that. On the phone he didn't mention what was going to happen at Project Number 7, but I can guess. No, I'm not just guessing, I know. I know Uday by now, I know he has a tendency to eccentricity. And the preparations over the past few days could hardly be ignored.

For a week, Namir Al-Tikritti, Uday's master of ceremonies, has done nothing but rearrange Project Number 7. He had champagne delivered by the case, had the chef make special dishes, and Hilal Al-Aki, a relation of Uday's, who always helps Namir Al-Tikritti when big events are planned, was forever moving back and forth between the palace and Project Number 7 to get decorations for the party.

Unlike myself, Uday has every opportunity to celebrate his 24th birthday. For years he has made 18 June a holiday, and his birthday parties were always talked about in Baghdad, because they mostly involved excesses which were not hidden from the public because Uday always celebrated in one of the clubs.

But it wasn't just his birthday parties that were escalating more and more – in fact Uday's whole life so far was one long excess, a ceaseless extravagance in the quest for his own self, made possible by the greatest financial opportunities that a person could possibly have. Uday has everything: money, power, influence. His world is one of decadence, recklessness and sin. There is no sexual morality, there is just the pursuit of pleasure.

If Uday goes a step too far, his colleagues cover up for him. If his errors can no longer be kept secret, he is protected by the powerful hand of his father or his influential mother.

Over the past few days I have thought time and again about why he became the son who went wrong, why he wants to suck in life like a drug, remaining quite unaware that his own excess of freedom is destroying him.

He was a dead loss at school, and he knew that. He knew that the teachers didn't accept him, and that he only got good marks because he was the son of Saddam Hussein. He probably didn't understand the consequences of his behaviour at the time. He was still a child, and children tend to glorify their parents. Uday glorified his father by acting in the style of his father and ordering around his subordinates, the professors. He didn't do any homework, turned up when he felt like it and went home when it suited him. He brought his girlfriends into class, his bodyguards did his dictations for him, his private teachers did his homework. He was constantly determined to prove that he was able to exert pressure on his teachers, and he could get away with it.

As a 14-year-old he roared into the school playground in his Porsche, at 15 he had his first employee, who found girls for him. At 16 he fired his Kalashnikov wildly into the air in the Al-Alwia Club and everyone applauded, probably including his father.

I carefully shave off my perfectly clipped beard and look at myself in the mirror for a long time. I open my mouth wide and inspect my new teeth, which fit very well and don't actually bother me at all. They belong to me, and by now my jaw has also got used to my slight overbite. Although I'm distracting myself by shaving, I can't stop thinking about Uday's ferocious devotion to the intemperate life, his addiction to hedonism.

He has barely changed his lifestyle for years. Every day at about two o'clock in the afternoon, after lunch, which he takes either in Project Number 7 or one of the Baghdad clubs, he and his personal guards go on their 'grand tour'. The convoy does the rounds of all the coffee-houses in Baghdad. After that they move on to the girls' schools and the universities. Uday parades up and down like a patrolman. If he likes a girl he hoots his horn, stops, drives on to the pavement and follows the girl at a walking pace until she agrees to talk to him. If she refuses, he sends one of the men he has engaged to find girls for him. If that doesn't work, he simply abducts his victim.

He needs sex almost every afternoon. Sometimes they bring three or four girls to one of his houses at the same time. Either he chooses one of them, goes to bed with her and throws the others out, or else he keeps them all and forces them to have group sex.

Uday starts drinking early in the evening. Mostly beer, cognac and whisky. Uday isn't the kind of person who just pours alcohol into himself, he drinks for the enjoyment of it. But there is hardly an evening when he goes to bed sober.

Before getting ready to go out, he has dozens of telephone calls with various girls. After that he spends an age wondering what to wear. He generally chooses whatever his personal tailor Yassem has laid out for him. But before that there are always violent discussions between the two of them.

The choice of accessories takes a similar length of time. Uday has far more than a hundred watches, and countless rings and gold chains. The contents of his jewellery boxes are quite unimaginable.

Although Uday has everything a person could wish for, he's envious of almost everything that other people have. If someone is better and more extravagantly dressed than he is, Uday has him removed by his bodyguards. If someone has a more exclusive Rolex, Uday wants it too. If someone has a better car, Uday loses control of himself.

Consequently, in the clubs Al-Darawich, Al-Said, Al-Sawarek and Al-Alwia everyone is careful not to have a run-in with Uday. Anyone who can't get out of his way would be well advised to behave obsequiously.

Things are much the same in the hotels of Baghdad. There is no hotel porter, no bar or night-club manager that Uday doesn't know.

When Uday's hordes arrive like a greedy swarm of locusts, all rules go out the window.

Uday usually appears with between eight and ten women, all of whom have to walk behind him when he walks into the hotel. His favourite hotels are the Babel Obri, the Al-Rashid and the Meridian.

When Uday walks into foyers, restaurants, bars or dance-halls, everyone present has to stand up and greet him.

If other men dare to dance in his presence, Uday sees this as an affront, and has the dancer carried off by his bodyguards, beaten up, or even, in the worst case, thrown into prison for insulting the President.

Uday wants the dance-floor for himself and his girls. He usually sends the girls alone on to the dance-floor. He only watches them greedily, occasionally shouting vulgarities at them. If he's in the mood, he takes his gun and shoots at the ceiling, the chandeliers, the walls, in rhythm with the music.

Sometimes he even shoots at the staff, particularly if they are Egyptian waiters, of which there are thousands in Baghdad. Uday hates Egyptian guest-workers. They're a plague as far as he's concerned.

On these drinking tours Uday feels big and strong and powerful. It's as though he constantly has to prove something. But who would Uday prove anything to with his self-destructive lifestyle?

His omnipotent father, who is celebrated like a god, and who has built 83 palaces throughout the country.

It must drive Uday crazy to see a picture, a statue, a heroic depiction of his father on every street corner as he roars through the country in his Ferrari. Or if he switches on the television and the loudspeaker booms: 'Saddam, the President, the supreme commander, the leader of the National Command, the hero of Kaddisiyeh, the knight of the Arab nation, Alfaris Al Mighwar – the bold knight. Saddam, the direct descendant of the Prophet. Saddam, the noble fighter, scion of a family to which the Imam Al-Hussein, the ancestor, the son of Imam Ali ibn abi Talib, belonged.'

Uday is the first son of the President. He was born into a world so absurd and unreal that a child could barely understand what was going on around him, what was happening to him. School was fun, architectural studies were a joke. He dashed his way through the phases of his life that shape other children's lives. He didn't stop in order to have his character shaped. He carried out his architectural studies in record time, with an excellent degree, in spite of the fact that he hadn't sat a single exam.

In spite of the fact that he hadn't handed in a single drawing of a house. Presumably he doesn't even know that a house needs a foundation.

I can still remember the day when all the important professors at the Baghdad universities were called to a ceremony in the Auditorium Maximum. We students were not allowed in, for fear of a possible row.

At the age of 23, Uday was appointed rector of the University. The President's son had financed the building of the Saddam Technical University. Of course he, Uday, hadn't financed the construction from his private treasury. The Iraqi people had paid for it. But officially it was said that 'Mr Uday Saddam Hussein' made the millions available.

He was not only appointed honorary director of the Saddam Technical University. One of the university professors, Mazen Abd Al-Hamid, suggested that Uday Saddam should also be elected rector of the university. The suggestion was accepted without an opposing vote. So a student who could barely string a sentence together became head of the university. It was a slap in the face for us ordinary students, and probably for the professors too, but none of them had the courage to complain. One false word in this context and they would have been removed from the university in a flash, perhaps even killed. Any criticism of the President's family was a punishable offence.

No less grotesque than his appointment as head of the university was Uday's appointment as President of the National Olympic Association. To this day he doesn't know how many players there are in a football team, what disciplines the decathlon consists of, or even when the Olympic Games are held.

While I am drying myself, and letting a time-lapse version of Uday's life story run through my head, I go into the sitting-room and make myself a drink. It's shortly after midday now, but I'm not hungry. I sit down on the comfortable sofa and make my first brief notes about Uday. I try to remember conversations and details, people I know from university, people I've met since my training.

'Munem Hammed,' I think to myself, 'is someone you can trust. He's correct, he's the only officer who can see through all this crap, and whose behaviour is at least halfway normal. He may join in with this sordid nonsense, but it pains him to do so and that makes him sympathetic.'

However I start not with Munem Hammed but with Abbas Al-Janabi. I write: 'Head of Uday's newspapers.'

I laugh as I write down Al-Janabi's name. He's a great softy, I met him once in the Olympic Club. They appointed him head of Uday's newspapers after Uday raped his niece the previous spring.

The newspapers *Babel* and *Al-Rachid* were placed under Uday's leadership because his father wanted to control the media and Uday suddenly took it into his head that he was a great writer. In a grand ceremony he was appointed chairman of the newspapers. In one of the first editorials, which I'm sure he didn't write himself but which bore his name, he even compared himself with the well-known author Al-Jawahiri, although he didn't come anywhere close to him.

In order to 'raise the intellectual level', Uday published so significant a work as the book by his grandfather Khairallah Tulfah. The title of the Ba'athist pamphlet is: *Three things that God should not have created: Persians, Jews and Horseflies.*

Khairallah Tulfah is a fixed point in the life of the Husseins. The *éminence grise* around which everything revolves. He has influenced them all, Saddam Hussein as well as Uday.

I take a new sheet.

At the top I write down the name of Khairallah Tulfah.

Then I wonder: 'Who is Khairallah Tulfah, who hated Persians, Jews and horseflies like the plague?'

It comes back to me: Khairallah Tulfah comes from Tikrit. He was an officer who took part in the uprising against the Hashemite King Faisal II in 1941. After leaving the army, he supported his clan with street-robbery and water fraud. So he started out as a little street-thief.

I jot down this association: 'Khairallah, first officer, then street-thief!'

Then comes the next step: Saddam Hussein's real father died before he was born. After his birth his mother married Ibrahim Al-Hassan, but he wouldn't have anything to do with him. At the age of nine Saddam was passed on to his uncle, that same Khairallah Tulfah.

So I write: 'Saddam passed on to Khairallah Tulfah.'

Suddenly I remember details that Uday told me about in school. But I set them aside so as not to lose the thread, and I go on spinning out my thoughts: Khairallah had a son, Adnan Khairallah. He was the only friend that Saddam had in Tikrit. When Khairallah Tulfah left Tikrit in 1955 to go to Baghdad, he took Saddam, Adnan and his daughters with him. Sajida is the eldest. According to Moslem rites, Saddam and Sajida were betrothed as children.

So I write on my notepad: 'Saddam's future wife Sajida is Uncle Khairallah's daughter.'

And on we go: the Tulfah family achieves wealth and power in Baghdad. In 1963, after the Ba'ath Party comes to power for the first time, Saddam Hussein marries Sajida Tulfah, his cousin.

In 1964 his first son, called Uday, is born. Saddam Hussein has no time to care for his son. Politics comes first. In 1966 his second son, Qusay, comes into the world.

I lean back and remember the relationship between Uday and Kusay. Even at school, Uday used to make disparaging remarks about his younger brother. Qusay was preferred by his father, mollycoddled and protected from the world. And in fact, unlike Uday, Qusay never did cause any kind of scandals during his schooldays. He was always considered the quieter one, the more balanced, the favourite son who had received much more attention from his father.

On the other hand Uday grew up with his grandfather Khairallah. So he too was passed on to 'Uncle' Khairallah Tulfah – just as his father had been in Tikrit.

And Uday constantly emphasised the close relationship between grandfather and grandson, for example when he crowed and thundered at school: 'My grandfather taught my father to kill any enemy that came his way.'

And then he would say menacingly, 'Just wait until I'm President. I'll be crueller than my father. You will often remember these words, and yearn for the days of Saddam Hussein.'

The memory awakens that oppressive sensation in me. After all I'm Uday's fiday, his serf.

I jump up, pace around, stare into the mirror that hangs on the wall by the sofa. I see Latif Yahia, who has ceased to be Latif Yahia for ten months, and is now Uday Saddam

Hussein. The double. If Uday were ever to come to power, my fate would be sealed. The people of Iraq already hate him: how much are they going to hate him if he's in charge of the country?

In fact it's all been decided already, and the clan dominates everything anyway: after Saddam Hussein's assumption of power in 1979 Adnan Khairallah became Defence Minister, and Uncle Tulfah was appointed governor of Baghdad. So Saddam gathered all his friends around him, at the summit of power.

On a piece of paper I write, 'Saddam President, Adnan minister, Uncle Khairallah governor of Baghdad.'

I'm sweating. Has the fan stopped working? Am I sweating with fear? My thoughts are exhausting me, I take another sip, set down the piece of paper, try to distract myself for a moment. I go into the bathroom and turn on the cold water. Twice, three times I splash cold water in my face. It feels good. A cool head is what you need in this situation, Latif, I warn myself.

Where does this madness come from? Why is Uday the way he is?

Uday has barely changed since we were at school. Even then, the most important things in his life were women and cars.

In order to assert himself, he always had to oppress others.

No wonder, when you think about what his grandfather was like. It's from him that Saddam inherited his tendency to violence, which he acts out in politics. Just like Uday, but he finds his safety-valve in Baghdad's high society.

But the key figure is his grandfather, Khairallah.

When Uday was 13, he was always telling us about his grandfather. How he was uncompromising in his fight against the British; how he built up the Tikriti mafia clan in Baghdad. The methods with which he tightened his net of violence and power, even though he was really nothing but a little street-thief in Baghdad.

The street-thief of Baghdad – he became a myth, a symbol, a spiritual father for Uday, just as he had been Saddam's mentor in violence.

He taught them both the law of murder.

The application of this teaching had brought Saddam Hussein to the summit of power in Iraq, and Uday knew that. It had been effectively drilled into him.

But Uday could never turn that knowledge into action. How could Uday have been better, from childhood, than his father, the President, the god, the direct descendant of the Prophet?

If Uday did something wrong as a child, he was beaten by his father with an iron rod. If he was fearful, Saddam forced him to watch videos of executions and tortures. Saddam was keen on these videos, and Uday didn't dare refuse to watch them, because cruelty is not a despicable character trait in Saddam Hussein's view of the world, but something positive.

If it all became too much for Uday, he fled to his grandfather, Khairallah. 'He understands me, he listens to me, he's interested in me,' Uday had always told us at school.

It's now shortly after three o'clock. I've got just about two hours before I'm collected to go to Project Number 7. I'm sorting out my notes, going through them point by point, when something else occurs to me.

Uday used to talk often and enthusiastically about his mother, both at school and later at university. He spoke of her as of a goddess, a fairy-tale creature, an ivory statue.

Uday's mother, Sajida, never appeared in public by

Saddam Hussein's side. She had to stand in the background and fulfil her duties as a wife and mother. In Baghdad it was an open secret that Saddam was always having affairs of various kinds. The women were always smuggled into the palace by Kamel Hannah, Saddam's loyal servant and food-taster. For a long time Saddam Hussein was able to keep it quiet, but when he had an affair with the tennis player Najida, everything came to light. Najida was the wife of the Minister of Culture and Media, Hammed Yusef Hammedi. Saddam Hussein was even supposed to have planned to leave his family for her.

At any rate it is a fact, and as a fiday I took this from many remarks of Uday's, that he, Uday, hated Kamel Hannah, his father's food-taster, with a passion: 'He brings women to my father, and it's destroying my mother,' he would cry, as he lay drunk at three o'clock in the morning by the pool in Project Number 7. He also said that his grandfather Khairallah wanted to kill the food-taster.

I spend a long time wondering who will come to Uday's party. His father and mother won't be coming. And his brother won't be there either, I'm sure of that. First of all the presence of the whole family outside of the palace would be too dangerous, because Project Number 7 can't be made as secure as the palace. And secondly, there's sure to have been a birthday dinner within the family circle over the past few days.

Not too many politicians would come, either, of course. Uday has a bad reputation; members of Baghdad society avoid the President's son, and have done for years, because they know how unpredictable he is and will do absolutely anything to avoid being drawn into an embarrassing situation that might have severe consequences.

And clearly Uday couldn't invite me, his double. Or is Uday so confident that he wouldn't care if people found out he had a fiday, I find myself wondering.

On the other hand it's no secret in Iraq that everyone in the President's family has a fiday, and that the ordinary people who are supposed to be deceived by the fidays never have the chance in any case to establish any small details. The public appearances are always such a performance that people concentrate more on the spectacle itself than on the people involved.

Almost all of Uday's personal friends have met me in Project Number 7. They are under the same obligation of secrecy as the rest of us. The same rules apply to them as apply to me: anyone who reveals anything about the President's family is a dead man.

They fetch me at about eight o'clock. We go to Uday's house. The masters of ceremonies have been hard at work. There are extravagant flower arrangements all over the place, there's a little stage with a sound and light system beside the pool. The party room on the first floor is filled with glitter. The staff are wearing radiantly white, freshly starched uniforms with gold buttons and the obligatory white gloves.

Uday only greets me in passing, saying 'Enjoy yourself.' His detached bearing is probably supposed to signal that I should stay in the background and not talk to anyone.

Everyone gradually arrives: Dafer Aref, the director of the Olympic Club. Dafer is a lickspittle of Uday's, and married to the actress Hanan Abdul-Latif. When he was a student, Uday would often have Hanan Abdul-Latif picked up by his bodyguards and brought to one of his farms outside Baghdad. She could never stand Uday, but gave into him because she had no other choice. Everyone knew at the time what Uday had done to the architecture student Nahle Sabet. Nahle Sabet had refused him; Uday raped her and threw her to his starved dobermanns and rottweilers.

Hanan Abdel-Latif greets Uday cordially, but he doesn't glance at her. She passes over that and turns to Abdel Akle. Abdel Akle is a small, curiously built man with crooked shoulders and a slack handshake. But Abdel Akle is a star in Iraq.

He is one of Uday's favourite singers, he has recorded countless records, is always on the radio, also appears on television, and is at all Uday's parties.

Abdel hasn't yet started to sing, and his band is playing pleasant instrumental background music.

Hanan Abdel-Latif sits down at a table with her husband and the singer Abdel Akle. I can't make out what they are saying, but see only that they are deep in conversation and burst out laughing a number of times.

The next person to arrive is Mohammed Al-Bhodadi, a friend of Uday's with the reputation in Baghdad of being a tireless skirt-chaser. As proof of his friendship, he made Uday a gift of his sister.

With him is Dureid Ghannaoui, the car dealer whom Uday made rich with his mania for cars.

I haven't counted them, but Uday must own more than a hundred cars: Maseratis, Ferraris, Porsches, Jaguars, Mercedes in every imaginable model and colour.

Cars are like guns as far as Uday is concerned: objects of devotion, mobile displays that are supposed to reinforce his confidence and make him into something special. In order to be sure that he is the only person in Iraq driving a Ferrari, Uday has even passed a law banning the import of Ferraris.

These cars are kept in two garages beside the Al-Hayat

block in the palace grounds. During my training as a fiday I was there a number of times, but even today I can't believe what I saw!

Dozens of mechanics have to look after this fleet and keep it in good condition. Mercedes stands next to Mercedes, in all colours, with all the latest equipment like anti-lock braking system and stereos that make you feel you're in a moving walkman, built-in bars made of polished walnut, televisions, telephones.

There isn't a single Mercedes lower than the 300 series. Almost all of them are top-of-the-range 500s. 500 SEL, the long version: six. 500 SE, the most powerful that Mercedes has to offer: ten. Open-top SL's in black, dark blue, bright red: 16. Not one of these cars would cost less than 100,000 dollars.

Then there's the fleet of Ferraris: several red Testarossas, an old Dino, four 348s. The cars gleam and flash, and there isn't so much as a speck of dust to be seen on any of them. Everything here is clinically clean, as sterile as it would be in an intensive care ward, but I doubt whether an intensive care ward would be as well equipped. The walls of the garage are tiled, the floor is specially covered.

Behind the Ferraris are the Lamborghini Countach series. Cars like aeroplanes, with top speeds of over 200 miles an hour. Uday rips through Baghdad in these cars, roaring down Palestine Street at 150 miles an hour. These luxury vehicles made him a star among his classmates even when he was at school, though I never much cared for his crazed desire to show off his wealth. It was still fascinating, though.

Uday must have got his mania for cars from his father. Saddam Hussein also has an enormous fleet of cars, although they are kept in other garages. Like his father,

Uday always drives his cars himself; he never drives with a chauffeur. As with his father, his tyres always have to squeal when he pulls up. 'Driving a car,' Munem Hammed told me repeatedly when I was learning to drive like Uday, 'is something sacred, something valuable, something special. Always remember that.'

Next to the Lamborghini sports cars are the silver-grey Maseratis. The Bi-turbos. Incredibly fast, although they don't look it. Classic sports-cars, but not turbo-driven monsters.

But the most impressive fleet is the gallery of Jaguars and Porsches. Uday has all the 911 series Porsches, in all models and colours. He's got open-tops, Targas, Porsche Turbos. He's got everything.

And it's the same with the Jaguar section: four E-types, those cigar-shaped classics, a car like a phallus. Two of them are open-tops. The burgundy-coloured pigs' leather seats are as soft and smooth as a woman's inner thigh. The spokes are gilded. The fittings are made of the finest chrome, and the engine sounds like a scud missile taking off. A few yards away there are 28 12-cylinder versions, both the latest models and British old-timers. A treasure-trove. Car fanatics shouldn't be allowed in here.

All these luxury vehicles need constant cleaning. Uday even checks the engines. He has no understanding of technology, but he loses his temper if a mechanic leaves so much as a single greasy fingerprint on the chrome cylinder-heads.

After an accident, the car isn't repaired but scrapped.

Uday tests all his new purchases for speed and performance. Before he carries out these tests, he has one of his bodyguards close off sections of the Al-Kadisya motorway linking Baghdad and Kuwait. The test itself is a ludicrous ceremony. In order to be sure that his new toy does what it's supposed to do, he organises car-races. Twenty-four hours before the test, the master instructs the head of the workshop, Tamal Al-Tikritti. New tyres have to be put on the trial car, sticky Goodyear Slicks, the kind of tyres used on Formula 1 racing cars. In addition, any 'unnecessary ballast', like the passenger seat and the back seats, has to be removed. On the day of the test itself, Uday appears in the garage, calls his bodyguards together and assigns them other cars. The trial team roars down the closed motorway in convoy.

Two cars always line up side by side. Uday sits in a Lamborghini-Countach, belted securely into the bucket-seat. Next to him stands a Ferrari Testarossa, with a serious-faced bodyguard. A referee counts down: 'Five . . . four . . . three . . . two . . . one!' Tyres squealing, the projectiles thunder off down the motorway, and who wins? Why, Uday, every time! Woe to anyone trying to beat the master! No one drives faster than Uday. The performance of the car is secondary, what's important is the 'driving ability and boundless courage' of the President's son.

The tests are followed by endless debates about road-holding, acceleration, technical details. Uday loves losing himself in technical details, although he hasn't the slightest understanding of them. He talks about oversteering and understeering, aerodynamics and slip angle curves.

Apart from his fleet of cars, Uday also has four helicopters, and he also has them designed according to various schemes in his painting unit. Uday doesn't like military colours. He wants his helicopters to look like those of Saudi and Kuwaiti princes: interior like a drawing-room, exterior like an elegant, sporty flying machine. He usually has them sprayed in his favourite colour, pale blue, with go-faster stripes.

But the high-point of the collection, the absolute incarnation of decadence, is a specially made vehicle, a one-off that only exists in the tiled garage of the Iraqi President's son: a 500 series Mercedes with a Rolls Royce engine. An Italian car manufacturer was flown in specially to Baghdad to design this amazing thing and oversee its manufacture.

It took Uday's mechanics two months to get the luxury car with the fiendishly powerful engine to work properly. The engine sounds like one of those rocket-driven racing cars used on world-record test-drives on the salt lakes of Utah.

Uday buys most of these luxury cars directly from European dealers, and Dureid just negotiates the transport. But Dureid makes a packet with each new acquisition. Money is irrelevant in Uday's life. None of his colleagues receives regular wages, myself included. At the end of my training I broached the topic of money with Munem Hammed. As a soldier, I received 22 dinars a month, a ludicrous sum: 22 dinars is barely 25 dollars. Munem Hammed gave me a tip: 'If you need money, go straight to Uday, and he'll give his paymaster instructions to give you as much as you need.' So far I hadn't taken Munem Hammed's advice. I didn't need any money. My staff supplied my food and drink, clothes were always available, and freshly washed and ironed every day. Toiletries like toothpaste, after-shave, soap and shampoo are renewed automatically, as in a five-star hotel.

Uday rushes up to greet the car dealer. He puts his arm around him and kisses him, and Dureid grins devotedly.

After Dureid, at intervals of about a minute, come Ali Asuad, Said Kammuneh, Muand Aani and Amer Aasami. These men play a special role in Uday's life. They're all involved, whether directly or indirectly, in getting hold of women and girls for Uday.

Ali Asuad is actually employed by Uday to get hold of fresh young girls from schools and universities if Uday's expeditions are unsuccessful.

Uday married him off to a girl he had previously raped.

Said Kammuneh is one of the chief pimps in Baghdad, a vile character. He controls the various bars and nightclubs, directs prostitution in Baghdad – he's the godfather of sex.

Officially Said owns an import and export business. But it seems only to be a disguise, and his chief import is probably girls. He imports them from Asia. Asian girls work in most of Baghdad's bars. Said controls these women, and Uday is involved in the trade in women. Uday invests his profits in hotels, bars, his private gambling. Said is said to own half of Baghdad.

Muand Aani is another dealer in women.

Along with the men comes a whole crowd of young ladies. They all wear wonderful, tight suits, some of them are even wearing short mini-skirts, unthinkable in other Arab countries.

But Uday doesn't care a fig for religion. He never prays, and his motto is, 'What did Allah ever give me? Nothing. Does Allah give me a single dinar? No, Allah gives me nothing. So stick with Uday, he has dinars, and that makes him greater than Allah.'

I have only seen him praying once since 1987, and that was when he visited the holy place of Al-Tekiia Al-Sufia. Of course the event was recorded by photographers and cameramen. The next day the media were full of the fact that 'Mr Uday Saddam Hussein, the great son of the President, had visited the holy place.'

Meanwhile the singer Abdel Akle has taken his place on the stage, and he will not leave it over the next few hours.

Uday doesn't want any other singers, and Abdel Akle is capable of performing for six to eight hours at a stretch.

To crank up the atmosphere, Abdel Akle starts with Uday's favourite song: 'Saddam, oh Saddam, you great and powerful man.' It's a gushing and hypocritical hymn to Saddam Hussein, which is played everywhere and all the time, but Abdel manages to bring something to the soft rhythm with its endlessly overstretched passages repeating over and over again how great and powerful Saddam is. Everyone joins in, and Uday swings his brandy glass along to the music.

He is sitting next to the stage with three women I have never seen before. He growls, drinks, growls. He's already slightly drunk. When Abdel begins the next song, Uday gets to his feet and pulls the girl in the tight dark-blue silk suit up with him. In her black patent shoes with their high, pencil heels, she is taller than he is. She has dyed her hair blond, and is wearing a lot of make-up, the way Uday likes it. Her lips are dark-red and shiny, and she has bluish powder on her cheeks, elegantly applied, and not all over the place like some other girls who look as though they've just been in a fight. She has large breasts which, when she moves rhythmically, look as though they're about to bounce out of her décolletage. Her dress is low-cut, and presses her smooth, white breasts rather obviously together.

'Dancing is like fucking,' laughs Uday.

Uday take the blonde in his arms, she closes her eyes and yields lasciviously to the rhythm. She writhes like a snake, her hips swaying in a circle, her belly trembling and thrusting with her pelvis as though she could already feel Uday inside her. Rhythm, sweat.

Uday dances with her twice before leaving her where she is and choosing another girl who is also a fabulous dancer.

Uday moves without elegance or grace, he isn't a streamlined jaguar on the black marble by the pool, more like a bulldozer, barging into everybody. But no one says anything, because Uday is clearly enjoying himself, and that's the point of it all.

He grabs the woman, presses his mouth to hers, his body against her body. He licks her face, his tongue is everywhere, and she doesn't like it. But she just giggles and everyone watches and laughs as well. Then she rubs herself along him, writhing as she does so. Uday groans theatrically and shouts, 'I love your mouth. I love your hair, I love your nose – I have to have you.' And he grabs her by the hips, reaches for her firm buttocks, pulls her to him and jerks his pelvis like a dog on heat. He roars with laughter and says, 'I don't know another arse like yours.'

The buffet is open.

The guests are asked upstairs to the party-room for dinner. The masters of ceremonies have acquitted themselves perfectly up here, too, and, with Jakob Al-Masihi and Said Al-Masihi, have conjured up a buffet that's a match for anything in the Rasheed Hotel. Jakob Al-Masihi is Uday's personal cook and food-taster, while Said Al-Masihi always accompanies Uday on his foreign trips.

On a table that must be 60 feet long, hundreds of different dishes have been elegantly constructed. In the middle is an Iraqi eagle made of butter, and around it melons, peaches, nectarines, apples, oranges, grapefruits, strawberries, pineapples. In among them are exotic fruits that I don't know, that I've never seen before. They have probably been specially imported from Kuwait for this evening.

On the left-hand side of the table stand the cooks, lined up like tin soldiers. In front of them flash the shining silver pots with the gold handles, engraved with Iraqi eagles.

There's something of everything, Arab, Chinese and European dishes. Pink duck-breast on red peppers, turkey-breast roulade with chicken-liver sauce, hare in a pepper sauce. The cooks cordially offer up their delicacies, asking whether they might create a menu, or whether the guests would rather choose for themselves.

The cold buffet is equally imaginative: salmon on silver trays, three different kinds of caviar in silver bowls. Transparent red salmon caviar. Silvery beluga, cleanly arranged on crushed ice. Shelled lobster and open oysters. Pale French foie-gras, Italian Parma ham, carpaccio, pink roast beef with various sauces, Barbary duck with plums and kiwi-fruit, sliced chicken and blinis with caviar. Salmon tartar, smoked trout mousse, asparagus salad with fresh herbs and shrimps. Between the dishes are artfully arranged vegetables, and carrots carved into the shape of roses, lemons and radishes cut into spirals, as well as the whole palette of Arab delicacies.

As instructed, I keep in the background, I avoid conversations and try not to catch anyone's eye. I push my way through the crowd and wander aimlessly about. Every time a waiter approaches me and holds out a tray of champagne glasses, I take one. I drink calmly, not hastily. I want to keep a clear head.

Abdel Akle sings without a break, and he must have performed the hymn to Saddam Hussein ten times now.

By now Uday is completely drunk, staggering through the crowd, and probably seeing everything through a kind of purple haze.

The girls are actually clinging to him. If another man wants to ask one of them to dance, he sees it as an impertinence, even though he can't actually dance with ten girls at the same time.

As I walk around the room I spot Ahmad Fadel. Ahmad is a lieutenant in Uday's troop of bodyguards and a dangerous man. If something goes against his will, he takes his gun and shoots, regardless of whether it's a man or a woman. He treats prostitutes like filth: 'They're scum.'

Deep in conversation with Ahmad is Hassan Sabti. Hassan is a goldsmith and a gold designer. No one seems to know if he's actually any good at it, but Hassan is Uday's friend, so people buy from him. Hassan is standing next to a tall, slim woman. She is wearing a pink pullover embroidered with pearls and a pink silk skirt. A beautiful woman.

It's already long after midnight, and the party is turning into an unbridled revelry. Uday is actually lying on top of the women, with Amer Aasami beside him. Amer is the son of a pimp, a transvestite. He has breasts like a woman, moves like a woman, dresses like a woman. He's lascivious, noisy and vulgar, shrill as a tropical bird. Uday is fascinated by him, because there's something of the animal about Amer. His whole person, everything about him shrieks about open, uncompromising sex. Uday loves having Amer beside him, he loves touching him. For him, Amer is indecency personified. Uday even had him released from military service so that he could be constantly by his side. Amer isn't the only bird of paradise in Uday's circle. Another member of his immediate entourage is the transvestite Issam Malla.

Issam Malla is the only person who has dared openly to insult Uday. Everyone knows that he has a relationship not only with Uday, but also with Sabaani, a young, fit secret service careerist. Issam Malla loves the secret service man, but he doesn't want to give up Uday, because he's his life insurance.

'Tear the whores' clothes off,' shouts Uday. Uday's friends

take it as an order: they harass the women, most of whom are now drunk, through the building; the prostitutes giggle and screech as the men rip their clothes off and throw them into the pool. Uday disappears into his room with two women – the room where I spent several months. He leaves the door open, doesn't even draw the curtains, and everyone by the pool can watch as he ties the women up, and beats them with his electric cable while looking repeatedly at the television. He has put a porn video in the VCR, so there are now sadistic pornographic scenes on the screen, men pleasuring themselves with leather-clad European women, who creep around in front of their 'trainers' and enjoy being tortured. Uday loves these video tapes, he has hundreds of them.

While Uday is amusing himself on the black silk sheets in his room, the birthday party turns into a wild orgy. The only people who aren't naked are the waiters in their white uniforms with the starched collars. The guests are even coupling in the toilets, standing up, and watching themselves in the baroque mirrors.

NINE

The Murdering Begins

After this party I don't hear anything from Uday for several days. No tasks, no training, nothing. Just waiting. I don't even know whether he's still in Iraq, or whether he's flown to Europe to recover from his birthday party. Only Munem Hammed phones every now and again.

To kill time I play poker with the secret service officers for small stakes. I don't know why, but I keep winning.

By talking to them I also discover something about the organisation of Saddam Hussein's security organisation.

Saddam divided his guards up into three units. Each one has to carry out its own tasks and missions, and the first troop always monitors the second, and the second the third.

The whole system is supposed to check and monitor itself at all times, so that it's impossible for potential assassins to creep into the group, as no one trusts anyone else and any changes must be reported immediately.

The first troop consists of officers that Saddam Hussein has known for years, and has either observed himself or placed under observation by men that he trusts. These officers escort Saddam wherever he goes, they are always nearby, even standing guard outside his door when he goes to the toilet.

They either belong to the Tikriti family or come from the area around the town of Tikrit. The group numbers between 1,000 and 1,200 men.

They are all masters of martial arts, and they have all had special training. They are also extremely well armed. Lower-ranking officers carry a high-calibre revolver, a machine-gun with two magazines and three or four hand-grenades on their belts. They have access to all the information services, have a high-tech walkie-talkie system with its own frequencies, and wear bullet-proof vests under their uniforms. Not heavy vests made of porcelain, but light ones made of carbon fibres that give far greater protection than conventional vests.

In normal service, the higher-ranking officers only need to carry a revolver or a pistol. They are considered privileged, and employed for life, as long as Saddam Hussein remains in power and they remain loyal and devoted to him. They earn vast amounts of money, and a new car every six months. If they don't want a car, they are given either financial bonuses or land and houses. A special administrative division deals exclusively with the award of presents and bonuses to these men and their families.

Anyone who wishes to rise to this first group must have an immaculate secret service career behind him. The commander of the first troop is the President himself.

The second brigade basically has a similar structure. In this one, too, most of the men are from Tikrit, the lower ranks have to carry machine-guns and hand-grenades, the higher-ranking officers carry handguns.

They're permanently on call. If men from the first department are killed or injured, a group automatically joins them from the second contingent.

There is no other chance of promotion to the first group. Only when a place has become free there does one rise to the higher and more attractive protection force.

It's a very tough system, and it means that the men from the second unit are waiting like vultures to get their chance. They spy, observe, record. Of course infringements of discipline lead automatically to expulsion from the first group. It's like a self-regulating measure. Almost everyone keeps secret archives about the activities of his comrades. Every instance of excessive drinking, every visit to a brothel – everything is recorded and monitored and employed to outmanoeuvre one's rival.

Saddam Hussein enforces this system of falsehood and denunciation as much as he can. He is constantly trying to play his people off against one another, and even to heap his enemies with praise. The better-known his victim, the greater the honours he shows him.

This was the case, for example, with General Salah Al-Kadi. In 1982, in Basra, Salah Al-Kadi had ordered his troops to retreat. Saddam, who considered this position untenable, had him discreetly killed the following day, and then gave him the title of a 'martyr'. His family, to whom he personally expressed his condolences, received all the favours associated with the title: a car, a plot of land and a long-term interest-free bank loan.

'Once,' my fellow-poker players tell me, 'the President had twenty-one senior Party officials and a hundred-and-eighty officers executed.'

They were supposedly guilty of conspiracy. The cameraman Chaker Yassin filmed the bloodbath; his films are actually used in the psychological training of Saddam's protection forces.

They show the following scenes: hundreds of officials are

sitting in the Party leadership's big Khulde Hall ('Hall of Eternity'). They're all there. All of a sudden Saddam Hussein walks into the hall. As elegant as ever, with a fat cigar in his right hand. He orders the secretary of the command, Abdul Hussein Machadi, to come to the microphone. The secretary is in a terrible state, as though he has just been tortured. Saddam shouts at him: 'Speak, reveal the deed of shame.' Abdul Hussein Machadi utters a series of names, and after each name is mentioned, Saddam yells, 'Out! Go!' The bodyguards are seen leading the men away.

The men are brought to the gardens of the President's palace, and lined up blindfolded against a wall. With the camera running, Barzan Al-Tikritti, Saddam's brother and current UN ambassador in Geneva, directs the execution. Before this happens, the condemned men are forced to wear red football shirts. Barzan Al-Tikritti has had the brilliant idea of dressing the victims in red, in the ancient Ottoman tradition.

The condemned men are shot not by the bodyguards, but by members of the bodyguards' families.

The video shows two children standing next to Barzan Al-Tikritti: Barzan's eight-year-old son, Mohammed, and Uday, who was just fifteen. Barzan says to his eight-year-old son, 'Take this pistol and choose the one you want to kill.' And the boy fires.

My fellow-poker players describe these video scenes down to the smallest details, as though they wanted to say, 'You don't mess about with the Issaba, the band. They'll make short work of you. All members of the protective troops are potential killers.'

By some way the biggest is the third protection force: the Republican Guard. The Republican Guard are recruited from the districts of Tikrit, Baghdad and Ninana. The guards only take people recommended by the secret service or the Ba'ath Party. They must be from good families loyal to the Party; no family member may ever have been found guilt of any crime.

There are more than ten battalions in the Republican Guard; each unit has been trained in the use of all weapons. They are the elite force of the Saddam regime.

The chief task of these guards consists in making sure that the places that Saddam visits are entirely secure. Forty-eight hours in advance the commander of the first protection force is informed of three destinations. He passes this information on to the head of the Republican Guard, and surveillance units are immediately put into operation. Then whole districts are cordoned off, searched, with a member of the Guard on every street corner.

Saddam doesn't decide which destination he's headed for until as late as possible. His entourage travel in ten identical Mercedes limousines. The limousine in which the President himself is to travel is also decided at the last minute.

Ambulances equipped with mobile operating theatres and blood supplies follow the convoy.

When he is visiting the front, Saddam chooses his helicopter or a Boeing. He also decides which type of vehicle it is to be at the very last moment.

In order to test his pilots and escorts on flights, Saddam is forever thinking up new and more refined tricks.

Before an official trip he once ordered his escorts to turn up at the airport in heavy winter clothes. They all arrived in thick shoes and fur coats and fur hats. Only Saddam turned up in a light-coloured summer suit.

'Why?' he was asked. 'Aren't we going to Moscow?'

To which Saddam replied, 'No, we're flying South.'

On his rare visits to the front, the Republican Guard always ensures that all weapons and ammunition are removed from all soldiers and officers before the President turns up.

The Republican Guard have at their disposal all the weapons that are used in the regular Iraqi army. Their pay is six times higher than that of a normal soldier. And at every opportunity, such as the President's birthday, they are heaped with gifts.

While the Republican Guard have their own barracks, the first two groups live and train in the palace grounds. They have their own gymnasiums to practise their exercises, their own shooting clubs, in which I myself was trained, their own canteens and a leisure area with billiard tables, bowling alleys, cinemas and table-tennis tables.

All of this equipment is available for me to use as long as I keep Uday's bodyguards constantly informed as to my whereabouts.

It makes my isolation easier to bear, and it also means that I'm always picking up new snippets of information. For example, I learn from a bodyguard that after the party Uday flew to Geneva to see his uncle Barzan Al-Tikritti in Geneva, and came back to Baghdad yesterday with a sensational announcement: at the United Nations in Geneva, Barzan Al-Tikritti has ceasefire negotiations with Iran into a new stage.

On television they are still showing the glorious deeds of our army at the front, but in truth we all know that Saddam has not accomplished his military goal, even despite the use of poison gas. At first our troops may have advanced deep into Iran, but they couldn't hold their positions. Our men are happy enough as long as the Iranians don't advance into our territory.

What do these negotiations mean, I wonder, is the war over now?

It isn't over, it's just stopped for a while.

On 18 July 1988 I am called to Project Number 7 early in the morning. This is very unusual, even unique. I've never been summoned there at this time of day.

I get a move on, and my chauffeur takes me to Uday at top speed. Bakr Al-Nassiri, the house administrator, is already waiting for me. He's excited, everyone there is excited. Uday most of all: 'We've won the war, they've signed.'

We later hear on the news what Uday means by that. After long and tough negotiations, Barzan Al-Tikritti agreed to UN resolution 598, and signed the ceasefire treaty with Iran. This brings to an end the longest conventional war fought by two sovereign states in the 20th century.

Uday is almost beside himself with joy. He puts on the tape of the Abdel Akle song about his father and turns up the stereo to top volume. He throws his arms around us, hugs us, kisses everyone.

Uday declares himself, his father and Iraq to be victorious, and we agree with him. 'Iraq has wiped the floor with the fundamentalists in Tehran.'

In fact the war has ended with a pact. Our forces are practically in the place they set off from in September 1980. Saddam had started the war because he wanted control of the Shatt Al-Arab, and in his boundless megalomania he wanted to prove that he was the greatest Arab leader of all time.

In 1979, Saddam had seen the fall of the Shah and the assumption of power by Saddam's deadly enemy Ayatollah Khomeini in Tehran as the only chance for Iraq to become the dominant power in the Gulf, and for himself to achieve immortality.

In Project Number 7 my doubts are, of course, quite irrelevant, and I'm careful not to give so much as a hint that might dim the sheen of our 'victory'. Uday has a waiter bring us champagne. Cold, sparkling champagne. We clink glasses, hug, clink glasses again.

Gradually large numbers of Uday's friends arrive, among them Dr Mahmoud Samrani. He is responsible for the preparation of interviews and newspaper transcripts, and directs all the interviews and meetings in which Uday is involved. Uday withdraws for a discussion with Dr Samrani, and then they both leave Project Number 7 for three hours, probably to give interviews.

The following days and weeks are filled with parties and drinking. The whole of Baghdad is celebrating, there are millions of people in the streets, no one can bear to be at home. It's like when Saddam Hussein came to power. Strangers are hugging and kissing one another with pure joy.

The absolute climax comes on 8 August. The end of the war is announced at midnight. All factories have been put at a standstill. It's a pointless decree, since no one is working at that time of day anyway.

Saddam's court painters and propaganda specialists have used the past few days to polish up the image of the great general Saddam Hussein. Whole armies of workers are busy preparing new pictures of Saddam and distributing them around the country.

In the early days of the war with Iran, Saddam had suddenly styled himself as a great military leader. He had hundreds of different uniforms tailored for him, and appointed himself Army Field-Marshal. Everywhere you looked in the country you saw huge images of Saddam, whether as a fighter in a trench, as a pilot or a battling Saladin.

He ensured that the myth of the successful warrior Saddam was spread far and wide, until he became the personification of war for everyone in Iraq.

But when the casualties mounted and Iraqi troops could no longer hold the Iranian bases they'd managed to conquer, the warlike images were swapped once more for normal images of Saddam: Saddam in a suit, Saddam with children, Saddam as a good Moslem, in the headscarf worn by the Southern Arabs, Saddam in Kurdish national costume.

Now that it's all over, the strategy can be changed once more. And once again the advertisers are presenting the President as a military genius. Over the past few days, posters have been going up all over the place showing Saddam as a brave fighter and a beaming victor. Hundreds of such pictures are appearing in all the papers. In some editions, his image is on almost every page.

And it's the same on television: Saddam here, Saddam there. His personality cult is unlimited now. You would almost get the feeling that the President had been taken in by his own propaganda.

Uday orders me to fly to the southern city of Basra on 8 August. I'm to visit the 3rd and 7th Units to congratulate the soldiers on their glorious victory. We go by helicopter, as we did before. This time I'm not in civvies, but in the black uniform bearing the monogram of Uday Saddam Hussein.

Some of my bodyguards had already travelled to Basra the previous day, taking a number of trucks laden with toys and presents. By the time our helicopter lands the companies are already lined up on the parade ground. We walk up and down the ranks with the commanders; I don't deliver a speech, but I pass on the President's greetings to the officers, and hand on decrees that Munem Hammed has issued to me.

The official visit to the soldiers is followed by the unofficial part. I am to leave the barracks' grounds and make contact with ordinary people. The 'ordinary people' have already been rounded up by my guards. There are perhaps three to four thousand people. Children, women, old people, hardly any men.

They shout 'Long live Saddam Hussein! Long live Saddam Hussein!'

The women sing and screech and keep bursting into cries of 'Long live Saddam Hussein!' My bodyguards surround me, and we march in a group towards the children standing in the front row with Iraqi flags. By now the trucks have driven up as well. My bodyguards hand me three packages, which I press into the dirty hands of the little children with the big dark eyes. I ask them how they are. Meanwhile the soldiers have started distributing the presents from the trucks. They just throw the packages to the people.

All of a sudden a shot rings out.

I have no idea where the shot came from, who fired it, or who it was meant for. My bodyguards dash towards me, form a living protective shield, hurry me over to the car and push me in. We dash back to the 7th Unit, where we climb into the helicopter and fly back to Baghdad as quickly as we can.

It's only during the flight that I learn by radio what had happened.

It was an attempt on my life.

I take several deep breaths, realise I'm drenched in sweat, and suddenly understand the danger I was in. That bullet could have killed me.

I lean back, stare at the back of the pilot in front of me, and allow myself to be distracted by the clatter of the rotor blades.

Then we have another radio announcement, the co-pilot writes it down and calls this new message out to me as well.

'They got Abdullah Al-Dalimi, a serious wound to the chest.' Abdullah Al-Dalimi is one of the youngest bodyguards, perhaps 18 or 20 years old. He was standing right beside me, and he was the one who caught the bullet that was meant for me.

'Will he make it?' I shout back. The co-pilot shrugs his shoulders and shouts, 'I don't know!' A third radio message informs us that the perpetrator has been overpowered and arrested. He is a young Iraqi deserter, 23 years old. Two of his brothers have been killed in the war.

In Baghdad I write a detailed report about the attack, and present it to Uday. He isn't interested in it, so I pass it on to Munem Hammed, and his reaction is icy cold. He orders the attacker to be shot immediately.

Thereis no trial, no interrogation of the prisoner.

The execution is carried out the following day. That's the end of the matter, and Munem Hammed asks me not to mention the assassination attempt again, and not to make a fuss about it. I agree.

For Uday, the whole business in Basra is clearly of no interest whatsoever, it's as though it had never happened. He's just interested in the celebrations in Baghdad, the triumphal processions in homage to the 'great victor Saddam Hussein'.

Despite all security precautions, Uday wants to be present at these unbridled celebrations. He wants to enjoy his triumph to the full.

We drive in convoy into the district of Al-Mansour. There are still thousands of people on Palestinian Street. There's a noisy great crowd, everyone's relaxed, the whole of Baghdad feels happy and liberated. Uday is sitting in an armoured Mercedes with a sunroof, and this time he is being driven by a chauffeur. He has a Kalashnikov in his left hand, and his revolver in his right.

When we turn into crowded Palestinian Street, Uday stands up in his Mercedes, stretches his torso out of the sunroof, points both guns at the sky and fires one salvo after another into the air. His bodyguards hold their Kalashnikovs through the opened windows of the car and fire until their magazines are empty.

From the security point of view, Uday's action was sheer madness.

Hundreds and thousands of people in that street were armed, and Uday was a perfect target when he stood up in his car and fired.

And anyway, with everyone else firing their guns into the air at the same time, Uday's volleys were completely drowned by the general hubbub.

In Europe you might let off fireworks to express your exuberant relief and joy. But Arabs prefer to use their guns. It's normal for us to fire salvoes of joy into the air. I too stick my gun out of the car window and fire until I have to reload. We drive through Baghdad for three or four hours, firing out of our cars and cheering. Even Saddam Hussein can't keep himself from driving through Baghdad in a convoy that night, and taking part in that orgy of shooting.

The spectacle continues for several days: motorcades push their way through the city, and the drivers and their passengers hold their guns out of the car windows and fire. These orgies of gunfire have a habit of getting completely out of hand, so Iraqi television often carries announcements calling for greater care. Several people have been injured and killed by crossfire.

People ignore these warnings, because shooting is like a

drug for them, an expression of their boundless delight in victory.

And why should the people behave any differently from their leaders? Uday must fire more than 10,000 cartridges on his triumphal drives through the city.

Sometimes our convoy also passes the street where my parents' house stands. I see the front door, my father's white Volvo, my brothers' cars. I'm only a few yards away from the people I haven't seen since September last year.

I hope I might bump into one of my brothers, my mother or my father. They might just be leaving the house or coming home, I think to myself. Then I would at least see them, because making contact with them would be impossible. It is strictly forbidden for a car to leave the convoy or even to stop unless Uday orders it to do so. All I could do, therefore, would be to wave and hope that someone might spot me.

But every time we drive along it the street is completely empty. None the less, that day I finally decide to talk to Uday and ask him if I can visit my parents.

I speak to Uday in the early afternoon of 14 August. His reaction is not at all what I expected. 'Latif,' he says, 'you've been with me for eleven months now, you've given one hundred percent in carrying out your duties. You are a good man.' Then he reveals to me that over the past eleven months I have been under constant surveillance, although I've never been aware of it. 'You haven't made a single mistake, so . . .' Uday assumes a considerate expression, 'you can see your parents.'

'When?'

'Tonight, if you want,' he replies, 'but talk to Munem Hammed first.'

Munem Hammed gives me very clear instructions for my visit. 'Not a word about your task, not a whisper about Uday, no hints, no hidden references, nothing. Is that clear, Latif?'

I nod.

The visit is fixed for eleven o'clock in the evening. I'm not allowed to phone my parents beforehand, but the secret service men tell me that my parents, my sisters Gallalha and Juan, and my brothers Jotie, Robie and Omeed are at home. This tells me that my parents' house is under surveillance as well.

At exactly eleven o'clock we drive up in front of our house in Al-Aadameed. I ring the bell, and my mother opens the door.

The light from the lamp is so faint that at first she doesn't recognise me. Apart from that, I'm wearing a dark djellaba, a piece of clothing that I would never have dreamed of wearing before because I preferred western clothes.

'It's me, your Latif,' I say, and throw my arms around my mother.

I feel her tensing, taking my head in both hands, almost pulling my hair. She wants to say something, but her voice breaks. She weeps, kisses me, and I feel her tears. I have trouble controlling myself, and bustle her into the house. My father and brothers and sisters dash out from the drawing-room when they hear my mother's sobs.

It's an indescribable feeling, having my family around me again. We hug for ages. I kiss my father, Juan, Gallalha, Jotie, Robie and Omeed.

We say nothing for minutes, we just kiss each other and stare at each other, and for the first time in many months tears come to my eyes. I can weep.

It's 20 minutes before we have calmed down enough to go and sit in the drawing-room. My mother hurls accusations at me. She tells me how she spent weeks desperately making phone calls, trying to discover whether I had been killed in battle or imprisoned by the Iranians. 'They didn't give us any information, all they ever said was that you had been picked up and taken away a year ago. Latif, my son, we have prayed for you, because we couldn't believe that you were still alive.'

And once again my mother bursts into tears. My sisters put their arms around her and try to comfort her, but she won't be consoled.

Now my father speaks for the first time. He is struck by the change in my teeth: 'What have they done to you, son?' he asks. But I shake my head and answer, 'Don't ask me, I can't tell you. I can only say that I'm well and that I've got an interesting job to do.'

'What job's that, Latif?' my little brother Robie interjects, 'are you a spy?'

It makes me laugh, we all laugh, and I repeat my little motto: 'I can't tell you, so stop asking questions. And don't talk to anyone about it, just tell my friends that I'm well.'

I'm allowed to stay with my family for two hours. At one o'clock I have to go again, that was the arrangement. My family walks me to the door; they watch my bodyguards picking me up, taking me to the Mercedes, and look on as we vanish into the night. I feel good, I feel liberated, and remember every detail, every word, every laugh of my sisters and brothers, my mother and my father. It was a lovely evening. I never lost control, I didn't say a word out of place, I didn't drop any hints, no one knows what I do. Perhaps my father has guessed something, I think to myself, because he spoke to me about my overbite. But he never mentioned the name of Uday. He knows the rules.

Four days later we head for Al-Habaniya with Uday. Al-Habaniya is about 50 miles west of Baghdad, and is a favourite destination for the Iraqi smart set when they go on outings; a tourist spot, a love-nest for honeymooners. There are discreet hotels here, a lake with all kinds of water-sports, restaurants.

Uday hasn't got a villa here, but he knows the area like the back of his hand. His father is a passionate hunter, and always used to bring Uday here to hunt deer. Saddam taught Uday how to kill a deer, and how to open up the dead animal. 'Some days,' Uday tells me on the way, 'we would shoot up to twenty deer. My father loves killing.'

During that short holiday, Uday went completely out of control. He spent his days doing nothing but enjoying himself beyond measure. He slept until about noon recovering from the previous day's alcoholic excesses.

After that came breakfast, then a conversation with Yassem. They discussed what Uday would wear, which of his hundred or so Rolex, Breitling, Patek-Philippe or Cartier watches he would put on. The most expensive item in Uday's collection of watches is an IWC Grande Complication from Schaffhausen in Switzerland. The watch is made from platinum, a complicated system of 659 individual parts and nine hands. It's a classic, worth more than a Ferrari Testarossa. After putting it on, he would always go to the Olympic Club, a tall building near the People's Stadium.

One thing is certain: once he got there, Uday wasn't organising sporting events. Under his leadership the club degenerated into a mixture of office, bar and amusement arcade. Uday's pimp friends go in and out, and some of them have set up their own offices there. The secretaries look like bar-girls, which is what most of them are.

Uday usually stayed at the club until one o'clock in the afternoon, then he went home and had spicy meat for lunch. After that he started drinking. Brandy, whisky, beer.

Then he directed his girlfriends to the various houses he

owns. Either his dream villa right next to the Olympic Club
or his house in Habbaniye, or one of his palaces in Mansour
or Al-Azmiye. Sometimes he would withdraw with the
women to his farm in Al-Rashdiya.

The evenings would always end up in one of the clubs in
Baghdad or the bars of the various hotels. After the war, it
was as though Uday wanted to drink and fuck himself to
death.

In Al-Habaniya we occupy several suites in the honeymoon
hotel of Al-Medina. The hotel has a majestic swimming pool
and elegant, well-tended gardens with lush green plants.

When Uday travels to Al-Habaniya, his bodyguards bring
his 'toys' along in a truck: a black Honda 750 with
magnificent chrome chassis and engine. Several BMWs.
Uday didn't like BMW cars, but he was fascinated by the
1000cc motor bike. Two Harley-Davidsons. A chopper.

Uday was always saying that he wanted to go hunting. But
his kind of hunting consisted of roaring through the
beautiful landscape on his motorbike, and, if he saw
someone out walking, drawing his gun and firing at the
people's feet. Uday's greatest pleasure came when they fled
in panic and he was able to go on firing at them from behind.

'Fishing' was much the same: Uday owns several water-
scooters, rapid Japanese mini-motor-boats made by Yamaha
and Kawasaki, which make a terrible noise.

For hours we dash across the lake on our scooters, and
Uday gestures to us to stop in the middle. We all stop and
switch off our engines, and from then on we have to be
quiet. When the water has calmed somewhat, Uday tries to
get fish out of the water. Of course the noise of the engines
has scared all the fish away, but he doesn't care: all of a
sudden he fires his gun into the water and shouts, 'I'm going

to get you, believe me, I'm going to get you, you little beasts.'

Furious that he hasn't hit a single fish, he orders us to jump into the water and swim back to the shore. None of us dares to contradict him. We jump into the clear water in our bodyguards' uniforms, swim back, and the water-scooters are picked up later on.

'I've got to educate you,' Uday explains to us when we reach the shore, exhausted.

We indulge in these ludicrous leisure activities for two or three days. Every now and again we go hunting for ducks, and each of us has to shoot down at least one duck. Saddam likes duck-hunting as well. He's an excellent shot, and often trains in his private shooting club. 'Once,' one of our bodyguards remembers, 'Saddam was hunting for duck with his political adviser. He handed his rifle to the secretary and said, 'You see that bird up there on the tree. Kill it.' When he refused, Saddam yelled at him, 'What? You've been a Ba'athist for twenty years and you can't kill?'

The ducks we shoot are fed to Uday's fighting dogs. On the way back from our duck hunt, Uday sees a young couple in the park in front of the house. They are clearly newlyweds, walking hand in hand through the gardens.

Uday likes the look of the young woman. He stops for a moment and calls out something to the couple, but they both stroll on as though they hadn't heard Uday's call.

That's an affront to the President's son. Uday dismounts, and nods to his bodyguards to come wth him.

I know what's going to happen now. Uday wants to have that woman at any price, regardless of whether she's pretty or ugly. He's greedy, and he's probably been made even greedier by the fact that the couple didn't react when he called to them. He hates people trying to stand up to him.

The couple notice us and quicken their pace, and Uday

starts running. His escort runs too. Uday overtakes the couple, takes the girl by the upper arm and says, 'You're much too good for a simple man like this.' The man is wearing a uniform, he's a captain.

'Come on, forget about him, I suit you much better. Come up to my suite.'

Until that moment the officer stands next to his wife, as though petrified. But now he yells at Uday, and is about to hurl himself at him. The bodyguards hold him back, beat him up and drag him away. He yells and tries desperately to fight them off, but he has no chance against the six bodyguards.

They drag the two of them into the foyer of the Al-Medina hotel. The man shouts and rages, but every time he tries to pull himself away, one of the bodyguards starts hitting him, in the face, the stomach, the kidneys. They aren't worried in the slightest about the fact that the spectacle is taking place in front of the whole hotel staff and the other guests. Everyone sees what's happening here. I'm ashamed, I feel sorry for the man, but what am I to do?

Uday has the young woman brought to his suite, and we follow him. In the lounge he tries to reassure the woman, who is too frightened and horrified to utter a word, and just goes on stammering that she got married the day before. He offers her a glass of whisky, she refuses it, and he asks her if she'd prefer champagne. She shakes her head again, fights back tears and cowers on the couch.

All of a sudden Uday's voice changes. Suddenly it is a hysterical shriek. His shriek is just as striking as his heeheehee staccato laugh. He yells at the woman to undress. She pleads, 'No, please sir, no,' but her desperate pleas only make Uday all the more furious. In front of our eyes he pulls out his belt, rolls the buckle end around his right hand and strikes the woman in the face with it. The woman screams and tries to run away, but Uday goes after her, catches her, throws the belt around her neck and pulls it until she chokes. Then he loosens it again. She falls on to the floor, begs him to leave her in peace, not to dishonour her. But he grabs her by the hair, pulls her behind him into the bedroom and throws her on the bed like a sack.

Uday goes on beating her until she bleeds; he is breathing heavily, intoxicated with his own violence. The blood, the lashes, the pain that his victim is feeling – the torture excites him even more, practically driving him out of his mind. He throws himself on to her and tries to kiss her, to put his tongue in her mouth. She keeps avoiding him, tries to fight him off, but her strength has given out. Her weeping is a quiet, desperate moan. He pushes her thighs apart. She is able to turn away two or three times. Uday strikes her in the face with the back of his hand, blood flies out of her nose, and he enters her. We don't hear any more screams, just his greedy, panting groans. It's the most degrading thing I've ever experienced.

After Uday has satisfied his lusts, he comes grinning out of the bedroom, pours himself a brandy, and goes on chatting as though nothing had happened, as though he'd just had dinner with a friend.

Suddenly we hear a long, shrill scream that seems to go on for ever. Then, all of a sudden, there is complete silence. I dash into the bedroom, see the open door to the balcony, dash outside and look down. She is lying on the concrete right in front of the hotel entrance, motionless. She is half naked.

Uday comes out on to the balcony as well. I stare at him, but he avoids my eye, and just asks, 'Is she dead?'

She is dead. She jumped from the sixth floor because she couldn't stand the shame.

I dash into the foyer with some of the other bodyguards. The people at reception already know about the woman's leap to her death. They stare at us, with sheer horror in their eyes. They don't say a word, but their expressions tell me how much they hate us. Uday, the bodyguards, me. They can't quite place me. Am I Uday's brother?

The victim's husband screams, 'You murderers! You beasts!'

We call Uday into the room and he orders that the man be taken to Baghdad, and imprisoned in the Kasr Al-Nihaja, the Palace of No Return.

A short time later the officer, whose name is Saad Abd Al-Razzek, is found guilty, by a military court in Baghdad, of insulting the President.

According to Paragraph 225, that crime is punishable by death. Saad Abd Al-Razzek is executed. The captain, who had served ten years in the Iraqi army, several years of them spent fighting at the front, is shot by a firing squad.

TEN

Death of the Food-taster

I'm ashamed of myself for being too weak to do anything. But what could I have done? I wouldn't have had a hope. Uday's bodyguards, who almost derived more pleasure from their boss's acts of cruelty than he did himself, would have killed me. The would have executed me on the spot.

In the palace, the woman's desperate act is of no importance, and neither is the execution of the officer. No one talks about it, the events are never mentioned, and only the bodyguards sometimes make unpleasant jokes about the captain: 'Why did he have to insult the President like that? The woman wasn't worth it.'

These remarks go straight to my heart. I imagine the same thing happening to me. What is a human life worth in these circles? Nothing. What would happen if I had a wife that Uday happened to fancy? Would I want to die for her, just as that young captain had to die?

Uday is strikingly absent during the weeks after our return from Al-Habaniya. His expeditions through Baghdad are reduced to two or three a week, and it almost looks as though his instincts have told him to get out of the firing line. Too many people witnessed what happened in the Al-Medina Hotel. It's impossible to put all of them under so much pressure that they wouldn't even talk to their immediate families. And stories like that are like dominoes. If you line them up it only takes a breeze to bring the whole lot of them down.

None the less I'm sure that Saddam Hussein never learned anything about the events in that tourist resort. The newspapers just carried a tiny report that a young officer had been executed for insulting the President.

During these days Uday concentrates more intensely than usual on the newspapers and his many business connections in Baghdad. He has a number of meetings with Al-Haj Khaled Al-Kabisi. Al-Kabisi is a close friend of Uday's, and is in charge of all imports from Jordan. His management office is near the restaurant Al-Saat.

But Uday avoids having discussions and negotiations in the offices of business partners. He's afraid of bugs and hidden video cameras. His motto is: 'Never negotiate in places that your business partner has chosen. Mistrust everything, ask about everything. Even friends can be cheats and blackmailers.'

So Uday conducts most of his business deals in his office in the Olympic Club. He can use his secret microphones there, and his 'business partners' must unconditionally fall in line with his ideas.

Uday has a share in almost all the international hotels in Baghdad, and controls all the imports from abroad. But his biggest business is food production. He has farms in all the fertile regions of Iraq. These agricultural industrial plants, working with the latest technical devices, were set up on the American model. They use only high-performance products such as a special sort of grain that gives three times the yield of the grains that ordinary Iraqi farmers have at their disposal.

Uday's farms are run by Afif and Yaudant, two specialists who studied agriculture in the United States. Bachar Al-Abdullah is responsible for the enormous herds of cattle and sheep. The farms are united in a kind of fraternity. Ordinary farmers must deliver their products to Uday's farms. They receive a pathetic price for them. In return they must buy all their seeds, fertilisers and machines from Uday. In this way, Uday's agricultural mafia control everything.

The goods are sold on in Baghdad at ten times their initial value. The businessmen, in turn, are obliged to take certain quantities from the farms of the President's son. Uday draws a profit from every egg, every piece of meat and every grain of corn. It's a perfect money-making machine.

The income from this business is administered by Uday's financial advisers Madhat and Salhan Al-Chahbandar. All profits are transferred to Switzerland. The only people with access to Uday's accounts in Switzerland are Uday himself and his uncle, Barzan Al-Tikritti, who also administers Saddam Hussein's money abroad.

A tight-meshed net, a corrupt system in which everyone has his own fixed place.

The financial side of this empire is run by Salhan Al-Chahbandar. He was married to an ophthalmologist called Samira, an attractive, successful, Western-oriented young woman. She created a scandal that even everyone in the palace found out about: Samira was introduced to the President. That conversation, the rumours went, was the initial spark for an affair that became a genuine crisis within the family. The President heaped his attentions on the ophthalmologist for weeks. He sent her jewellery, cars, clothes and expensive perfumes. He was crazy about her.

The ladies of Iraq see Saddam Hussein as a handsome,

attractive, fascinating man. He's powerful, strong, dangerous. Brutal and unscrupulous – attributes that would be
repellent under normal circumstances, while with Saddam
they become magically attractive. The ladies of Baghdad's
fine society fall over themselves for private audiences with
him. There are endless lists of requests for an audience with
him. A photograph with Saddam Hussein is worth more
than any wealth. During the war against Iran, Saddam
Hussein even put himself at the head of a campaign to
persuade the population to give up their valuables to reinforce Iraq's dwindling financial reserves. Evening after
evening Iraqi television showed elegantly dressed ladies of
Iraq's high society, calling on them to come to the palace to
deliver rings, necklaces, jewels and family heirlooms. Of
course this produced pressure, fear of the shame that at least
the wealthiest families would bring down on themselves if
they refused the President's appeal.

But it was generally the narcissistic greed of the ladies
who were desperate to meet the leader, appear on television
with him, pay homage to Iraq and praise Saddam Hussein's
policies. Saddam Hussein kissed the women's hands before
the cameras, flattered them with his considerable charm and
brought all of his personal charisma to bear.

Dr Samira reacted differently. She was coy with Saddam,
refusing him for a while, and he sent his closest bodyguard,
friend and food-taster, Kamel Hannah, to her practice with
presents almost every day. He besieged her, he flattered her,
and the contrast couldn't have been starker: on the one hand
the murdering despot, on the other the refined charmer. And
that contrast had its effect. After weeks of wooing, Samira
accepted an invitation from Saddam. They met in one of his
83 palaces. For more than six months the President was able
to keep the relationship secret.

Kamel Hannah was perfect, he kept everything secret from Saddam's wife Sajida. Just like the time when Saddam had an affair with the tennis-player Najida, the wife of the minister of culture and the media, Hamad Yusef Hammedi. On that occasion, Saddam had wanted to leave his wife for Najida but had then, for reasons of state, given up the idea and ended the stormy, passionate affair.

This time Saddam acted differently. He secretly married Samira, taking her as his second wife. Only Kamel Hannah and Samira's husband, who had been informed by Saddam's officials, knew about it.

It was only when Samira fell pregnant and gave birth to a son that the first rumours started trickling out, and couldn't be hidden even from Saddam's first wife Sajida.

Sajida had always been the steady character in Saddam's family, although she too has a tendency to eccentricity. Like Imelda Marcos, she loves shopping more than anything else in the world. She is almost addicted to consumption, she jets around Europe every month with her fashion advisers, and regularly visits Dior, Yves Saint Laurent and Chanel. She doesn't visit the big fashion designers in their salons, but has them fly to Geneva with their collections and models.

In one area Sajida even outdoes the clothing fetishists Uday and Saddam Hussein: she changes her clothes almost once an hour. If she gets bored, she has her ladies-in-waiting drape jewels around her and wanders through the palace, turning around in front of long baroque mirrors.

She has only one worry: how to get hold of more – and more exclusive – jewellery. At the rare parties that she attends, her jewellery is the sole topic of conversation. She will talk ecstatically about where she bought which ring, and in which city she acquired this or that pair of ear-rings.

Like the President, she too has her own bodyguards,

secret police employed to protect her. And like her son Uday, Sajida uses her bodyguards as serfs. Once she planted tomatoes in her palace garden, in the blazing sun. She wanted to be an ordinary housewife. When the tomato seedlings looked pitiful after a few days, she had six of her bodyguards, who had been detailed to water them, whipped and thrown into prison for ten days.

Sajida learned about her husband's secret marriage, and turned to her father Khairallah Tulfah, whom Saddam had appointed governor of Baghdad. That set a ball rolling, which was to damage even the tight-knit Saddam clan. Khairallah complained publicly about the behaviour of his son-in-law, whom he had brought up as his own. He advised his daughter to move out of their palace. She moved into a feudal villa in the President's grounds, very close to the villas of her daughters Rena, Ragdh and Hala.

Uday is beside himself when he is informed that she has moved, and learns what his father has done to his beloved, honoured mother. Uday was always Sajida's favourite child. She covered up his scandals, protected him against his father's anger, forgave him everything.

And now this.

But Uday's hatred wasn't directed so much against his father, but against the bodyguard and food-taster Kamel Hannah: 'He's the one who has always acquired women and girls for my father. If only he hadn't dragged this whore into our palace. If only he'd killed her, like all the others,' he rages at every opportunity.

Until then Saddam had had most of his playmates removed by Kamel Hannah and his men once he no longer wanted them. They were run over, cast in concrete and sunk in the Dayla River to the east of the palace.

Once, by chance, I witnessed such murders. Our convoy with Uday was en route for Project Number 7 when Kamel Hannah's men chased two women in black limousines and drove over them. They reversed a number of times to drive over the lifeless bodies again. Then they dragged the corpses to one of the slip-ways connecting Saddam's palace with the steam-ships on the Dayla River. On that occasion Uday stopped, got out of the car and spoke to Kamel Hannah. 'My father's whores,' he told me later.

After Sajida's dramatic move, Samira moves into a side-wing of the palace, along with her child. Saddam, the child's father, calls this palace Project 2000. The castle was designed by an Austrian architect, and the building work, which swallowed up more than $500 million, was carried out by French firms.

It was a terrible scandal that Saddam had taken Samira in, it was a humiliation for the whole family.

But the humiliation affects Uday more than anyone else. I have come to know Uday by now. Every day I have to dress as he does, I have to change when he changes, have my hair cut when he has his hair cut. These external features also give me an insight into the man himself. I notice when he's happy, I sense when he is in pain – and in any case Uday generally makes no secret of his thoughts and feelings: he boasts about his affairs, talks dozens of times about the guns he has fired in the clubs, praises himself when he has had another hotel guest beaten up by his bodyguards.

Uday is an open book to me, even when he tries to be as discreet as possible.

As he is doing now. We notice that the family council is being called with striking regularity. Normally these meetings, each of which is held in a different palace, barely occur more than once a week.

Now they're happening almost every day. The meetings are arranged by phone shortly beforehand, for security reasons.

Every time Uday returns from the family council he seems frustrated, furious. He speaks contemptuously of Kamel Hannah, he calls him the 'spineless lickspittle who destroyed my mother'. Uday's rage is also directed against Farouk Abu-Omar. Farouk is considered to be Saddam Hussein's private pimp. He always procures the women, whom he passes on to Kamel Hannah. Uday is never dismissive about his father. I am struck that Uday no longer wears his favourite watch, a specially made gold device with a picture of Saddam Hussein on the face. And he no longer comes out with the ravings that had previously been degenerating into a real deification of Saddam. I remember one scene during Uday's birthday party. When the party became an orgy, Uday picked up a 25 dinar note, set it on fire and yelled at the naked men and women who were pleasuring themselves in the pool and all around it, 'Do what you will, but always remember one thing — if any one of you speaks ill about my father, I will burn him like this banknote.'

And Uday has no qualms about anything. Why should he? From childhood his father had taught him that rivals must be eliminated. Uday sees Samira as a rival to his mother. He can't get rid of Samira, but Kamel Hannah . . .

For weeks Uday has no tasks for me. My job is monotonous, sometimes even desperately boring. Although Uday has made no public appearances, I am constantly receiving my special instructions. The evening before, my three permanent guards give me instructions about which suit I'm to wear the following day. This clothing rule applies equally to all the bodyguards. Uday likes everyone to be dressed to match. This means that dressing and changing becomes a daily ritual, because Uday doesn't just own suits in every colour, but in every shade of every colour. The absurdity of our everyday life blots out the tensions within the Saddam clan. Everything seems to have its order again – until the day when it is announced that Saddam Hussein has given Kamel Hannah the task of organising a party in the garden of the ministerial assembly.

That happens early in November 1988.

Invitations to the party are sent out to all ministers, leading party members, the whole of Baghdad society. Even Suzanne Mubarak, the wife of the Egyptian president Hosni Mubarak, is expected at this jamboree. Kamel Hannah has also issued an invitation to Qusay, Uday's younger brother – but not to Uday. Uday is furious when he finds out, seeing it as an absolute provocation and a complete lack of respect that he hasn't been invited to the party and is therefore undesirable. For days Uday works out a plan of action to shake off this ignominy. He informs Namir Al-Tikritti, his master of ceremonies, and together they come up with a ludicrous and childish strategy: Uday wants to hold another, rival party at the same time, in a nearby part of the garden.

He sets up sound systems there, has his cooks create a huge buffet that must be more elegant and opulent than that of Kamel Hannah. Invitations to this counter-party are sent to all of Uday's friends; he even wants to have the Baghdad demi-monde there. 'We need the most beautiful, attractive and interesting women in Baghdad,' Uday tells Ali Asuad, his procurer of women. Uday even invites me to the party.

It's a pleasant, warm night, the liveried staff are serving cold champagne and canapés. The music from Kamel

Hannah's party is barely audible, although the two parties are only separated by low hedges. Uday has instructed Abdel Akle and his musicians only to play respectable background music. Uday is out for a fight, and everyone at the party can feel that.

But he is sufficiently controlled not to take the first step. We eat, we exchange small-talk, the mood is awkward and quiet, and by no means as relaxed and vulgar as Uday's parties usually are, except that Uday starts drinking spirits early in the evening. Even before dinner he has drunk a few glasses of whisky, without ice and water. With his dinner he didn't have wine like the rest of us, but brandy. He isn't drinking for pleasure, he's just knocking back the spirits.

How unlike Kamel Hannah's party. Although almost everyone in the world of high politics is gathered there, his party is relaxed and atmospheric, and his guests are enjoying themselves hugely. Even Suzanne Mubarak has come, as has Qusay Saddam Hussein with his wife Zainab, a general's daughter.

Qusay can be heard laughing. He doesn't have his brother's giggle, his laugh is loud and hearty.

Qusay is the second-born, two years younger than Uday and me. He was born in 1966. Unlike Uday, Qusay didn't cause scandals of any kind during his schooldays. Certainly, his daily appearance in the Baghdad college was no different from that of Uday. Qusay came to school with his bodyguards as well, and they sat inside and outside the classroom. But during break-time Qusay was always very reticent. He hated his elder brother's noisy, boorish, exhibitionistic behaviour. Qusay did also come with a convoy that brought him to the front door of the school; but he didn't come roaring through the playground like Uday, in an open-topped sports-car with booming music. Qusay always seemed introverted, intellectual, sensitive. At first glance he was a peaceful young man. In his British made-to-measure suits he was the precise opposite of his brother. Uday was always the young savage. Our school uniform was a pair of dark trousers and a white short-sleeved shirt. Uday wore jeans and a t-shirt with a printed picture, on the American model. He always wanted to be different.

Qusay left school with very good marks, and in 1984 he began to study law and public administration at the University of Baghdad. Like Uday, he wasn't a good student, he barely attended more than fifteen to twenty lectures a term, and he sometimes left those lectures after half an hour. But his extravagant behaviour wasn't as provocative as Uday's. He just got up and left, quietly, head raised, posture straight. Qusay was always a personality, he had a charisma of his own.

He knew that he was something special, but he didn't have to prove it to anyone, you could sense it from his facial gestures and the way he used his hands, his way of speaking. Not a single loud word, no screeching, no adolescent bragging. A gentleman, although not one that anyone wanted to get too close to, not that they could have if they'd wanted to.

Because he couldn't bear it in the lecture halls among his sweating fellow students, he always sat in the office of the dean, Dr Mohammad Al-Douri. Al-Douri was a slimy, contemptible, careerist person. Whenever he met Qusay outside on the way to university, he bowed obsequiously. Qusay always nodded briefly, walked quickly on with his eyes straight ahead, followed by his group of bodyguards, which generally consisted of between 20 and 25 people. Like a faithful dog, Al-Douri tried to keep pace with Qusay. The dean even personally opened the door to his office if Qusay preferred to study in the university offices. Everyone at the university used to talk about the fact that Qusay always sat at Al-Douri's desk and the dean had to stand while the President's son got on with his studies. Qusay didn't even sit his finals in the examination room, along with the other students, but in the dean's office.

Like Uday, Qusay had a clique of his own. It consisted solely of the sons and daughters of ministers and high-ranking Party members. Young people from 'more lowly' social strata had no chance of being included in this clique, or even to come anywhere near them. Qusay's closest friends are:

- Bassem Latif Nassif Yassem, the son of the minister of media and culture
- Sael Souheil, a general's son
- Marwan Adnan Sharif, a minister's son
- Aiad Saadam Ghaidan, a minister's son
- Ali Ghateb, the son of a Party officer.

None of Qusay's friends had achieved the marks (85 percent) required for attendance at a university in Iraq. Qusay managed it for his friends none the less. In 1988 Qusay graduated with an excellent degree. His result was even published at the university: Qusay Saddam Hussein, the best graduate of 1988, achieved 99.9 out of a possible 100 points in his exams.

Saddam Hussein clearly paid more attention to Qusay than to Uday.

Even during his studies he tried to shape his son, to lead him to higher tasks. Under all circumstances, they had to ensure that Qusay didn't slide into the demi-monde as Uday had done. Saddam married Qusay to Zainab, a daughter of the excellent general Maher Abd Al-Rashid. General Maher Abd Al-Rashid had won many great victories for Iraq during the Iran–Iraq war. Among others, he won the battle of Tahrir Alfan. After the war the general was celebrated as a glorious hero.

Saddam Hussein values the general, he needs him, he knows about his abilities. The President's well-calculated consideration is that he needs the general's loyalty, and the respected, scandal-free Al-Rashid family is of greater value to Qusay than any education.

Nine months after Qusay's and Zainab's wedding, their daughter Zaina is born. After his studies, Qusay is appointed president of the Iraqi riding club. At the same time, Saddam Hussein puts him at the head of the secret service: Qusay becomes deputy head of Al-Khass.

Since my training as Uday's fiday I have only seen Qusay once. Qusay had a fiday as well. Unlike me, Qusay's double is a member of his family. He is a distant cousin who looks deceptively like Qusay. I have no idea whether this distant cousin had to go through the same training as I did.

Qusay and his wife left Kamel Hannah's party shortly before midnight. Uday's bodyguards watched him drive off. By now Uday is completely drunk. He no longer cares whether he disturbs the food-taster's party or not, and tells Abdel Akle to turn up the music.

Uday prowls from table to table like a tiger. He doesn't talk to anyone. In his right hand he clutches his 'magic wand', a special instrument with which Uday always prunes his roses. It's a kind of battery-operated electric knife. The blade is as sharp as a scalpel. Uday has been holding it in his hand all evening. He switches it on, off, and on again, cutting through the cloth napkins, fruits from the buffet, even his cigars.

Shortly before midnight, when Uday's party is completely drunk, we hear shots coming from nearby. A few salvoes, one after the other, followed by loud laughter and more salvoes from a Kalashnikov.

Uday immediately sends his bodyguards to Kamel Hannah's party, one of them Saddam Al-Tikritti. A few moments later Saddam Al-Tikritti comes back with his people, laughing. 'What happened?' Uday snarls at Saddam Al-Tikritti. He replies with a grin, arms outstretched: 'Kamel Hannah is standing on the table firing celebratory salvoes into the air.' When he says that, we hear it again: Ratatata. There's nothing unusual about people firing guns into the air at parties. Uday does it on almost every expedition he makes through Baghdad.

But this time it's different. It isn't Uday who's letting himself go here, but Kamel Hannah, the food-taster, Saddam Hussein's loyal hound. Uday yells: 'Go back and tell that son of a whore to stop. Tell him the President's son doesn't want him to do that.' In less than two minutes Al-Tikritti comes back. His face is blank, and you can tell that what he's about to say is going to lead to a furious row. Uday shouts: 'What did he say?'

At that moment we hear gunfire again.

Al-Tikritti: 'Sir, Kamel Hannah says he only responds to orders from the President.' Now, like a lunatic, Uday storms towards the hedge separating the two parties. He forces his way through it, and walks angrily and defiantly up to Kamel Hannah's table. Kamel Hannah is standing on the table, legs spread, with a Kalashnikov in one hand and a reserve magazine in the other. When he sees Uday he fires off another salvo. He holds the gun casually with one hand, and the kick shakes his body. Hannah laughs loud and long.

Uday yells at him: 'I order you to stop.' In a flash the murmur of voices at the table stops, the musicians stop playing and Uday goes on raging: 'Come down.'

Kamel Hannah jumps down from the table. Everyone stares at him, he's wearing a serious expression. He pulls himself up to his full height in front of Uday and comes very close to him.

'I only listen to orders from the President,' says Hannah, who is clearly also drunk. Uday is shaking with fury. For the first time in his life, someone is openly contradicting him. A food-taster, a favourite of his father's, a slimy creature is daring to insult him, the first-born son of the direct descendant of the Prophet, openly and in front of the society of Baghdad, before the eyes of Suzanne Mubarak. Uday is lost for words. He feels wrong-footed, and is too furious to be able to control himself. All of a sudden everything that Uday has ever seen in the way of licentiousness and violence bursts out. No one knows what's going through his head during those seconds, but the humiliation has extinguished the last spark of rationality in his brain. There is no longer any morality, there never has been any morality in his life. At the age of five his father took him to executions of opponents of the regime; he witnessed acts of torture as a ten-year-old.

Uday brings up his electric knife and strikes Kamel Hannah heavily on the head. Once, twice. Kamel Hannah wasn't expecting the attack. He staggers two paces, and Uday goes after him like a lion. He darts towards him like a fencer and with a well-aimed, powerful blow he slits the throat of the President's food-taster.

Kamel Hannah groans, with blood spurting out of the

gaping wound in his neck. He opens his eyes wide, topples sideways on to the table, the cutlery crashes to the floor, women shriek in horror. Suzanne Mubarak is immediately taken from her chair and led away. The President's wife is so distraught that she can't even pull her hands away from her face.

Kamel Hannah rolls sideways off the table and falls on to the floor. Blood is everywhere. Uday hurls himself on top of him once more, and plunges the blade in again and again. Kamel Hannah tries to fight off Uday, he tries to lift up the Kalshnikov that he's still clutching, but Uday pushes the weapon aside and kicks and punches until Kamel Hannah has stopped moving.

Kamel Hannah's brother, a senior officer in the secret service, tries to hurl himself on top of Uday, shouting, 'I'll kill him, I'll kill him.' But Uday's officers hold him back, press him to the ground and try to put handcuffs on him.

It's as though Uday is in a trance; he doesn't hear the man's screams. His breathing is heavy, he spreads his legs, stands right over the dying Kamel Hannah, draws his gun and fires. The first nine-millimetre projectile shred's Kamel Hannah's belly, and the second hits him in the chest.

Suddenly everything in the garden is completely silent. The people stare in horror at Uday and the dead man, and no one dares say a word. Only some of Uday's officers leave the table, run to the telephone and tell Saddam Hussein.

Uday stares at the dying man for several minutes. He stands motionlessly by his hated victim. Then he raises his head and looks vacantly into the faces of the guests. He can't see the people around him any more. At that moment Uday is quite far away, he probably hasn't yet realised what has happened here. All of a sudden he grins, drops the gun and dashes through the hedge into the other garden, runs into one of the upper storeys of the ministry building and locks himself in an office. His bodyguards follow him.

A few moments later Saddam arrives. He is wearing trousers, his shirt is unbuttoned. He is wearing shoes and no socks. He looks as though he as only taken a few seconds to get dressed. Saddam is shocked. He runs over to Kamel Hannah, bends over his friend and shouts, 'Where is the doctor?'

The ambulance is there within minutes. They load Kamel Hannah on to a stretcher, but it's too late, he can't be saved. Saddam refuses to believe it. He urges the doctors on, gets into the ambulance and dashes with his friend to the Ibn-Sina, Saddam's private hospital. Kamel Hannah is already dead by the time he is loaded into the ambulance.

I only learn what else happened that night the following day, from Azzam, Uday's first bodyguard. Uday, who has now officially become a murderer, tried to take his own life with tablets that he had brought to him by his bodyguards. 'He took a whole tube of sleeping tablets,' says Azzam. When he tips groaning on to the floor, Azzam and his people also bring him to the Ibn-Sina hospital.

'The doctors informed Saddam that his son was also being brought in.' Azzam shakes his head and goes on talking: 'Uday stammered – don't tell my father, I want to die.'

When Saddam learns about this, he storms furiously into his son's room in the hospital. The doctors are about to put a plastic tube down his throat to pump his stomach. Uday vomits and retches, the picture of misery. Saddam tears the tube out of the hands of the doctors, pushes them aside and hits Uday in the face, twice. As he does so he yells, 'Your blood will flow, as my friend's did.'

So the bestial murder of his friend is even enough for

Saddam. Uday isn't let out of hospital for several days. No news is allowed to leak out of the presidential palace, there isn't a line in the papers. Within the palace it is argued that the murder was 'the action of a perfectly normal, unstable, short-tempered and uncontrolled man. Uday has always been guided by his aggressive emotions.'

We know that this attempt to play matters down is craven. Everyone in the palace knows it. Uday has always been an animal, a sadist who enjoyed violence and killing.

But this murder of an opponent was more than just working off a sudden rage. Uday was carrying out an indirect instruction from his mother: 'I want Kamel Hannah, that procurer, to be destroyed,' Sajida had said on a number of occasions. She certainly didn't want Uday to take it as an order. But by uttering these words she had spurred her son, whom she loved and revered to distraction, to even greater fury.

Uday had been out of hospital for two days when he flew to Geneva with Yassem, his fashion adviser. Saddam Hussein was sending him to his uncle, Barzan Al-Tikritti, this time as a punishment. Saddam made it known that Uday would have to appear before a court and pay for his crime, but at the same time he applied pressure on Kamel Hannah's family. As a result of this, Kamel Hannah's brother, whom Uday also wanted to shoot during the party, suddenly appears in public to request that the perpetrator be treated with mercy. So the charge against Uday is dropped.

None the less, discussions of the murder produce a new and hitherto unknown dynamic within the politics of the family. Until this point the family itself had played the most important part in maintaining control over the state institutions. Sometimes it was even more important for

Saddam Hussein to clear up obscure arguments in the marriage negotiations between two clans than to do serious economic politics.

Saddam took the attitude towards the family that has shaped social life in the Arabic-speaking world for centuries, and cultivated it to excess. Political associations were deepened by marriage, and the most important members of the regime were inevitably personally connected to Saddam. So far that had been to their advantage.

But after the murder of Kamel Hannah and Uday's departure for Geneva, the cabal within the Saddam clan emerged into the open. Something that began with Samira moving into the palace developed into a tragedy on the scale of *Macbeth*.

Sajida, her father Khairallah Tulfah and her brother Adnan Khairallah, all levelled severe accusations at Saddam Hussein because of the murder of Kamel Hannah. But Adnan Khairallah reacted most violently of all.

Adnan Khairallah had been a close friend of Saddam Hussein since childhood. If Saddam Hussein had anything like a friend, that friend was his cousin Adnan Khairallah. When Saddam Hussein became President, he appointed Adnan defence minister. At the end of the war with Iran Saddam appointed him General Chief of Staff.

Adnan is popular in Iraq. The people revere him as a war hero – a great general who is also concerned about the well-being of his soldiers. After the war he came up with many plans to bring invalids back into society. Soldiers who were particularly brave and successful in battle were awarded bonuses in the form of plots of land, apartments and tax benefits.

With these social programmes, Adnan Khairallah became

a star, the darling of the masses. He was celebrated in Baghdad as the second man after Saddam Hussein. That was his first mistake. But reverence for him was so great that this egocentric self-presentation remained at first without consequences.

Saddam's chief advisers precisely registered these currents of sympathy. But until the murder of Kamel Hannah the President didn't react to this development; this was quite unusual, because otherwise Saddam had no scruples, and even had his close relations eliminated if he saw them as competitors.

Adnan's second great mistake was to highlight the feuds within Saddam's family to such an extent that it looked as though he wanted to discredit, or even to topple the President himself.

Adnan referred constantly to the scandal that Saddam Hussein had brought down on the head of his sister Sajida. He found it infuriating that Samira lived in the palace and Sajida had to move out. He openly accused the President of destroying the peace of the family for the sake of his mistress Samira.

The row became so violent that it could no longer be concealed, even from the bodyguards and the palace staff. Neither Sajida nor her father Khairallah Tulfah appeared at the weekly family meetings. Sajida even instructed her bodyguards to keep Samira away from her villa within the palace grounds. Adnan went there pointedly almost every day in order to visit his sister.

Saddam Hussein reacted in his own way. First he sent Samira and her son Ali to Europe. Then he delivered his first blow against the family. The secret police raided all the businesses of his adopted father Khairallah Tulfah. Seventeen of his managers were arrested and pilloried. They were accused of cheating the people of millions with criminal skulduggery. Although everyone in Baghdad knew that Saddam Hussein was behind these, he was bold enough to praise Khairallah Tulfah as an excellent businessman and politician in a television interview the day after the raid.

Saddam waited a few months to deliver a truly deadly blow, when he invited his whole family on an 'outing' to Northern Iraq: Ajida, Qusay, the three daughters Ragdh, Hala and Rena; Uday, who had by now returned from Geneva; the husbands of the daughters and Qusay's wife Zainab; Adnan Khairallah and Ali Hassan Al-Majid – 'Chemical Ali' – who was responsible for the use of poison gas against the Kurds. They flew in a number of helicopters.

In one of them sat Saddam Hussein, in another Sajida with the daughters; Uday and Qusay took their private helicopters. Ali Hassan Al-Majid also had a helicopter of his own, as did Adnan Khairallah. The take-off of all the helicopters was something of a spectacle, and was even shown on television. Twenty-four hours later, Saddam and his close family were still in Northern Iraq when the headline was announced on Iraqi television that defence minister Adnan Khairallah, who had had to return early to Baghdad on urgent business, had flown into a sandstorm and crashed. He and his bodyguards had lost their lives.

Saddam Hussein's whole family was at Adnan Khairallah's funeral. Sajida was supported by her father Khairallah Tulfah. Everyone cried, even Saddam looked grave. The funeral ended with an insult: Khairallah Tulfah shouted at Saddam Hussein: 'You have destroyed my daughter's life and had my son murdered. For that I swear eternal revenge.'

In the days that followed Khairallah Tulfah gave Baghdad

society his own explanation of his son's helicopter crash: not an accident, but murder.

1. When Adnan Khairallah flew back to Baghdad, there was no sandstorm in the whole of Iraq.
2. Adnan had had no cause to return early to Baghdad.
3. He, Khairallah Tulfah, had received information that four explosive charges had been fixed to his son's helicopter.
4. These explosive charges had been applied by a secret agent with the code name Karim.
5. Karim had received instructions for the assassination from Hussein Kamel, who was married to Saddam's eldest daughter Ragdh.
6. Ali-Hassan Al-Majid had been in charge of the operation.
7. Karim had travelled to Paris on an Iraq Airways flight on the day of the assassination.

Saddam reacted in silence to all these accusations. He went bird-hunting with his bodyguards.

ELEVEN

The Mute Girl

August 1989, and Uday is in a rage. Azzam has just brought him the news that there's a shoot-out going on at the bus station in the centre of Baghdad, involving 50 soldiers recently released from the border troops. Dozens of civilians have been killed, Azzam pants, and the Republican Guard, along with the secret service, are trying to bring the soldiers under control. The battle has been going on all night.

The next morning Uday sends me to the bus station with my bodyguards. My task is easy, but also dangerous: I'm to check out the situation from first hand, and then return to Project Number 7 to deliver my report. Yassem brings me Uday's black uniform, I change into it, and about 20 minutes later our convoy of 10 identical black Mercedes limousines sets off. The situation at the bus station has calmed down again, and it's been cordoned off by special units. There are tanks and soldiers in the square in front of it, and among them hundreds of people waiting for the bus. It's a gloomy picture. When our convoy drives up, the crowd shrinks back. I get out, and so do my 12 bodyguards. An eerie silence descends. I walk up to the people. They stare at me in silence, their faces blank. There's suspicion in the air. The last time I was here was exactly a year ago. The war against Iran had just come to an end, and thousands of people had celebrated euphorically in the streets of Baghdad. There had been a great feeling of relief, boundless joy. And now.

The eight-year conflict with Iran left our country bankrupt. Our army, numbering just about a million, went into decline. Among the demobilised and unemployed soldiers, disorder and criminality were commonplace. Marauding soldiers were forever attacking and robbing people. In the palace, we heard of the existence of these terrible conditions, but we didn't really want to believe them. Now I am seeing them with my own eyes. The dead have been cleared away, but there's still dried blood on the hot asphalt.

The war with Iran has made the country poor. I walk up to four women who are waiting with their children for a bus and ask how they are. They respectfully fall to the ground before me, but I have nothing to give them, so I ask them what is making them so unhappy. 'Sir, we don't know where to find a roof for our children. It's all so expensive.'

I tell them I'll look after them, and have one of my bodyguards write down the woman's address. Then my bodyguards hurry me back to the car. Our convoy drives back to Project Number 7. I write a report for Uday, telling him what the woman said to me. That they have no money to get by with their children, and that I think the soldiers who started those gun-battles are in much the same state. After all, a regular soldier earns only 22 dinars a month. That's just enough to keep you from starving.

Uday is furious about my behaviour. He strikes me in the face with his length of cable, shouting, 'It isn't true, say it isn't true!' He lays into me again, ranting, 'Why didn't you stick to my instructions, why did you talk to the people? No one ordered you to do that. You're my fiday, never forget it.'

*

The next day Uday's newspapers carry lengthy reports about the events at the bus station: 'Police arrest car thieves,' is the headline. Then there is some mention of an exchange of fire between the Baghdad police and a group of car thieves, in which some people were unfortunately killed and a number injured. There are identical accounts on television and on the radio. These falsified reports are designed to maintain the fiction of a peaceful post-war life.

The reality is rather different. Saddam is having terrific difficulties maintaining his large and highly developed military-industrial infrastructure, and feeding an army of one million in peacetime.

Iraq is bankrupt, but that doesn't interest Uday. After the furore surrounding the murder of Kamel Hannah, he's only concerned to show that he's the same old Uday. Uday Saddam Hussein, the powerful President's son. He is a stranger to any sense of responsibility, and he adheres to Marie Antoinette's line: 'If they have no bread, let them eat cake.'

He now begins to display his wealth even more pointedly than before. He even tells us that he completed his watch collection during his stay in Switzerland with his uncle Barzan Al-Tikritti. He now has over a thousand watches, he boasts, waiting for our applause.

The course of Uday's day is much as it was before. Expeditions through Baghdad's clubs and hotels, excess of alcohol, wild public appearances with 20 women and more in his wake. On these outings Uday now finds a new group on which to vent his hatred. Previously it was only the Persians, Jews, Egyptians and horseflies. Now he hates the Kuwaitis as well. On Thursdays they fly in from Kuwait City in their thousands, to enjoy themselves in Baghdad. In

Kuwait, alcohol and prostitution are forbidden, as they are in Saudi Arabia. The desert-dwellers use the freedom of Baghdad to enjoy and amuse themselves. 'They descend on the hotels like locusts,' curses Uday. 'They boast about their petro-dollars, and they're only alive at all because they steal from us.' Of course the truth is quite different. Iraq was only able to survive during the war because throughout those years Kuwait supported Saddam's regime with billions of dollars of credit.

On one of his expeditions Uday meets his old friend Fahd Al-Ahmed Al-Sabah, the brother of the Kuwaiti emir, in a hotel. Uday has known him for years, and always described Fahd as 'my brother'. As chairman of the Olympic Committee and president of the national football associations respectively, they have stayed in permanent contact with each other.

Of course I wasn't present at their meeting, and only learned of it the following day: Uday ran up to greet Fahd and kissed him like a brother. But the effusive delight at their chance meeting lasted only for a short while. Fahd, Uday's bodyguards tell me, immediately started talking to Uday about Iraq's debts. 'Iraq owes us $11 billion. When are you going to pay us?' he said. The next day, Uday was still furious about this unbelievable piece of tactlessness on the part of his Kuwaiti friend. 'They're thieves, common, devious thieves. They've been stealing from us for years.'

Uday paces up and down in his office like a tiger. Munem Hammed comes in and hands him a folder containing large numbers of documents about relations between Iraq and Kuwait. Uday sits down at his desk and reads impatiently, skimming over the documents, nodding repeatedly. All of a sudden he leaps to his feet and deluges Munem Hammed with his words: 'You know just as well as I do that they're stealing our oil. They're pumping our oil out of Rumaila. Rumaila belongs to us,' he rants, 'Munem, you know that's true.'

The Rumaila oil field is divided by the Iraq–Kuwait border. The larger part is on Iraqi territory, the smaller belongs to Kuwait. It is exploited by both sides. But more efficient technology puts Kuwait's quotas considerably higher than Iraq's.

'Yes, that is true. They are stealing our oil out of Rumaila and daring to behave like Iraq's creditors,' says an unusually obsequious Munem Hammed, adding, 'Sir, they are taking oil from a field that lies entirely on our territory. The border was drawn in completely the wrong place, and Rumaila belongs to Iraq.'

Uday nods and says, 'The day will come when we will prove it to them. Father has spoken of it several times.'

Uday takes out a map on which Kuwait is shown as one of three governmental districts of the Ottoman Empire in what will later be Iraq. He stares at the map for a long time, then quotes an inscription on it: 'We will extend the borders of Iraq to the south of Kuwait. Iraq and no one else concludes treaties about Kuwait, so we consider the treaty between Kuwait and Great Britain, from the day on which it came into effect, as illegal. No one, either in Kuwait or elsewhere, has the right to rule the Kuwaiti people, because they are the people of Iraq. The age of the sheikhdoms is at an end.'

This text was written by General Karim Kassem, later Iraqi President, six days after the declaration of Kuwaiti independence. Uday isn't interested in the fact that Kassem was a deadly enemy of his father, and that Saddam Hussein tried to have Kassem assassinated. For him, all that counts is that Kassem's words bear out his convictions of the moment, and document the fact that Iraq's claim on Kuwait is not a new one.

On 19 June 1960, under the government of Abd Allah Al-Salim Al-Sabah, Kuwait received its independence. In the years leading up to that there had been repeated border disputes between Kuwait and Iraq. Iraq, which had joined the League of Nations in 1932 as a formally independent state, justified its claims to Kuwait with reference to the fact that Kuwait had formerly been a part of the Ottoman administrative district of Basra. And since Iraq was the legitimate successor of the Ottoman Empire . . .

Uday waves the map wildly around, saying that back in 1961 Iraqi troops had crossed the border to Kuwait, and had marched as far as Mutla, 30 miles outside Kuwait City. Six thousand British soldiers, immediately dispatched to Kuwait, repelled the Iraqis.

This attempted invasion did nothing to alter the vague definition of the borders of Kuwait, which dates back to Sir Percy Cox, the British High Commissioner for the region. In 1922 he called a meeting in Baghdad, because he had had enough of constantly arguing with marauding Bedouins and selfish rulers about borders. So he forced both parties to the table, took a red pencil and drew a line from the top of the gulf to the trans-Jordanian border. Then two more lines to create neutral zones which Saudi Arabia, Iraq and Kuwait were to share between them.

These schematic boundaries, with their randomly established, geographically unidentifiable starting-points, satisfied no one. They gave a piece of Kuwaiti territory to Saudi Arabia, and Saudi land to Iraq, and created two neutral zones which were to become a source of endless quarrels and feuds. And yet these decisions, made in 1922, had remained effective until the present day. Although, in the meantime, the question of oil had come into play.

In 1963, after the fall of Kassem, Iraq officially recognised

Kuwait as a state. But not its borders: 'It is true,' says Uday, suddenly revealing himself to be an international political player, 'that we have sat alongside the Kuwaitis in the UN and the Arab League. The borders are wrong, and the best thing would be to merge the two countries together.'

What he doesn't say is that by 'bringing Kuwait home', Iraq would be relieved of its debts at a stroke. The marauding soldiers would once again have something to do. Iraq would be able to satisfy its own people with the treasures from the banks of Kuwait.

During this discussion between Uday and Munem Hammed I don't say anything, sit quietly on the couch listening, and trying not to disturb anyone. I know that Uday is just coming out with his father's words. In conclusion, he says, 'If my father had been in charge in 1961, Kuwait wouldn't exist anyway.'

This is the first time that an invasion of Kuwait has been openly discussed in Project Number 7, but it won't be the last time. But for the moment that's enough of Uday's transformation into a statesman. He returns his attention to his hedonistic pleasures.

I record the most important points from this discussion, complementing them with extracts from Iraqi newspaper articles about Kuwait and the border problem. The tone is more or less as follows: 'There has never been accord about the borders between the two countries. Baghdad would accept the border only if Kuwait were prepared to concede the islands of Warba and Bubiyan to Iraq, and Kuwait has so far refused to do this.'

Other articles denounced the immeasurable wealth of the Kuwaitis: 'Emir Jaber Al-Ahmad Al-Sabah's garage holds more than forty luxury limousines. As a private hobby he keeps hunting falcons worth five million dollars. There are gold fountains in the Dasman Palace, a temple to pleasure with two hundred rooms in which the infidels hold orgies.'

I can't help sniggering as I write that down. Uday's garage alone is bigger than that of the Kuwaiti emir, and Uday has orgies almost every day, with his transvestite friends always in attendance.

The newspaper articles are pure provocation, to distract readers from the terrible economic situation in Iraq and the excesses of Saddam's family.

None the less, not everything can be hushed up. And that's Uday's fault.

Autumn 1989, Hotel Rasheed. Uday is very drunk, as are his bodyguards. All of a sudden a little girl appears. Her name is Linda, her parents are from the Lebanon, Palestinians. Linda is selling fresh flowers, and her mother is standing beside her. Uday sees the girl, he likes her, and he orders his bodyguards to take Linda away. Everyone in the hotel sees her and her mother being led away.

A week later the corpses of Linda and her mother are found near Al-Maghreb Street in Baghdad. Uday had forced himself on Linda, and handed her mother over to his bodyguards.

A short time afterwards, Uday gives a party in the Said Club, with Abdel Akle. As always, he orders Abdel Akle to sing the song about his father: 'Saddam, you great and powerful man, may God preserve you for us, may God preserve your youth.'

Uday hums devotedly along, and so do his bodyguards, but Asra Hafez, a pretty young girl, suddenly explodes with laughter. She's drunk and doesn't know what she's doing. The President's son jumps to his feet, pulls her by the hair and screams at her: 'What are you laughing at?'

Asra isn't intimidated by this mistreatment. She laughs, shouts, and then giggles mockingly, 'How old is the young President that Abdel's singing about?' She tries to push Uday away. He lets go of her, and she arranges her hair. She cheekily sweeps back her mane, and looks at Uday, who is standing in front of her trembling with rage. She looks him in the eye. For a few seconds nothing happens. Then Asra suddenly starts laughing again. She yells with laughter, almost bent double, and then tries to suppress her laughter again by pressing her hands to her mouth. She laughs so heartily that a few other people can't help joining in.

Uday isn't one of them. He grabs Asra, drags her out of the club, draws his pistol and, before the eyes of the shocked guests of the club, he fires three bullets into her chest. Asra dies on the spot.

Although everyone has seen Uday shooting, his friend Sirwan Al-Jaf, who imported cars for him from abroad, is charged with the crime. Sirwan Al-Jaf is sentenced to eight months' imprisonment.

I have recorded five further crimes committed by Uday.

Crime number 1: One fine late autumn day Uday decides to take his friends to the Mansul district. Saddam Hussein has a magnificent castle there, near the tourist hotel Nenaua Obri.

When Uday's convoy passes the hotel, he orders them to stop for a moment so that he can look around the hotel. In the foyer he discovers a family with a pretty daughter. The girl is hardly older than 15, 16 at the most. Uday likes her.

And once again the sadist's work begins: he orders his bodyguard – this time it's Ahmad Souleiman – to abduct the girl and bring her to him.

The girl is brought to Mansul Castle. Uday rapes her and

throws her out: 'And don't you dare say a word!'

She drags herself back to the hotel. Only there does the true extent of the tragedy become apparent: the girl desperately tries to explain what has happened, with her hands and feet. She has been deaf and dumb since birth, and can only come out with croaking, incomprehensible words.

Uday's men look at the child turning desperately to all the hotel guests in the foyer, gesticulating, silently weeping. No one can understand her. The bodyguards take her to a nearby wood, and they rape her as well. Then they tell Uday that the girl tried to tell people in the hotel about the rape. Uday orders that the girl be executed and buried in the forest. The order is carried out.

Crime number 2: At irregular intervals, Uday invites Beida Abd Al-Rahman to Project Number 7. Beida Abd Al-Rahman is a successful chanteuse and television presenter with her own children's programme. Uday supports and encourages her. Beida Abd Al-Rahman even describes herself in public as Uday's girlfriend.

One day she comes to Project Number 7, complaining that Sana Al-Haidari, a young student, has also claimed to be having a relationship with Uday.

Uday pretends to be furious, has his bodyguards fetch Sana from the university and questions the girl: 'Is what Beida tells me true? You're claiming to be my girlfriend?'

Sana begs and pleads and implores: 'Please, sir, I never claimed that, it's a lie. I swear I never said I was your girlfriend.'

Uday calmly listens to the girl's pleas. He just looks at her, without stirring. Then he orders her: 'Get undressed, lie down on the bed and ask for me!' Sana hurries to undress and does what Uday has ordered her to do. Uday brings his

electrical cable down several times on the student's naked
skin. She groans loudly with each blow, and that is exactly
what Uday wants. It puts him in an intoxicated state that
excites and satisfies him. Uday beats her as hard as he can,
the cable comes down on her skin, it breaks, blood flows.

Then he enters her body.

After that he shouts, 'Bring me a razor blade!' Two
bodyguards have to hold Sana, a third presses her jaws apart.
Uday takes the blade, pulls Sana's tongue out and slits it
open. 'So that you can tell your stories all the better.'

But that isn't enough. His bodyguards take her away, load
her into one of Uday's helicopters and throw her into the Al-
Sarsar Lake near the district of Anbar.

Crime number 3: The Al-Zanarek Club in Baghdad. Uday is
giving a party. Once again all the President's son's friends
from the demi-monde are present. This time Uday instructs
his bodyguards Numair Al-Tikritti, Hilal, Muaed Alaani and
Ali Asuad 'to get as many pretty girls as possible together'.

About 100 girls come, including Weam Tabet Al-Kabisi.
She is the daughter of one of the wealthiest businessmen in
Baghdad. Her father also gives Uday's mother financial
advice.

Weam doesn't come on her own: she is accompanied by
Uday's uncles Maan and Luai Khairallah. Weam is Luai
Khairallah's girlfriend.

The party starts and, as always, Abdel Akle sings for hours.
Uday dances with lots of women, and behaves as always: he
grabs the women by the breasts, imitates sexual intercourse
as he dances, is vulgar, excessive and noisy.

He could have all the women he wanted on this particular
evening, apart from one: Weam. And it's Weam that he
chooses. He says straight out: 'I want you, and you want me

too.' As he does so he grabs her by the hips, pulls her to him, and tries to press his half-open mouth on hers. Weam shrinks back and tries to pull away from Uday's embrace. When he doesn't let her go, she calls her boyfriend.

Luai jumps on Uday and forces him from the dance-floor, and all of a sudden three shots ring out. It isn't clear who has shot at whom, because Uday's bodyguards carry Luai off, and disappear with him in the club's extensive park.

The President's son leaves the party, and has Weam 'delivered to him'. She spends the night with Uday, and I don't know whether she's forced to or not. I just see them talking the following morning, and hear Uday shouting theatrically, 'I love women more than I love my father, I love them more than God.'

Days later, Weam is found shot. Luai has killed her. He couldn't bear the fact that she spent the night with Uday. Because he can't take his revenge on Uday, he avenges himself on the girl.

Crime number 4: Baghdad, in the district of Mansour. It's between six and seven in the evening. We are on our way towards the Olympic Club with Uday. All of a sudden a car overtakes our slowly moving convoy. A couple are sitting in the car. Uday is enraged, because no one is allowed to overtake his convoy. By radio, he orders Namir Al-Tikritti, Salam Al-Aousi and Saadam Al-Tikritti to stop the couple and bring the woman to him, regardless of what happens.

They drag the woman out of the car and force her to get into one of our cars. While Namir Al-Tikritti is taking her husband to a police station, we drive with the woman to one of Uday's farms on the edge of Baghdad. Namir Al-Tikritti accuses the man of 'insulting the president of Olympic Club'.

The innocent man, whose name is Hassan Abd Al-Amir

Janabi, is imprisoned for six months and tortured, while his wife is set free after a week.

When he is released, Hassan Abd Al-Amir Janabi is warned: 'Keep your mouth shut, or Uday's men will cut your tongue out!'

The woman's husband ignores the warning, tries to contact President Saddam Hussein and acts in an incredibly naïve manner. He turns up at the entrance to the presidential palace and tells the sentries what he wants. Of course they call Uday: he has Hassan Abd Al-Amir Janabi brought to him. Three days later passers-by find the man's corpse in the Al-Umma Park. He had tried to save his honour, and sought help from the guardians of the law. That was his crucial mistake.

Crime number 5: Miss Iraq is chosen every year; it's a big event, and a particular gain in pleasure for Uday. The initiators are Uday's henchmen, his business partners. In the past, Uday has invited every Miss Iraq to see him, and always had what he wanted. Things are different when Ilham Ali Al-Aaazami, a student, is chosen. She refuses to obey him. Uday reacts as he always does: a nod from him, and Ahmad Souleiman, the karate fighter, Muid Fadel and Mohammed Baghdadi will know what's to be done. They take the girl to Project Number 7. She is held there for a week, and raped by Uday and all his bodyguards. He even offers the woman to me – 'Take her, she's good.'

I refuse, but the others greedily join in. Day after day the student is passed from one filthy man to the next.

After that she is thrown out, and Uday puts rumours about that Miss Iraq is a prostitute who would do it with 'the nearest soldier'.

Ali Al-Aaazami is an only child, the only daughter of a

respected businessman, who is driven practically to distraction by the rumours about his daughter. He first kills his daughter, and then wants to question Uday in the Olympic Club.

Uday even lets the desperate man into his office, and talks to him. He offers him money and advises him 'just to forget the dead little whore'. Uday is sitting casually in his President's chair, smoking his Havana. He gives a super-cilious grin and says, 'God has given her so much beauty, but unfortunately no morals. She enjoyed it.'

That is too much. Ali Al-Aaazami's father, who has not yet had the courage to shout at Uday, begins to scream at him. Uday glances at Dafer Aref, and he knows what to do. The bodyguard grabs the old man and throws him into a room. I hear two shots. In the evening the body is carried away.

I have to stop writing a number of times as I draw up this list. Uday, the crimes, my job as a double, which I hardly ever perform. What have I done so far? I've been to the football stadium a few times – but what about the rest? I'm nothing but a silent witness to terrible crimes. I see murders and intrigues, I'm an accomplice in horror. Now that I'm writing it down I'm even becoming a book-keeper of atrocity.

'Latif,' I shout at myself, 'you've got to get out of here. You're twenty-five, you want to start a family, you want to work for your father's company, take over his factory and his import and export business. But what are you doing? You're living side by side with a crazed criminal, wasting your days by the pool or watching idiotic videos.'

I must have seen *The Godfather* 30 times now, and all the porn films in Uday's archive as many times.

But how am I going to get out of here? Who can I turn to? Uday?

No, no, out of the question. What about escaping? Where to?

For the first time I start hating Uday. I hate him because he's a merciless criminal, and in spite of that there's nothing anyone can do. But I hate him even more because he's put me in this golden cage, which I can't get out of. I don't care if he hits me now and again with his electrical cable or his iron bar because at regular intervals he thinks I need *educating*. The physical pain is bearable. It hurts, it stings, there's a wound that will heal.

But what about my soul? Have I come to resemble Uday internally as well as externally? No, internally I'm completely different, the exact opposite. My parents nurtured me when I was growing up, as the eldest my brothers and sisters treated me with the same respect as my father. If my father was busy, I helped my brothers and sisters with their tasks and problems. We all treated one another well, and religion was a fixed component of our life. I regularly went to the mosque to pray. But now? We don't even keep Ramadan.

I light a cigarette and inhale it deeply. I never used to smoke. My father didn't like it. But now? I smoke two packs of Marlboro a day, and drink, sometimes to the point of unconsciousness. Drinking makes this life bearable to some extent.

And what am I supposed to do but drink? My life consists of nothing but waiting, observing. I'm driven to various appointments in luxury limousines, as bait for assassins. Why, back in Basra, did the bullets hit that young officer and not me?

It's 26 December 1989, shortly before four o'clock. I hide my piece of paper with my jottings in a niche in the wall behind the built-in wardrobe in my bedroom. Then I go into the bathroom, pick up a razor blade and look at it for a long time. It makes me think of the way Uday slit Sana's tongue with just such a blade. I see the blood swelling from her mouth and dripping on to her clothes.

I slowly run the blade along the vein in my right wrist. At first no blood comes. I cut deeper, then I slit open the vein in the other wrist.

I feel the warm blood flowing over my palm, hear it dripping on to the floor. I lie down on the bed, and am about to slit my wrist, but I don't have the courage or the strength to do the job properly. I start a number of times, but I only manage a few little cuts which break the skin but don't get to the artery. I cry, and try again, but I can't do it. I slowly let my head fall on the pillow. I'm breathing with difficulty – all of a sudden the phone rings beside my bed. It sounds a long way away.

TWELVE

The Kuwait Plundering Raid

Azzam has to strip naked, and so do my four bodyguards. They do it without a word of contradiction, stand in front of Uday's big baroque desk and cover their private parts with their hands. They stand slightly bent, with their shoulders drooping forwards, their heads and eyes lowered. Uday comes silently out from behind the desk, takes his electrical cable, pulls it through his hand a number of times as though to clean it, then throws his hand back. His body tenses like a spring, he looks like a tennis player about to serve. With a swish, the cable comes down on Azzam's naked back. Uday beats him until he bleeds. Then he beats my bodyguards. Once again his torture instrument comes crashing down. Ten times, twenty times, but he doesn't groan as he usually does.

Uday is punishing the men, humiliating them, for not having prevented me from slitting my wrists. If Azzam hadn't called me to tell me that Uday was leaving for Geneva in the next few days, I'd probably have bled to death. I don't know how long I'd been lying on my bed when the phone rang. I just know that it sounded very faint, as faint as though it were coming from another apartment.

Azzam had them storm my room because I didn't pick up the phone.

They broke down the door of my apartment in the Al-Hayat House, saw me lying on the blood-smeared bed and had me brought to Ibn-Sina Hospital.

The doctors sewed up the wounds on my arms with six stitches each. Two days later I was reasonably fit again.

Now I'm standing in Uday's office watching him punishing my bodyguards. He would really like to be punishing me. The best thing for him would probably be if I were dead, but he needs me. So his concern over the past few days has not really been for me; Uday has principally been concerned with himself. I am his most important security factor. Without me as his double, he would have to put himself in all those risky situations, and Uday has every reason to fear that these risky situations will shortly increase. For weeks it's been an open secret that 'something is shortly going to happen'.

The atmosphere is tense. That's apparent from the fact that Munem Hammed has hardly any time for me now. The instructor-in-chief has a new trainee fiday: a double is being initiated for Qusay, Uday's younger brother. This double comes from Saddam Hussein's family, a remote cousin.

Further rumours about the murder of Adnan Khairallah are also going around the palace. All of a sudden it is being said that the reasons for his death were not only personal (Adnan's criticism of Saddam Hussein's mistress) but political as well.

Defence minister Adnan Khairallah is said to have warned the President against an Iraqi invasion of Kuwait. 'It would provoke the West too much. An invasion of Kuwait can be nothing but a protective measure against American imperialism in the Gulf.'

But Saddam has already decided long ago to 'bring Kuwait home'. His threats on the subject are veiled, but in the palace we hear suggestions that his plans for annexation were already complete at the beginning of 1990.

Publicly, he tries to cover this up. He rouses people up against Israel to distract from his intentions, to pull the Arab world behind him. A refined diversionary tactic that hardly anyone outside of the palace can see through.

In Uday's newspapers and all the other Iraqi media Saddam issues massive threats against Israel. He is constantly delivering reminders that the Jewish people launched a military attack against Iraq in 1981. On that occasion Israeli fighter planes destroyed the atomic reactor in Osirak. Now Saddam declares that Israel and America have recently been planning an attack on Iraq: 'If it comes to that, we will destroy the whole Jewish people with poison gas.' Uday's newspaper *Babel* bears the headline, 'Our missiles are strong enough to reach Israel.'

In his naïvely egoistic way, Uday is forever putting his foot in his mouth. Once he declares – patriotically, and with a whisky glass in his hand – to his astonished friends, 'Everyone knows that Iran's aggression against our people has cost a great deal of money. They forced this war on us, but couldn't defeat Iraq. Now other people want the proud Iraqi people to starve. It is a black conspiracy against our country. A conspiracy among the rulers in Kuwait.'

Uday pauses for a moment, picks up one of his newspapers and quotes from a speech by his father: 'Sometimes war is fought with soldiers, they inflict damage on one another with explosives, steel and attempted putsches. At other times war is waged with economic means.'

Everyone in the room knows what Uday is getting at with this quotation. Our state is bankrupt, we can't pay the debts we have with our main creditors, Kuwait and the Emirates. Either we persuade our creditors to drop their claims, or we demand further help from Kuwait, which we will be able to declare as compensation for the oil stolen from the Rumaila oil field.

'As we all know,' says Uday, repeating his standard phrase on this subject, 'Kuwait has stolen oil worth twenty-eight point eight billion dollars from Rumaila. The southern tip of the oil field is only five kilometres inside the Kuwait–Iraqi border. So we would only need to move the border a few kilometres and all our worries would be over.'

Once again, this observation confirms that people in the palace are seriously considering war against Kuwait. Because even I find it hard to imagine Kuwait voluntarily allowing the border to be changed. And Saddam is telling us on television every day that Kuwait isn't just stealing oil, but also waging a hidden attack on Iraq through chronic overproduction of oil.

The resulting excess is bringing the price of oil down from 20 dollars a barrel to 14. 'As a result of this aggression on the part of Kuwait, our country is losing more than a billion dollars a year,' explains Uday, adding, 'It's like a stab in the back with a poisoned dagger, and a direct attack on my father.'

I have never seen Uday like this before. All of a sudden he seems politically involved, and is even trying to acquire some knowledge about the current situation.

Two days after those declarations, his political involvement has ceased again. He tells us he's going to fly to Geneva with Waadallah Abu-Sakr. I'm surprised that Uday is taking Abu-Sakr on this journey. Abu-Sakr is the most senior head of security in the presidential palace. A powerful man. He controls all of Saddam Hussein's bodyguards, and is responsible for the personal training of the bodyguards.

The two men stay in Geneva for two days, on a secret mission. But once they come back, news of what they were up to is circulating around the palace in no time: Abu-Sakr has employed Cubans in Geneva, elite soldiers who are to be used as additional bodyguards for the ministers and leading party members. These mysterious men are occupying four storeys of the Al-Hayat building in the palace grounds. When they have shooting practice, the shooting ranges are closed to the rest of us. All contact with them is most strictly forbidden. It trickles through that the Cubans are being paid in US dollars and not in dinars. They are supposed to be getting millions, but precise figures aren't mentioned, and I don't try to find out. It seems too dangerous. The Cubans are just one more element in the murky and overstretched system of surveillance in the presidential palace.

June 1990. Once again, Saddam Hussein is summoning his family together with unusual frequency. After these meetings Uday used to chatter about their conversations, sometimes in considerable detail. Normally he just gives derisory hints like, 'Iraq has a million soldiers, Kuwait only has seventeen thousand, a pathetic air force and an apology for a navy with twenty patrol boats. All the navy does is help some of the princes to smuggle alcohol into the country. The sons of bitches in the Al-Sabah family forbid their people alcohol, while they themselves have orgies and a monopoly on the smuggling of alcohol.'

In every other sentence Uday tries to stress the military superiority of Iraq and insult the Kuwaiti royal family.

Kuwait was governed by the Al-Sabah family. On 31 December 1977 Sheikh Jabir Al-Achmad Al-Jabir Al-Sabah became the 13th Emir of Kuwait. The Crown Prince and head of government was Sheikh Saad Al-Abdallah Al-Salem Al-Sabah. Finance Minister was Sheikh Ali Al-Khalifa Al-Sabah, Foreign Minister Sheikh Sabah Al-Ahmad Al-Jabir Al-Sabah, Minister of the Interior Sheikh Salim Al-Sabah Al-Salim and Defence Minister Sheikh Nawaf Al-Achmad Al-Jabir Al-Sabah.

So all important positions were held by members of the Emir's family. Uday is furious about this, but his fury is ludicrous, because things are exactly the same in Iraq. Saddam surrounds himself exclusively with family members. But even these family bonds are not a guarantee of survival, as the example of Adnan Khairallah showed.

And unlike Iraq, a strong opposition was permitted in Kuwait. Even open criticism of the Emir is allowed. In Iraq one word out of place against the President can mean death. So by Arab standards Kuwait is one of the most open and tolerant countries in the region. What it lacks is the national assembly that would give the citizens of Kuwait a say in the running of the country.

Just such a national assembly did once exist, but because of the openness with which many members criticised the ruling family the Emir dissolved it again. But in early 1990, many former Kuwaiti members of parliament began to wage a massive campaign to put through new elections for a revived national assembly, with extended powers.

This was widely reported in Iraq. There was talk of mass demonstrations against the Emir, uprisings and radical repressive measures on the part of the Kuwaiti police.

The Al-Sabah family yielded to pressure, and in June 1990 elections were held for a 75-seat national assembly. 'A farce,' said Uday disdainfully, 'because a third of them are going to be appointed by the Emir. And in any case this farce will be boycotted by the opposition. We in Iraq must support that opposition with all the means at our disposal.' Uday goes on to explain in greater detail how he envisages this: 'The people will have to take to the streets, because the bigger the gatherings the greater the pressure will be on the government. If thousands of people take to the streets, they will lose their nerve and make the police shoot into the crowd.'

Uday doesn't say it out loud, but I know what he's thinking: in comparison to Iraq, Kuwait is a dwarf state (17,818 square kilometres). Only 800,000 of the country's two million inhabitants are Kuwaiti citizens, and only 100,000 of those are actual Kuwaitis, or members of the ancient Bedouin nobility. The Al-Sabah family has just 1,000 members.

The bulk of the population of Kuwait consists of the foreign workforce (1.2 million). A good third of those (460,000) are Palestinians. The rest are Arabs from the whole region, as well as Asians, Europeans and Americans.

This population structure produces big social differences, because only Kuwaitis have full citizenship.

So in the event of an invasion, a massive defence operation on the part of those foreigners in Kuwait is hardly to be expected. Certainly not from the Palestinians who, as we know, have good relations with Iraq, hate Israel and see Iraq as the only power with the strength and the will to destroy Israel.

'We must support our Palestinian brothers in Kuwait in all matters, because they are the true Kuwaitis. Without them the country could not survive economically,' Uday philosophises. 'They will have to resist the exploitative regime of the Al-Sabahs.'

Uday also mentions some names, confirms that members of the Iraqi secret police have been trying for weeks to persuade Kuwaiti politicians and opponents of the regime to fight openly against the corrupt government. 'We also talked to Ahmed Al-Sadoun,' says Uday. Ahmed Al-Sadoun is one of the best-known opposition politicians in Kuwait. Another person to talk to is Mohammed Al-Quadri of the Democratic Forum. 'They're both of our opinion,' lies Uday, 'they are both openly calling for an invasion by Iraq in order to topple the fiendish system in Kuwait.'

Uday neglects to tell us that both politicians have categorically rejected the idea of any kind of collaboration with Iraq, and have no intention of taking part in this transparent game. Uday stresses once again: 'We will hurry to our brothers' aid, and drive out the corrupt government which takes its pleasure in London with homosexuals and whores.'

Uday interprets Saddam Hussein's plan for Kuwait as follows: rapid invasion of Kuwait to support a 'revolutionary opposition group' that has asked Baghdad for help. Elimination of the Emir and the whole government.

The Republican Troops will attack the Dasman Palace as quickly as possible to overpower the Kuwaiti ruler. If he declares himself willing to co-operate, and to remain in office as head of a puppet regime receiving its orders from Baghdad, his life will be spared. But if he refuses, as might be expected, he will be shot on the spot for resisting the friendly Iraqi forces, along with his whole clan.

Saddam Hussein was already one step further along the way, and had already begun to get his units ready: At the end of June 1990, everyone in the palace knew that the first troops were being mobilised towards Kuwait. Thirty thousand men were moved to the Kuwaiti border. In the Al-Said Club, businessmen who had just come back from Basra in

Southern Iraq stated openly, over their gin and tonics, that when driving along the Al-Kadisya motorway linking Baghdad and Kuwait, they found themselves stuck in endless traffic jams behind columns of south-bound tanks and artillery. Huge camps are said to have been erected beside the roads.

I ask Uday about this, and he confirms that troops have been sent to the south. 'Purely as a precautionary measure,' he argues, 'in case our Kuwaiti brothers need our help in their struggle against the corrupt Al-Sabah regime.'

'How many units have been moved?' I ask, and Uday says, 'More than one hundred thousand.'

This makes it clear to me that zero hour is just around the corner. The countdown is running.

First of August 1990. Uday set off unusually early this morning, supposedly to the Olympic club. He calls me at about nine o'clock and tells me I'm going to have to keep myself ready over the next few hours. A crackling noise on the line tells me that Uday isn't in the Olympic Club, because the lines there are always excellent. It sounds more as though he is further away, or in a bunker of some kind. I don't give it another thought. But when I hear the news early that afternoon, my suspicion is confirmed: Uday and the whole leadership of Iraq have withdrawn to safe areas. The newsreader informs us: 'Discussions in Jeddah between an Iraqi delegation led by the deputy president of the Iraqi revolutionary council, Izzat Ibrahim, and the Kuwaiti prime minister, Crown Prince Saad Al-Abdallah Salem Al-Sabah ended with open provocation and aggression against Iraq.'

The speaker pauses for a moment, then continues: 'Kuwait did not agree with Iraqi proposals that they concede territory in the border region of the Rumaila oil field. And in addition Kuwait refused to pay compensation for the damage that Iraq incurred as a result of Kuwait's increased oil production, and the striking of the credit from the time of the war against Iran. The discussions were broken off after two hours.'

Izzat Ibrahim flew back to Iraq immediately after discussions were terminated. When he landed in Baghdad, the borders between Kuwait and Iraq were closed.

Meanwhile, all hell has broken loose in the palace grounds. Convoys of ministers, party officials and their bodyguards are turning up every minute. Helicopters land and fly off again. The security troops are on red alert, the numbers of sentries at the palace have been trebled. All soldiers are absolutely grounded, the phone lines from the Al-Hayat building are blocked, and conversations with people outside are only possible via radio. Everyone is tense and rushed, but not particularly nervous. Everything is going according to a plan that has been practised and trained for hundreds of times.

In the evening I go back to the shooting club. Two of my bodyguards come with me. The shooting club is almost empty; the only people there are some members of the security service. I practise shooting my pistol. My aim is good this evening. Shortly after midnight, another of my bodyguards suddenly hurries into the shooting club. He's very excited, and orders me to come to my apartment straight away. On the way there he says, 'Saddam is going to Kuwait, in the next few hours.'

'How do you know that?' I ask. He pants, 'We've just found out from Project Number 7.'

On 2 August at about two o'clock in the morning our tanks cross the Kuwaiti border at Al-Abdali. Three hundred and fifty tanks are heading for Kuwait City at a speed of 60 miles an hour. As Uday predicted, and everyone in Iraq expected, there is hardly any Kuwaiti resistance.

But I only find that out the following day. The Kuwaiti border troops have fled in a panic. The only gun-battles were on the edge of Kuwait City. Individual defenders tried to stop our tank columns, but they were simply rolled over. Even the Kuwaiti air force didn't put up any resistance: their best pilots drove to their bases, started up their 36 Mirage fighters and flew straight to Saudi Arabia.

I don't sleep a single second that night. I'd like to celebrate with my bodyguards, but we hold back and wait tensely for news and orders from Uday. But he doesn't phone. He finally calls me to Project Number 7 on the evening of 3 August. The villa is full to bursting. All Uday's friends are there. Hundreds of vehicles stand outside the house. Azzam tells me that Uday has planned a big victory celebration in the Al-Said Club, and the masters of ceremonies have already prepared everything. We drive to the club in a huge convoy. Even on the way there, some people fire their Kalashnikovs wildly into the air through the open car windows.

This evening the Al-Said Club is the most bizarre thing I've ever seen. Outside the front door there's a parade of cars that would make you think you were in a showroom specialising in luxury vehicles. There are crowds of people in the club itself. The whole of Baghdad's fine society is there.

Everything is elegantly lit, the summer and winter pools shimmer in every imaginable colour. At every corner there are buffets, liveried servants pass through the crowd balancing their trays of champagne glasses. The mood is relaxed.

When Uday comes into the club with all his bodyguards,

about a hundred in all this evening, a sudden silence falls. Then everyone bursts into thunderous applause. Everyone claps, bows down before Uday, some of them even kiss his hand. Uday is surfing on a wave of enthusiasm. He is wearing his Ray-Bans, and a black uniform with the golden inscription 'Uday Saddam Hussein'. He doesn't walk, he strides. In his left hand he holds the Havana, with his right he waves to his subjects, as though in slow motion. Sometimes he stops for a moment, walks over to a girl, runs his hand over her hair, and then walks on, followed by hundreds of pairs of eyes.

I keep myself in the background, wearing my normal bodyguard's uniform. It's curious, and although I look very similar to Uday even this evening, hardly anyone glances at me in my bodyguard's uniform. Everyone concentrates on the radiant hero, the great son of the President.

After immersing himself in the crowd, Uday comes to the microphone. As though announcing the opening of the Olympic Games, he shouts into the microphone: 'We have achieved our aim.' Then he puts the microphone down again, grabs his bodyguard's Kalashnikov and fires it into the air until the magazine is empty. While doing this, he shouts and howls and encourages all the men to do likewise. All of a sudden they all have weapons in their hands, and fire off into the clear, starry night over Baghdad. The reports sound like gunfire at the front, and I'm almost inclined to think that more shots have been fired this evening in the Al-Said Club than during the whole invasion of Kuwait.

Naturally enough, the invasion is on everyone's lips. I gradually discover from scraps of conversation what the situation is: our troops had occupied all the key positions in Kuwait within four hours after the invasion. Nine hours after the start of fighting, our soldiers were able to celebrate their victory in the streets of Kuwait City. They have control of everything: the Dasman Palace is occupied. Radio and television stations have been taken over by our people. The only serious resistance came near the Dasman Palace at the northern end of the peninsula on which Kuwait City was built.

It was here that the Kuwaiti resistance formed. These brave fighters were led by Uday's friend Fahd Al-Ahmed Al-Sabah, the Emir's brother.

Fahd had been in Baghdad only weeks before. When Uday learns that Fahd lost his life fighting for the Dasman Palace, he says cynically, 'What an idiot. He was like my brother. Like myself, he was president of his country's Olympic Committee, and president of the football association. Why didn't he yield to our will? He could have been my deputy. What was he trying to prove by being stupid like that?'

Fahd Al-Ahmed Al-Sabah had tried to repel the attacking Iraqi soldiers with the Emir's guard, but he hadn't a chance. When he stepped out towards his attackers on the top of the palace steps, pistol drawn, a 21-year-old Iraqi killed him with a volley from his Kalashnikov. When Fahd fell, the Kuwaiti resistance completely collapsed. The sheikh's corpse was dragged into the road and run over by a tank. Then three soldiers simply threw his remains at the side of the road.

That didn't disturb Uday at all. 'It's war,' was his arrogant justification. 'We didn't want to kill anyone, we just wanted to support the revolutionary forces in Kuwait.'

There's one thing that Uday doesn't mention that evening: the fact that the Emir and all his ministers were able to flee. Even before our troops reached Kuwait City, the guarding Kuwaiti officers had actually been able to warn the whole government. By the time the Republican Guard stormed the palace, the Emir and his ministers were already on the way to the Saudi Arabian border.

I learn about the second disaster the following day, the 4 of August. None of the members of the Kuwaiti opposition will declare themselves willing to join a new Iraqi government. Everyone in the palace knows what that means: the great declarations to the world's media that Iraq had only been supporting a national revolution in Kuwait against a corrupt regime are thus revealed as a lie.

But Saddam Hussein is not greatly concerned about that. On 4 August he has a transitional government installed in Kuwait. At the same time Kuwait is declared a republic. In a press conference in Baghdad, the world is informed that the head of this government is a certain Colonel Alaa Hussein Ali, officer in the Kuwaiti armed forces. But no picture of this mysterious officer is published.

And we know why: no Kuwaiti officer of that name exists.

In fact, this officer is Hussein Kamel Hassan, who is married to Saddam's eldest daughter Raghd.

I can hardly believe it! Hussein Kamel Hassan, known in Baghdad as 'Saddam's loyal hound', started out as an ordinary police constable. Later he became chauffeur to the former Iraqi president Hassan Al-Bakr. He kept that position until Saddam Hussein replaced Al-Bakr as president in 1979. (As I mentioned before: officially, Al-Bakr died of heart failure. In fact, he was poisoned by Saddam Hussein's men, and everyone in Baghdad suspected that Hussein Kamel had poisoned his master's food.)

Hussein Kamel, like Saddam Hussein, comes from Tikrit, and is closely related to Saddam. After the death of Al-Bakr, Hussein Kamel rose rapidly under President Saddam, and these suspicions were reinforced. Saddam now appointed him as his first bodyguard, a position more important than any ministerial post. Hussein Kamel received the title of lieutenant, although he had never trained as an officer.

But that mattered not at all, the only important thing was complete loyalty. In order to bind Hussein Kamel even more closely to him, Saddam married him to his eldest daughter Raghd.

Hussein Kamel has two brothers: Saddam Kamel and Hakim Kamel.

So that everything was kept in order and the family stuck together, these two also had to marry into Saddam's clan. Saddam Kamel was married to Saddam's daughter Rena, and Hakim Kamel, the youngest, was wedded to the youngest member of the Saddam family, Hala. The three brothers received dream villas within the palace grounds.

But to return to Hussein Kamel: after his marriage to Raghd he was given complete responsibility for Iraq's entire armament programme. A special arms ministry was founded for that purpose. Hussein Kamel, the former chauffeur, became the minister in the department, and also took on the Ministry of Industry, which was at this point responsible for arms production.

Even that didn't satisfy his craving for power: he also had his eye on the oil ministry. For his sake, Saddam Hussein forced his oil minister to issue a public self-denunciation. During the television news he had to declare that he had broken the laws of Iraq, and sold oil in order to enrich himself.

His whole body was trembling so much that it was clear to everyone in Iraq that the man was under pressure. Shortly afterwards he died in a Baghdad hospital. Heart failure was the official cause of death.

The following day Hussein Kamel also took over the oil ministry. In addition, he was given the defence ministry that was left vacant by Adnan Khairallah's helicopter crash, as well as the transport ministry.

Hussein Kamel, the man without a degree or any other kind of qualification, had thus become a minister four times over – and now all of a sudden he was head of the Kuwaiti government as well.

THIRTEEN

Everyone's Been Stealing

Just days after the invasion, Kuwait City looked like a ghost town. Our troops were in control of the whole region, the oil ports of Shuaiba and Ahmadi and the airport. Thousands of abandoned cars lay scattered about the empty streets. All the shops were closed, their owners having mostly fled. Our soldiers drove the Kuwaitis' luxury cars, chiefly Mercedes, in triumph through Kuwait City. The streets and pavements in some parts of the city had been ripped open by the cater-pillar tracks. Radio, television and all other means of communication were under Iraqi control. Only individual skirmishes flickered when Kuwaiti snipers opened fire on our patrolling soldiers.

The new government, since no member of the Kuwaiti opposition could be found who was willing to take part, consisted entirely of middle-ranking Iraqi soldiers. None the less, Baghdad television proudly announced that the new head of the Kuwaiti government, Alaa Hussein Ali, alias Hussein Kamel Hassan, had, in an official letter to the Iraqi head of state, declared the provisional Kuwaiti government willing to enter into negotiations with Iraq about the position of their shared border – pure eyewash, because the new head of the Kuwaiti government was Saddam's son-in-law, a favourite who would never contradict Saddam.

Now the border problems could be solved, so to speak, within the family council. Izzat Ibrahim, another puppet of Saddam's, was appointed leader of the Iraqi negotiation delegation. At the same time all senior officers in the Kuwaiti army and police were dismissed with effect from 4 August.

While this transparent political display was going on, behind the scenes plans were being drawn up for one of the biggest private plundering raids of modern times.

It is 8 August 1990, a day to remember. First of all, US President George Bush showed strength and resolution in sending the first contingents of troops to the Gulf: the 18th Marine Corps. The aircraft carriers Independence, Saratoga and Eisenhower set sail for the Persian Gulf with 50 escort vessels. US F-111 fighters are moved from Great Britain to Turkish NATO airports, B-52 bombers are being moved from their bases in the Indian Ocean to Dahran in Eastern Saudi Arabia. The big Allied Gulf campaign is under way.

And at the same time, in Kuwait City the independent state of Kuwait is being officially dissolved. In a television address, Saddam Hussein announces the union of Iraq with the former Emirate: 'Thanks to the help of God we are now one people, one state, which will be the pride of the Arabs. The new Iraq extends from Zacho (Northern Iraq) to Ahmadi (Kuwait's oil port on the Gulf).' In Baghdad the speech prompted frenetic celebrations, and the Party brought hundreds of thousands of people into Palestinian Street to demonstrate their joy. The crowds have no idea that at the same time the first US troops are arriving in the Saudi Arabian desert. The Iraqi media say nothing about that. The people are intoxicated and feel like victors, and no one seriously thinks that the Western world could possibly be preparing to counter-attack.

But the most important event for us that day takes place in Project Number 7: Uday Saddam Hussein has summoned all his bodyguards and colleagues to explain his 'Operation Kuwait' to them. He brings with him our schedule for the coming days, lays his documents meaningfully on his desk, stands in front of us and begins: 'Kuwait now belongs to us. Its possessions are our possessions.'

As he speaks he picks up his lists again and walks back and forth in front of the desk, taking big strides. Then he stops again, turns towards us, draws on his cigar, looks over our heads and says in a dramatic undertone: 'Tomorrow our Operation Kuwait begins.'

Uday pauses for a long time to emphasise the importance of his moment. Then he explains, like a manager at a directors' meeting, what he means by Operation Kuwait: 'Azzam is going to be putting together twenty-man teams,' he says, and proceeds to explain the tasks of these teams.

Number one: 'Car Team'. Every Mercedes and BMW abandoned in Kuwait is to be requisitioned and brought to Baghdad on car transporters. Uday stresses that for the time being he doesn't want any Cadillacs or Rolls Royces, just German quality cars. Any cars for which no keys can be found are simply to be hot-wired or lifted by crane on to the trucks. If Kuwaiti dealers or owners cause problems, they are to be executed immediately for 'resisting the forces of the state'.

Number two: the 'Buildings Team' is to requisition all abandoned villas and put them under the administration of Uday's companies. The furniture, the household utensils and air-conditioning systems, marble floors and valuable objects are to be loaded up and brought to Baghdad. A subdivision of the 'Buildings Team' will assume the task of dismantling and transporting large air-conditioning systems and kitchens from hotels, valuable hospital equipment, machines, office fittings, computers and telecommunication systems.

Number three: the 'Hi-Fi Team' is to go through all shops and supermarkets in Kuwait and carry off electrical goods; only valuable equipment, nothing cheap.

Uday doesn't actually mention jewellery shops, which surprises me, because jewels and watches could be transported without difficulty.

Then Uday and Azzam assembled the three twenty-man teams.

Things get going 24 hours later. I drive south with my team along the Al-Kadisya motorway. It's congested with army vehicles transporting soldiers and military material towards Kuwait. We travel along the motorway without any difficulties. At the checkpoints it's usually enough for my bodyguards to say that our convoy's working for Uday, and if not then we've always got our papers from the most senior secret service officers to say that we're carrying out a 'special mission'.

We're even obsequiously offered a police escort, although I reject it, pointing out that my own escort is enough. Our convoy consists of four identical Mercedes limousines and six two-tier car-transporters, as well as five ordinary tractors and trailers.

Our first destination that day is only 15 miles across the border. We park our car-transporters outside Gahnem, the biggest car dealership in the city. The forecourt is full of European and American cars.

Before the invasion, most cars in Kuwait were enormous

gas-guzzlers, because petrol was as cheap as water. There was no road tax, and every household had at least two or three cars. Especially popular were European luxury cars like Mercedes, BMW, Porsche, Jaguar and Rolls Royce, and heavy American cars. Seven hundred thousand cars were registered in Kuwait at the time.

When our convoy stops, an officer guarding the car-show-room comes over to us. I leap out of my car, and my bodyguards come after me. My black uniform bearing the name of the President's son is identification enough. The officer, a slim man with dark skin, salutes and stammers his name and number. I tell him that I, Uday Saddam Hussein, am going to take away all the Mercedes and BMWs. The officer salutes again, kisses my hand and bows a few times. As he does so I see that there are some soldiers taking everything that can be taken out of the bullet-riddled abandoned cars. Radios, aerials, headlights, wheels, mirrors – they're taking anything, like scavenging hyenas. When they see us they drop everything, and disappear behind the big showroom building. The officer is aware that I've noticed the soldiers. His embarrassed expression tells us that he's in league with them. I manage a friendly smile, and order him to clear off immediately, or else I'll have to have him and his men punished.

The slim officer makes off just as fast as his men.

On the journey here I'd noticed hundreds of vans and buses coming towards us, all full to the brim with spare car-parts: it's as though every single occupying Iraqi soldier had called all his relations into Kuwait to carry off their plunder.

Kuwait is one great big self-service shop as far as the soldiers are concerned, and clearly none of the officers have done anything about it so far, as though they were all in it together. It's common knowledge that everyone is stealing, but no one reports anything. Who would they report to?

Everyone's looting as though it was the sole purpose of this war. I don't have a sense that we really want to keep Kuwait. Would we go on plundering so brazenly if we did? And on top of that, none of the soldiers seem to be at all bothered by the fact that a few miles away, in the Saudi Arabian desert, a massive army is preparing to tear into our troops.

No one is seriously giving any thought to that, the only thing they're concerned with is getting as much booty out of Kuwait as they can. I can understand the soldiers' point of view: normally, men at the front earn 22 dinars a month, barely 25 dollars. Too little to live on, although not too little to starve. Here they can multiply their meagre wages a thousand times over if they can somehow get the goods out of Kuwait and into Iraq. The roads towards the border are full of soldiers and refugees. In huge columns the Asian and Arab workers who have earned their money in Kuwait are leaving the country. There are endless columns of refugees heading northwards. More than a million people are trying to reach the Jordanian border to the west, or the Turkish border to the north of Iraq. Mixed in among the refugees are Iraqi soldiers carrying off their loot.

At the same time, thousands of Kuwaitis are trying to leave their country for Saudi Arabia. The Iraqi soldiers aren't stopping them, but they are demanding to see the Kuwaitis' papers and extorting a kind of toll from them, generally exploiting their misery. The whole campaign is nothing but the most unbelievable, shameless robbery. The only people who have had to stay behind as hostages in Iraq are about six thousand foreigners, Europeans and Americans, representatives of the countries whose governments have sent troops to the Gulf. They are obliged to report to various hotels in Kuwait, and are then brought in groups from there to Baghdad.

We load 42 Mercedes 500s and big BMWs on to our transporters. My bodyguards are enjoying themselves in their own way. They are hot-wiring luxury cars, doing handbrake turns on the showroom forecourts. They're especially delighted when they crash the vehicles.

It takes us two hours to load all the cars. During that time I feel as though I'm constantly being watched, even though I can't see a single Kuwaiti.

The whole region seems completely dead.

The next day we bring our first load to Uday's Al-Rashdiya farm in the Baghdad district of Al-Jasira Al-Siahia, the farm where Uday breeds his fighting dogs, his rottweilers, mastiffs and Alsatians. He even keeps a young tiger and two black panthers in cages there.

Our transport isn't the first one. Azzam and his men were faster than we were, as was Captain Siad. The exploitation is there for all to see: on the farm alone there are already more than 100 German luxury cars.

Uday is happy with us and our troops. There have been no problems, and no one has had to fire a gun. He tells us proudly that yet more transporters are going to arrive tonight, and that we're to start over again the next day.

On 11 August I drive with my men to the districts of Shuwaikh and Hawalli in Kuwait City, where we've been told that most of the car dealerships are based. The information is correct. But there are problems: in Hawalli we come across a group of other Iraqi officers who are loading up cars as well. They're Hussein Kamel's men.

'What's going on here?' I ask the commander. He replies, 'Sir, we have been given the task of bringing European cars to the farms of Hussein Kamel Hassan in Tikrit.'

I don't say anything, just turn away, thinking, 'So Hussein

Kamel Hassan is another of these hyenas.'

But there are plenty of cars around for both teams. We load up, and watch an officer from another group stopping a Kuwaiti who happens to be passing in his car, ordering him out of the vehicle and chasing him away. He vanishes without resistance, presumably happy not to have been shot.

It takes us considerably less time to load up the cars than it did on the previous occasion. By now my men have a certain amount of practice in breaking into cars and hot-wiring them.

When I get back to Baghdad I tell Uday about my meeting with Hussein Kamel Hassan's men. He flies into one of his rages, shouts and gives away one important detail: 'We'd agreed exactly who was to requisition which cars.'

It's clear what's going on here. The whole Hussein clan is joining in the looting of Kuwait. They're so greedy that they're even getting in each other's way, like wild animals fighting over their booty. But there's also a kind of ranking involved: first come the hyenas (the Hussein clan), and then the vultures (the ordinary soldiers) to take away what's left.

Saddam Hussein carries off the biggest coup of all: he carries off 3,216 gold bars from the treasuries of the Kuwaiti National Bank, as well as 63 tons of gold coins and whole helicopter-loads of foreign bank-notes, and all the art treasures from the National Museum.

The ordinary Iraqi people are also profiting from this plunder. Although the United Nations have imposed an embargo, you can get anything you want in Iraq. During this time Baghdad, like all other Iraqi cities, is being deluged with goods from Kuwait. All of a sudden the shops are full of the finest commodities, most of them with their Kuwaiti price-tags still attached. There is chicken liver paté and Norwegian salmon, alcohol-free beer that you could never

get in Baghdad, and preserved meats from all over the world.
There are video cameras, video recorders, cameras and all
kinds of electrical goods, from food mixers to hair-dryers,
from washing machines to ordinary light-switches. There's
everything, basically, and it's all for sale at knock-down
prices. This renders UN sanctions completely ineffectual,
and there's enough food stored in the Kuwaiti supermarkets
to keep the whole of Iraq supplied for months.

Most of these shops are kept supplied by the men of
Hussein Kamel Hassan, who has assigned several units the
sole task of looting goods from the supermarkets in Kuwait
and bringing them to Iraq. It's a business worth billions.

Our troops are operating more discreetly than that, but
they're equally efficient: by 10 September they've managed
to bring more than 10,000 luxury cars from Kuwait to
Baghdad. There is no free space left on Uday's farms for us
to store any additional cars. Even the car parks and garages
at the Olympic Club are full to the brim with luxury cars.
The rest of the stolen goods, like electrical appliances, make-
up and furniture, are either sold in Iraq by Uday's business
partners, the dealers Mohammed Kora Ghauli, Khaled Al-
Kabisi, Said Kammuneh and Dureid Ghannaoui, or
smuggled to Jordan.

Now comes the next step. The stolen cars have to be sold
on, so full-page advertisements start appearing every day in
the Baghdad newspapers: 'Auctions of Mercedes and BMW
limousines', followed by the time and the place. The stolen
cars are being sold at rock-bottom prices. The auctions are
held in the car park outside the Olympic Club building.
Payment is to be made in US dollars. The auctioneers are
alternately Azzam and myself. Uday stays discreetly in the
background, studying the view from his office in the

Olympic Club. On average we sell 60 to 70 cars a day.

The buyers aren't worried about the fact that we have no ignition keys for the cars. We offer to hot-wire them so that the buyers can drive to the nearest garage and get themselves a key. There are no problems with new papers and registration plates, either: for 100 dinars everyone gets a new plate. We come away from the first auction with a profit of $8 million. We throw the money in great bundles on to the desk in Uday's office in the Olympic Club. The whole club is like one big safe, and everyone takes a piece of the pie, because Uday and his financial managers have long since lost control of this unexpected windfall.

New girls are forever turning up in the club, everyone's drinking and partying every day. The offices are basically turning into flophouses and being used for wild orgies. The lives of Uday and his men were already pretty wild. But what's happening now goes beyond anything that went before. Naked girls roll screeching with bodyguards on the floor. At one point Uday has a girl jump on to a table on which various lamb dishes are laid out for a warm buffet. The girl rolls about in the pilau rice, smearing curry and all kinds of sauces over her breasts, and demands that we lick them off. Some of the men do.

By 10 September Uday has achieved the fabulous profit of $125 million from his car sales. In the streets of Baghdad, where a Mercedes or a BMW was once a rarity, these luxury cars have now become a familiar sight. And in the past Uday had punished anyone with a more stylish car than his own. Now Baghdad is inundated with them. Even a Jaguar, a Rolls Royce or a big American gas-guzzler doesn't particularly stand out any more.

Unfortunately, the glut leads to a drastic drop in price.

Above all, Hussein Kamel Hassan's men are selling the cars at discount prices: Chevrolets for $5,000, Cadillacs for $4,000, BMW's for $8,000. Their particular enticement: free registration plates which the buyers can collect directly from the Ministry of the Interior. Hussein Kamel Hassan's car sales in the Baghdad districts of Alnahda and Algaya are turned into enormous motor shows, attracting thousands of people.

This represents major competition for Uday. He has Hussein Kamel Hassan's retinue shadowed, and comes upon a scandal: the huge incomes from the sale of cars, electrical goods and make-up aren't actually enough for Hussein Kamel Hassan. On the basis that in times like this everything is possible, he has set up printing machines on his farms in Tikrit, with which he has been printing 25 dinar, 50 dinar and 100 dinar notes. There are about 80 million forged dinars from Hussein Kamel Hassan's workshop circulating in Baghdad alone.

Even before he knew of Hassan's involvement, Saddam Hussein had announced that he was taking radical steps against the counterfeiters. First of all two Baghdad businessmen, Maker Al-Dlimi and Naser Al-Basrani, were arrested and charged. When Saddam learned shortly afterwards that his son-in-law was behind it, he drove to his farm in Tikrit. Seven forgers, all members of the secret service, were arrested and shown on the television evening news. A week later they were executed. The President shot them in person, using the revolver that belonged to his bodyguard Abed Hamed.

At the same time, the minister four times over was relieved of his offices. Iraqi television announced that Hussein Kamel Hassan no longer had his job. In addition, all his property was requisitioned, and Saddam forced him to divorce from Raghd, the President's eldest daughter.

But after a short time and some internal discussions, these radical measures are revoked, supposedly because all the ministers have spoken up for Saddam's son-in-law and guaranteed his innocence. One of the usual television spectacles is organised to announce that Hussein Kamel Hassan has had his offices restored to him. The divorce is also revoked, and the President pointedly assures his son-in-law of his complete trust.

But back to Kuwait: on 28 August 1990 Saddam Hussein declares Kuwait to be the 19th province of Iraq. Two weeks later, on 15 September 1990, Ali Hassan Al-Majid is appointed as the new governor of the province of Kuwait.

So one criminal follows another. And Ali Hassan Al-Majid, 'Chemical Ali', who had ordered the poison gas attacks on the Kurds in 1988, is even stricter than his predecessor in Kuwait, ordering rigorous punitive actions against supposed resistance fighters. Saddam Hussein had given 'Chemical Ali' complete freedom of action. And he was reckless in his application of martial law.

Once, when an Iraqi patrol was fired on in a residential area, all the inhabitants were taken out of their houses. Men and women had to line up separately, along the walls of the building. An officer counted out the women and made each tenth woman step forward. Another counted out the men, and made every fifth man step forward. They had to line up against different walls. Then a jeep mounted with a machine-gun drove up. A burst of gunfire and it was all over. An officer ordered the survivors to carry off their dead.

In another punitive action, 15 Kuwaitis were massacred. The survivors were beaten on the soles of their feet until the bones were visible, and then they had their heads pushed into a bathtub filled with water and human excrement, until they drank the brew to avoid drowning.

Al-Majid also tortured any Kuwaitis who refused to describe themselves as Iraqi citizens. To count as a traitor or an *agent provocateur* it was enough to have coins or notes in the now-invalid Kuwaiti currency.

Al-Majid's men had complete licence. The rigid disciplinary regulations of the army didn't apply to them. They murdered, raped, committed arson. Al-Majid was in his element.

In Baghdad we hear next to nothing about these punishments. We're concentrating too much on our plundering raids. By now we're taking any cars that strike us as at all valuable. We've thrown caution to the winds, and are now acting just like the men of Hussein Kamel Hassan. We stop cars in broad daylight, throw out the drivers, and that's that. Or we simply force our way into shops and requisition everything in sight.

Of course, I know that we're committing a crime. But I have to carry out Uday's orders.

Soon we start going beyond car theft. One day Uday orders me to loot the private villa of a jeweller in the Kuwait City district of Shamiya. There are large amounts of gold hidden there, 600 kilos of gold, as well as rough diamonds, jewellery and watches.

By the time we storm the building another group of looters is already at work. The jeweller has been killed, and is lying in a pool of blood. In the middle of the room there is a coffin in which the men are stowing all the jewellery. They are led by Ali Hassan Al-Majid, the new governor of 'Province 19'. While his soldiers think that I am Uday Saddam Hussein, he knows immediately that I'm only his double.

Al-Majid yells at us and chases us away. As we leave, I see his men draping an Iraqi flag over the brimming coffin.

The coffin is officially brought back to Baghdad the following day, escorted by an officer. They call it 'the return of the hero'. But it actually ends up on Ali Hassan Al-Majid's farm outside Baghdad.

The officer and the three soldiers who had the task of officially handing over the coffin were hanged two days later. Al-Majid charged them with the crime of robbing a jeweller in Kuwait. Their corpses hung in the streets of Baghdad for seven days, 'to encourage the others'. The pictures of the dead were broadcast all around the world. Al-Majid duplicitously declared that any soldier caught looting will be executed immediately, without trial.

Uday isn't at all impressed by this. He knows just as well as we do that this applies only to ordinary soldiers and officers, but not to members of the presidential clan and the people who work for it.

By now the bodyguards of Uday's mother Sajida are also taking part in the plundering expeditions to Kuwait. Sajida, who was already one of the wealthiest women in the world, has truck after truck of marble brought to Baghdad. Shortly before the invasion she had had a high-rise building erected near the Babel Aubouri hotel, and is now having its walls and floors clad with marble from Kuwait. The tall building will house exclusive shops and offices, which will be rented out via agents from 300,000 dinars per unit.

I'm barely aware of developments in Saudi Arabia and the arrival of the Allied troops. Certainly, we have heard of catch-phrases like 'Desert Storm', and of course we know that new troops are constantly arriving in the Gulf. But none of us seriously believes that there will be a massive strike against Iraq. I'm aware that Saddam Hussein is constantly calling for a 'holy war' against the West, and trying to draw the Israelis into the conflict by threatening to fire poison gas missiles into Israel, but I don't take these threats seriously; I see them as mere attempts at distraction.

And apart from that, we still have the 6,000 Western hostages. A security to ensure that nothing will happen.

Most of these 'special guests', as Saddam calls them, stand around in the bars of the big hotels, spending their time playing cards, and after a few weeks hardly anyone pays them any attention.

When I'm not in Kuwait with my team, I'm either in the Olympic Club or at auctions. The trade in plundered goods has by now assumed such proportions that it isn't even hidden from the foreign journalists posted in Baghdad. There are only a few foreign journalists here, and their movements are severely restricted – but all those Rolls Royces and Mercedes, Jaguars and Cadillacs in the streets of Baghdad speak clearly enough. Soon reports about them are appearing in the Western media.

And in Baghdad, everyone with a spark of decency and self-regard has begun to get annoyed that the President's son is filling his own pockets in such a contemptible way.

It's a precarious situation for Uday. On the one hand we have many hundreds of cars to sell, on the other the pressure of public opinion is intensifying from one day to the next. Even Western politicians who are coming to Baghdad to plead for the release of the hostages learn what the President's son is up to. The Ministry of Information has its hands full coming up with lies ('The goods were brought to Iraq by the refugees') to cover up what's going on here.

Saddam Hussein is annoyed by these reports. The whole Gulf region is facing a war that could go either way – and now he has to deal with the fact that his own son and his closest colleagues are being accused of robbery.

On top of that, a critical discussion has begun in the army about the fact that ordinary soldiers are being hanged or shot on the spot if they are caught looting, but Saddam's son can plunder with impunity. Uday has always been hated, but now his reputation has plummeted.

Furthermore, hundreds of people in Baghdad are now aware that Uday Saddam Hussein has a double. He uses me as he sees fit, whether as Uday or as Latif Yahia, his bodyguard. He is constantly taking me to his parties, and I'm even allowed to accompany him on his expeditions through the hotels of Baghdad. So I'm no longer just his fiday, but also his drinking companion and friend. Things couldn't go on like that for long!

Uday is aware of this. Late in September 1990 he speaks openly about getting rid of me. The simplest thing, he says at one point in conversation with Azzam, 'would be for you to murder Latif and dump his body in the lake.' My death sentence? No, my quiet death would be of no use to him. So Azzam replies, 'There would be no point, people would continue to talk. It wouldn't save your reputation, sir.'

But most of the guilt for the plundering raids was still placed on the shoulders of Uday, both in Iraq and in the West.

So it must be possible to find another solution. On the day after his conversation with Azzam, which I listened in on from the next room, Uday calls in Munem Hammed and all the other officers who have trained me to ask their advice about how the gossip about him and his plundering raids to Kuwait can be stopped. Shukr Al-Tikritti, an officer in the secret service, has a bright idea: 'I've come up with something that will deceive everyone . . .'

*

Shukr Al-Tikritti's idea is both bizarre and brilliant: Uday
has access to all the Iraqi media, including the state
television channel. 'Using those media,' he explains, 'we
should be able to get you out of this.' Uday is sceptical and
is about to interrupt Al-Tikritti, but then he lets him
continue, and his friend goes on: 'You've never appeared
anywhere in person, have you?'

Uday shakes his head and asks naïvely, 'What has that got
to do with anything?'

Al-Tikritti: 'Wait a moment and I'll tell you. You weren't in
Kuwait, you haven't stolen any cars anywhere or auctioned
them off. So no one can have seen you, Uday Saddam
Hussein, committing any criminal act.' Al-Tikritti takes a
short pause, runs his left hand over his moustache and then
continues: 'So if it wasn't you who carried out the
plundering raids in Kuwait, you can't have been lining your
own pockets – you see?'

Uday and the other officers still don't understand what
he's trying to say. Al-Tikritti explains his plan even more
precisely, and it chills my blood: I, Latif Yahia, am to appear
on Iraqi television, in the main news bulletin, and declare
that it wasn't Uday Saddam Hussein who undertook the
plundering raids in Kuwait, but me. I, Latif Yahia, exploited
my resemblance to the President's son in order to deceive
honest officers and bring thousands of cars to Baghdad.

Uday is speechless, and so are Munem Hammed and the
other officers. They shower Shukr Al-Tikritti with compliments and laugh. Uday says, 'Brilliant!'

He gets to his feet, stands in front of Al-Tikritti, grabs his
shoulders with both hands, pulls him violently to him, kisses
him three times and exults, 'My brother, this is brilliant,
simply brilliant ... we will also be able to print the
declarations of the wicked rogue Latif Yahia in all the

newspapers, and publish a photograph of him. The whole world must know that I have been dishonoured by an underhand trickster.'

I'm speechless. They've got me, and there's nothing I can do about it. Uday grins at me, claps me on the shoulder and hisses, 'We're going to condemn you to death, Latif, and you're going to play along.' They all look at me and burst out laughing. I grin with embarrassment.

Preparations for my television appearance begin the next day. My apartment in the Al-Hayat building is turned into a television studio. Shukr Al-Tikritti draws up the text that I'm to learn by heart.

'I, Latif Yahia Latif, born on fourteenth June nineteen sixty-four, have exploited my resemblance to Uday Saddam Hussein to steal goods from Kuwait in his name and sell them in Baghdad. I did this all for my own gain. I was the one who was enriched, not Uday Saddam Hussein. Uday is completely innocent. He is the most honest person in the world.'

I have to deliver this text time and again for 12 whole days. We make hundreds of recordings. I always have to sit on a presenter's chair in front of a grey screen, always in Uday's uniform. In my presentation I have to stress the word 'I'.

First we practise without accessories. I just sit upright on my chair and say what I have to say. But Uday thinks it would be more authentic if I held a Havana in my hand and sat in an armchair with my legs crossed. Then everyone would immediately see how much I looked like the President's son, and that I had even adopted his habits in order to cheat him.

We rehearse the scene a few times. I have to hold the cigar pointedly in my left hand, slump in the armchair, take a few drags on the cigar and then deliver my speech. Everything is recorded on video, and Uday always objects to something or other. Either I'm smoking too pointedly, or I'm slumping too much in the chair. Finally they agree that I should only hold the cigar in my hand, as Uday does, when delivering my text.

On 9 November 1990 I have my make-up applied by Ismail Al-Azami, Uday's private barber. He also precisely trims my moustache and my hair, cutting each hair individually. After that it's the turn of Yassem Al-Helou, Uday's dresser. He comes with a brand new uniform with the Iraqi eagle and Uday Saddam Hussein's monogram on the chest. It takes them just under an hour to get me ready.

Then it's time to get going. I sit on the presenter's chair, with the cameraman in front of me. He gives me a sign and I start: I hold the cigar as I've been instructed to do, my legs are crossed, I look straight into the camera. Although I'm quite calm, I fluff my lines during the first recording: 'I, Latif Yahia Latif, born on eighteenth June nineteen sixty-four in Baghdad . . .' Al-Tikritti interrupts me: 'You fool, you weren't born on eighteenth June nineteen sixty-four, that was Uday.'

We laugh, have another try, and this time it goes according to plan. I don't stumble over a single word, and nothing about me is artificial or tense. I come across as casual and relaxed, and not at all as though anyone were forcing me to make this statement.

It's ridiculous: I'm declaring my guilt, and at the same time I'm proud that I can deliver my self-accusation perfectly and without a single mistake. I'm making an effort, I'm joining in, doing everything for my master. A true fiday, I say to myself, feeling awful.

Eleventh November 1990, the evening news. The speaker announces in a patriotic voice: 'Over the past few days a criminal by the name of Latif Yahia Latif, son of a wealthy Baghdad businessman, was arrested. Latif Yahia Latif is responsible for the smuggling of stolen goods out of Kuwait. This son of an affluent family has sold the goods in Baghdad and exploited his resemblance to the President's son in order to carry out these criminal acts. He has sullied the name of his family and the name of the great son of the President.'

Then the screen fades into the video that we recorded the previous day.

I am sitting with Uday, the bodyguards and Shukr Al-Tikritti in Project Number 7 when the programme goes out. The bodyguards clutch their sides with laughter when they see the video, and so does Uday.

After my self-accusation the speaker declares in a sepulchral voice, 'With this crime Latif Yahia Latif has undermined the reputation of Uday Saddam Hussein. He has been condemned to death by hanging. The execution will be carried out over the next few days.'

And that's it. Uday and his bodyguards cheer, clap and congratulate each other for such a fantastic show.

I feel terrible, because after this announcement Yahia is dead, for good. I no longer exist. Previously, as far as my friends were concerned I was just someone who had dis-appeared, and now I'm a hanged man, covered with shame. And my shame also falls upon my family, my father, my mother, my brothers, my sisters. Will my family have seen that? What will my mother think? If she hasn't seen it herself, her friends and neighbours will tell her about it. They'll phone her up, tell her that her son has just declared on television that he's a criminal. I don't want to make myself out to be better than I am. Of course I was greedy for the goods from Kuwait. I also admit that I swiped a few cars for myself. But Uday never found out about that, and I had no scruples about it because the true criminal was Uday. He was the one who had the idea in the first place, and he ordered us to carry it out.

'What happens now?' I ask Uday, 'what's supposed to happen after this television show?'

'You'll be informed,' laughs Uday. Before he leaves the room I ask him whether I can inform my parents and let them know I'm still alive. Uday replies with a stern, 'No. From now on you aren't going to leave the palace and the grounds of the Al-Hayat building.'

At that moment it becomes clear to me that if I'm ever to escape Saddam's clan alive, on no account can I stay in Iraq. My existence as a citizen has been destroyed, and that's worse than death. I think about the fact that there have been hundreds of incredible show trials in Iraq, and rely on the intelligence of the Iraqi people: 'They must have been able to tell that that was nothing but a staged spectacle to leave the President's family looking whiter than white. No, no, they won't have believed this story. Everyone in Baghdad knows that Uday has been lining his own pockets. He's been doing it for months. How could I have done it without his knowledge? There's no way that my parents, my friends could be deceived by my declaration on television!'

For the first time I think of escape, but things are to take a different turn.

FOURTEEN

The Bombs Fall

After my public declaration of guilt I am more or less under house arrest. I have bodyguards around me at all times. I'm allowed to go to the pool and the shooting-range. But I have no information about what's going on outside.

I don't learn that the situation in the Gulf is getting more and more critical, despite the fact that Saddam has freed all the Western hostages. My bodyguards just tell me that the United Nations Security Council, a 'pseudo-council black-mailed by the Americans', has given Iraq an ultimatum: either our troops have withdrawn from Kuwait by 15 January 1991, or the Allied troops will attack Iraq to free Kuwait by force.

In their blind arrogance, my bodyguards parrot everything they are told. Just like Saddam Hussein, they talk about the 'Jihad', the holy war, although they have no idea what that really means. Laughing and swinging their Kalashnikovs, they threaten 'to strangle any American soldier who should fall into their hands'. Or, 'If Bush attacks us, we'll be ready to teach the aggressor a lesson. We will win the mother of all battles.'

Empty words. I ignore all these outpourings, particularly since I know that the men are really thinking something quite different: 'Nothing but empty words. How are we going to stand up to the rest of the world?'

Almost everyone in Iraq is thinking like that. Everyone is frightened by the prospect of war.

And because I know that Saddam has a strong sense of the popular mood, I'm inclined to suspect that our President will withdraw from Kuwait at the last minute because he can no longer be certain of his people.

He's behaving like a poker player who keeps on bluffing until the last minute, but then passes after all because he has a bad hand. Saddam can't have failed to see that more and more people are leaving Baghdad for their summer-houses in the country, because they're frightened and think that in the event of an attack they might have a greater chance of survival there.

Every now and again I hear from my bodyguards that incredible figures are circulating about our fighting capacity: 'According to the American media,' my bodyguards say, 'there are more than half a million Iraqi soldiers in Kuwait, with thousands of tanks and the latest military technology. You were in Kuwait, what's the truth?'

My answer disappoints them: 'I was in Kuwait, and I can only say that there can hardly be more than a quarter of a million soldiers in Kuwait. Probably even less than that. Their bases are primitive, and none of them want to fight. What they'd really like to do is throw away their weapons and clear off home.'

If anyone in authority learned that I'd been saying such things it could mean the death penalty for me. But my bodyguards keep my outburst to themselves. They're probably thinking much the same things as I am.

January 1991. I happen to bump into Munem Hammed outside the Al-Hayat building. He asks me how I am, and I reply that I'm reasonably okay, but that I'd like to have some new tasks to do. 'For weeks I've been doing nothing, absolutely nothing,' I complain.

Munem Hammed nods sympathetically, and answers cryptically:

'You're going to be used sooner and more often than any of us would wish.' Then he walks on.

I don't know what to make of Munem Hammed's answer. What did he mean? What information does Munem Hammed have?

It isn't until a few days later that I learn what Munem Hammed already knew at this point: from one day to the next, almost the entire family of Saddam Hussein had left Iraq via Jordan in several convoys. Uday and his bodyguards were travelling in one. In another were his mother Sajida and Saddam's daughters Raghd and Rena, in a third the President's youngest daughter Hala with her husband Hakim. The families of numerous ministers had fled as well. The whole clan had travelled on from Jordan to Algeria, and from there to Brazil. Uday flew back from Brazil to Geneva, to stay with his uncle Barzan Al-Tikritti. The ministers' families fled to Mauretania. Only Saddam Hussein and his son Qusay stayed in Iraq.

This information is confirmed in principle by the statements of my bodyguards, although not in every detail. At one point I'm told that Uday has fled straight from Amman in Jordan to Switzerland, and on another occasion that he first went to Brazil with his family, and from there to Geneva.

These details don't matter much in my present situation. The only important thing is that the families have gone. That actually confirms that the Iraqi leadership is fully expecting war, and the negotiations of Foreign Minister Tariq Aziz and General Secretary of the United Nations Perez de Cuellar are already of no importance.

Saddam Hussein has no intention of withdrawing from

Kuwait. He wants war, and threatens countless times that in the event of an attack by Allied forces he will fire missiles at Israel.

In this situation I think of my parents. Where will they go? There are hardly any bunkers in Baghdad, and the few that do exist are reserved for Party members. With any luck they will travel to relations in Northern Iraq, or else book a room in one of the tourist hotels in Baghdad for the next few days.

Time and again I talk to my bodyguards about the growing threat of war. I want to know what's happening in the country. They confirm that public information films about mass evacuations are being shown on television, and all of a sudden the bodyguards aren't nearly as cocky as they were even a few days ago: 'My father,' says one whose name I don't want to mention because he always behaved decently, 'said that Iraq couldn't withstand a second war. That Iraq has no chance of survival. The Americans and Europeans will destroy us.' In that conversation he even admits that some members of his family had wanted to emigrate to Amman, but they couldn't get any papers to leave the country. For the first time I notice a rising tide of fear.

Sixteenth January 1991. A crucial day. The countdown begins. The Allied ultimatum has expired. War could start at any moment. My bodyguards bring me back the television that they took away from me weeks ago. One of my guards even has a short-wave radio. We turn it on, hoping to hear what the world thinks, but we only manage to get Radio Monte Carlo for a few moments. We can't pick up the BBC World Service.

We turn on the television. Of course we can't receive CNN. We can only get the Iraqi news. The announcer says that President Saddam Hussein is staying in the bunker at his headquarters, and that the Iraqi people will launch 'deadly strikes on the aggressors'. I can't bear to hear another word of that evil propaganda. But don't I hear fear in the announcer's voice? Certainly, our people are familiar with war, they know how terrible it is when missiles strike and bombs explode. But now? Iraq against the whole world? Where's my bunker?

My bodyguards reassure me, saying that we're certainly not going to be staying in the Al-Hayat building if there actually is an attack.

We concentrate on the television images again. They show thousands of demonstrators moving down Palestinian Street. They are waving pictures of Saddam Hussein, and shouting 'Down with Bush, down with Bush'. In among them there are young people aiming their Kalashnikovs into the sky as though to bring down fighter planes.

Amongst the demonstrators you can make out Party members, spurring the people on. I detest those *agents provocateurs* – you can see the fear on the people's faces! And they don't even know that Saddam Hussein's whole family has headed for the hills long ago. They aren't aware that all the important units are being withdrawn from the palace grounds, and that this has been going on for days. Project 2000, Saddam's headquarters, is empty. Files are constantly being carried off by special units. The atmosphere is tense and quiet. Everyone is nervous, but no one wants to admit that they're afraid of what's about to come. My main fear is: how will Israel react if we launch our Scud missiles on Tel Aviv? Will the Israelis use the atom bomb if Saddam sends poison gas?

Shortly before seven the phone rings. One of my guards picks it up. He turns white as a sheet, jumps to his feet and shouts, 'We've got to get to the bunkers under the next-door building, right away!'

I ask, 'Why?'

'Secret service men in Saudi Arabia have information about intensifying activities in the airports in Dahran. It looks likely that they're going to bomb Baghdad tonight.'

On the way from the Al-Hayat to the bunker I see that Baghdad and the palace grounds are brightly lit. Why would they light everything up if they were expecting an attack? There's no logic to it. Aren't they taking the information from Saudi Arabia seriously? I find myself having doubts again: 'Will they really do it?

They do it: there are 16 of us in the bunker. The atmosphere isn't bad, although we all know that the palace grounds will be the main target of their attack. They will bomb this part of Baghdad until not a stone is left standing. We are the main target.

Painful hours of waiting. At a quarter to three the first explosion shakes the palace grounds. It must have been a big one, because our bunker trembles and creaks, and there is a smell of petrol. We're not going to get out of here alive, I think. Then there's a second explosion, a third, a fourth. The bombs must have come down very close to where we are. Probably in Project 2000. We can only guess what's going on over our heads. We are sitting under an 18-foot thick reinforced concrete ceiling in a nuclear-proof bunker. All that we feel is a vibration, from the strength of which we can just about guess whether the missiles have landed nearby or further away.

The attacks come in waves. For five minutes there is an explosion every second, then a short pause, then that vibration again. None of us would admit it, but we're all frightened. We over-compensate for our fear. We laugh, joke, some of us make a point of playing billiards although we've lost power by now, and have only emergency lights. Someone says sarcastically, 'I hope the Frenchmen who built this bunker didn't skimp on the reinforced concrete.'

Then there's another dull rumble, a quake. It's as though the concrete walls were amplifying the rumbles and making them even more dull and terrifying.

One wave after another rolls over us until shortly after five o'clock. Then, all of a sudden, everything is dead silent.

An officer comes into the bunker. He orders us to take off our uniforms as quickly as possible, and put on brown djellabas which other soldiers will bring us. We're ready in less than five minutes. They take us up. There's a dense pall of smoke above the palace grounds, a burnt smell. The damage is surprisingly slight. To judge by the noise in the bunker, you'd have expected everything to be razed to the foundations. But that isn't what happened. Only Project 2000 is completely destroyed. An officer tells me that the first bomb hit Saddam's palace.

We are hastily loaded on to the military transporter, and leave the palace grounds. The quiet is ghostly. We drive towards Al-Degel (a small place about 40 miles from Baghdad). There's still hardly any damage to be seen. 'What's been going on here, what did they bomb?' I ask the officer, but he doesn't reply.

In Al-Degel we are lodged in a little estate of terraced houses. There's nothing to suggest that this is a military installation. The buildings look like private houses, they're furnished like private houses. Among the one-storey buildings there are some bunkers. Their entrances are some way away from the estate, and so well disguised by trees that they can't be seen from the air, although they are so big that you can even drive a tractor through them.

We stay in Al-Degel until early February. Four days after our arrival, we suddenly learn that Saddam Hussein is staying there too. Saddam Hussein was really in Al-Degel. Like ourselves, he isn't wearing uniform, and his convoy consists only of four ordinary small cars. No Mercedes limousines, no escort to attract attention to him. Just four small cars. And I'm quite sure that it was Saddam Hussein himself, and not his fiday, Faoaz Al-Emari.

Saddam spends three days in Al-Degel. Then he suddenly leaves; we don't find out where he goes.

Late January 1991. The war from the air is in full swing. We got used to the raids long ago. Fear has made way for a kind of apathy. A few days ago we heard reports that Saddam Hussein had been visiting his troops in Kuwait, despite the constant attacks by the Allies, who control the whole of Iraqi air-space. Everyone knows that. Since then the American bombers have been flying over our territory at an extremely low altitude, and our anti-aircraft guns seem to be almost powerless. The weather seems to be our only ally. Only on days when the weather is bad does the air activity subside.

For the soldiers, the only days of celebration are the ones when the Scud missiles hit Saudi Arabia and Israel. At this point we don't know that the Scuds are completely insignificant from the military point of view. We're just told that we've managed a crucial strike against the Zionist enemy, and that every such attack will cause frenzied jubilation among out Palestinian friends. The reports about the celebrating Palestinians in the streets are supposed to suggest to people in Iraq that we actually *have* some friends.

None the less, the morale of the Iraqi army is sinking from day to day. It's simply frustrating to watch thousands of people dying helplessly because they have practically no defence against the air attacks.

Rumours seep through that morale among our troops is almost down to zero. No food's getting through, because all the supply routes are being constantly bombarded. Some of our men are even supposed to have deserted.

I don't find out anything precise. It is, however, a fact that morale is as bad as anyone could imagine. Not only in Kuwait, but in Iraq as well. And to a certain extent that is because everyone knows by now that almost the whole of Saddam Hussein's family is abroad.

The short-wave broadcasts by the Western radio stations report several times that Uday has been enjoying himself in Geneva night-clubs while people have been dying in Iraq.

Iraqi radio counters: this is pure propaganda by Western news services and their broadcasters in Saudi Arabia.

Those broadcasters really do exist, and they can be received in Iraq. They are forever calling to us to put down our weapons, to give up, to put up open resistance to Saddam Hussein.

Twenty-eighth January 1991. Rokan Al-Tikritti, one of Saddam Hussein's closest confidants, picks me up in person. He takes me to an underground bunker, about 15 miles away from Baghdad International Airport. The entrance to the bunker is cleverly disguised among private houses, with a few trees in front of it. Although we're in the middle of war, the place emanates a sense of incredible peace. Not a single building has been damaged, there isn't a crater to be seen.

Rokan Al-Tikritti takes me inside the bunker. First there's a hangar, with two MiG-29 fighter bombers. Next to them are some military vehicles, personnel carriers.

We walk through four rooms. They have steel doors,

painted reddish brown. Then we go a floor lower via a kind of spiral staircase. The sort of checkpoint I saw when I was introduced to Saddam Hussein. I am searched briefly, then taken to a kind of conference room. A long table, two dozen wooden chairs with dark green upholstery. The door to a side room is open. I see electronic equipment, telephones, computer screens. Rokan closes the door, and I wait.

All of a sudden the door to the side room opens up again. Qusay Saddam Hussein comes in. Shortly after him, Hussein Kamel Hassan and the President himself come into the room. Everyone sits down. Hussein Kamel sits on the left of Saddam Hussein, Qusay on his right. I stand next to Rokan, about five metres away from Saddam Hussein. He glances at me, and I am horrified at how ill he looks: sunken eyes, spongy face, his hands trembling slightly.

The President says, 'I want you to go to our troops with Hussein Kamel. Do your job well, my son.' Saddam's voice, already quiet and whiny, sounds like the voice of a sick old man. It sounds tremulous, exhausted, as though he were fighting for breath.

Then Rokan leads me out again. Saddam remains behind, and I can see him bending down to Qusay and explaining something to his son.

Twenty-ninth January, shortly after nine in the evening. Our journey to Kuwait is beginning. We travel in convoy, our lights out. Only the driver of the first car keeps flashing his headlights, which are taped to a tiny slit. The other vehicles take their bearings from the brake-lights of the cars in front. If one driver loses the others, he's allowed to flash his lights briefly.

Our chauffeurs are such masters of this kind of wartime

driving that the moonlight is almost all they need to avoid collisions.

Hussein Kamel and I are escorted by 75 bodyguards. The drive is peaceful. Only sometimes do we see the orange glow of flames on the horizon, as though the horizon itself were on fire. The bombardment of the Republican Guard, who have retreated from Kuwait into Iraq.

In the small hours we reach Basra. The city has been badly damaged. From there we go on to Safwan, the big Iraqi airforce base on the border with Kuwait. But we drive to a camp outside it. I am wearing the black uniform of the President's son and a pair of Ray-Bans. All that's missing is the Havana.

The most senior camp commanders welcome us. I have to stay somewhat in the background. We are taken to the underground operations rooms, which seem to be more or less intact despite the fact that the Allies have been flying raids against these positions for more than two weeks now. Hussein Kamel is informed about the state of the troops, and the commander gives him some plans and documents. The plans are in a brown briefcase. Hussein Kamel glances through them briefly. None of the commanders mentions that morale among the men is as bad as it could be, and that food supplies have reached disastrous levels. And no mention is made of the acts of terror that Shi'ite deserters have been carrying out against their own troops.

Tea is served, and we are shown the food rations and the weapons that the troops have at their disposal. The commanders also mention tabun and sarin, chemical weapons that can be placed in all kinds of warheads.

But not a word about the fact that none of the ordinary soldiers are equipped with gas masks.

Before we leave the positions, our propaganda men have

their job to do. We are filmed by two cameramen, and four photographers record the whole visit: Uday in conversation with the soldiers, Uday on an anti-aircraft gun, Uday on the radio, Uday eating with the soldiers.

My cameramen have chosen the soldiers whose uniforms are reasonably clean, and who don't look too exhausted. They shout 'Saddam Hussein, Saddam Hussein' into the camera, and 'Down with Bush, down with Bush'. I deliver a short prepared speech to the soldiers, say a few morale-boosting words. When I speak to 11 Magawir Company, I discover a former comrade in the first row, someone I fought with in 1987 in the Iran–Iraq war. He was with me in the observation post in the marshes of Basra. My friend stares at me for a long time, acting as though he recognises me. I return his gaze and smile, and he smiles back. For a split second I think of putting my arms around him, but then think better of it.

The pictures of my visit to the front appear in all the Iraqi newspapers, particularly in *Al-Iraq* and *Al-Thawara*.

They are full of the visit of the President's son to the brave troops at the front. Uday's courage is praised to the skies, and much is made of the fearless way in which he ate with the troops in the middle of terrible air-raids that are a crime against the Iraqi people. This suggests that the men have enough to eat. 'Look,' says one headline, 'Uday the great son of the people, fights with the brave troops against the imperialist American enemy.' Shoddy, unimaginative propaganda.

We spend the following night in a school, a few kilometres away from Basra. Hussein Kamel Hassan avoids this city, which has been in chaos for days. There are repeated attacks from fundamentalist Shi'ites against the Republican Guard there. Many supposed assassins have been arrested and either killed immediately or taken to the prisons of Baghdad.

The Shi'ite insurgents are led by Iran-based Mohammad Bakr Al-Hakim. There isn't a word in the Iraqi papers about problems with the Shi'ites in the south of the country. It's a quiet night, and Hussein Kamel Hassan sets off again during the hours of darkness, to get back to Baghdad as quickly as possible to deliver his report to the President. I stay behind with 17 bodyguards. The next day we drive to Basra, a suicide mission. At one checkpoint we are informed that several resistance groups have formed in the city. There are also supposed to be demonstrations. But we want to get to the city anyway. Then it happens: gunfire from the dunes on the side of the road, the rattle of machine-guns, exploding hand grenades. We stop and return fire.

The vehicle that was supposed to be covering my left flank is hit by a hand grenade and bursts into flames. Then there's a terrible explosion, and the armoured windscreen of my car explodes in a thousand pieces. I, Uday Saddam Hussein, the hated President's son, the target of the attack, am hit by shrapnel from a grenade, in my shoulder and my right hand. Two fingers of my right hand are hanging by a scrap of flesh. There's blood everywhere. I don't feel any pain, I just hear the crash and rattle of my bodyguards' Kalashnikovs. My men have been returning fire for some time.

I slump under the steering wheel. As though through a grey veil I see someone pulling open my car door. Bodyguards bundle me out of the Mercedes and into their car, and off we roar towards Baghdad. Only now do I feel the pain in my shoulder, my head, my hip, my right hand.

After twenty or thirty kilometres at top speed my bodyguards stop and bandage me as best they can. The worst thing is the injury to my hand. They bandage my arm so that I don't lose too much blood.

I can't remember how long the journey back to Baghdad took. They bring me to a normal hospital, and I undergo an operation. When I come round from the anaesthetic, the doctors tell me that the little finger on my right hand will probably have to be amputated.

It's a disaster. Not for me, but for Uday Saddam Hussein, who is still enjoying himself in Geneva. I have three further operations over the next few days. The surgeons do every-thing they can to save my finger. The operations, or at least this is what the doctors tell me, have gone well, but because of the poor hygienic conditions in the hospital I develop a serious inflammation in my right hand.

But even worse than that: news gets out about the attack on the President's son's convoy. Presumably the Shi'ite rebels have reported their attack to their headquarters in Iran, or to the Americans themselves.

At any rate, about ten days after the assassination attempt, the American news channels Voice of America and Radio Monte Carlo, which can be received on short-wave in Iraq, reported 'that Iraqi President's son Uday Saddam Hussein was killed during an attack by Shi'ite rebels in Basra'. These reports are then carried by all the big international news agencies, and cause panic in the propaganda department of the President's clan, first because they boost the insurgents; secondly because they confirm that there is open resistance against the President in Iraq, which has always been denied; and thirdly because a ground offensive against our troops in Kuwait is just around the corner, and in this situation reports such as these, which could shatter the myth of the indestructibility of the President's clan, are the last thing Saddam wants.

FIFTEEN

Torture

Captain Sabri Kamel Matar was a good man. He's dead now. So are First Lieutenant Hussein Fath-Allah Mohammed, Lieutenant Basehir Yunes Al-Tikritti and Lieutenant Nazem Hilal-Al-Douri. Since my self-denunciation on television in November 1990, these four men have been guarding me. Perhaps 'guard' isn't exactly the right word. They have lived with me, they've been my bodyguards, observing my every move, friends and enemies at the same time. We were together in the bunker when the bombing of Baghdad began, we fled together to Al-Degel, they were there when I visited our troops in Safwan, and they were the ones who opened fire when we were ambushed by Shi'ite rebels in Basra.

The four officers died trying to protect me. They jumped out of their cars and tried to charge into the hills behind which the rebels had holed up. The first to fall was Sabri Kamel Matar. He was hit by a salvo from a Kalashnikov. The other three were so badly injured by splinters from hand grenades that there was nothing to be done for them. Even today I don't know how many rebels my bodyguards killed. And if two of my bodyguards had not visited me and told me the whole Basra story all over again, I wouldn't even know that those four officers had lost their lives.

I'm still lying in hospital. The inflammation in my right hand still hasn't got any better. But the injuries to my head and hip have healed to some extent.

Rokan Al-Tikritti urges the doctors on. 'Latif must be ready to work again as soon as possible.' If necessary, I would go to the front with my hand in plaster.

Saddam needs successes, positive reports in the media, and as part of that the President's son has to appear with the soldiers. But Uday is still in Geneva, although the telegram telling him to come back to Baghdad as soon as possible must have reached him ages ago.

In the hospital, in the whole of Baghdad, everywhere in the country, people are already discussing the fact that soldiers are deserting daily and going over to the other side. The reports we are getting from the front are of sheer horror. The Allies are flying up to 800 raids a day against the Republican Guard and the front positions of the ordinary army. For days the soldiers don't come out of their bunkers. They have dug themselves in with their tanks, just like the units I visited in Safwan.

I learn another detail in the hospital: when I was in Safwan on 29 January, the 5th Motorised Division carried out tank attacks against Allied positions in three places. One column of tanks was beaten back relatively quickly, while the others managed to get as far as Al-Khafji, an oil processing plant on the Saudi coast, eight miles south of the Kuwaiti border. So Iraqi units had occupied Saudi soil for the first time. And our troops were able to hold the town of Khafji for a few days, defying the world. Saddam sent almost 400 tanks and armoured troop-transporters into that encircled area. An utterly senseless action from the military point of view, but perfectly viable from the public relations point of view. First the pictures of the President's son with the troops at the front, then the report that Iraqi troops have taken Saudi territory, including a whole town. At this point no one in Iraq knew that Al-Khafji was a ghost town whose 20,000 inhabitants had fled.

So Saddam's media machine is still in perfect shape – it's only the attack on me that throws the whole propaganda strategy into confusion.

Sixteenth February 1991. Uday is ordered back from Geneva to Baghdad. He flies via Rome to Amman in Jordan, where he is picked up by Iraqi secret service men. They take him to Baghdad in an ordinary car along the motorway linking Iraq with Jordan. It has been seriously damaged by all the bombing raids, but it is still manageable, although it is dangerous because of the constant air raids. After a conversation with his father, Uday is immediately taken to the hospital. He isn't interested in me or the many other casualties, but in my little finger. He visits the doctors who are treating me. They have been working incredibly long hours for weeks now, they've operated on thousands of people and tended to thousands more. He couldn't care less. He has them explain to him at very great length and in very great detail what the problem with the treatment of my finger is. The doctors point out to Uday a number of times that the little finger on my right hand can only be saved by costly plastic surgery.

They don't actually say it, but it isn't hard to guess what they're thinking: 'There are children, women, soldiers dying here, and you want us to save a little finger?'

Uday remains completely silent during the whole conversation. He pretends to be interested. Then he stands up and declares in his supercilious way: 'If you can't save this little finger I'm going to kill you all, with my own bare hands.'

Then he disappears.

His threat isn't about concern for me. It's all about him. If his double loses a finger – doesn't that mean that he'll have to lose one of his own?

Four days later, on 20 February 1991, they come to the hospital early in the morning to collect me. I'm still unsteady on my feet, but they order me to put on the black uniform of the President's son anyway. We have to get back to Basra. If the situation allows, a visit to the bases of the Republican Guard in Northern Kuwait is planned. The Tawakalna, Hammurabi and Medina tank divisions have been under very heavy fire for more than a month. A visit to these units, the elite of the Iraqi army, would be of the greatest importance, my commanders stress. That's not what happens: it takes us until sunset the next day to get anywhere near Basra. Time and again we have to leave the road; the Allies are flying one raid after another. It's complete chaos. We are constantly coming across units withdrawing from positions on the Iraq–Kuwaiti border. The retreat is not orderly but unplanned, haphazard and over-hasty. It looks more like flight than retreat. No one can tell us exactly which bridges are still intact, or whether there is the slightest chance of reaching the Republican Guard.

We hear on the car radio that Foreign Minister Tariq Aziz has come back from Moscow to Baghdad, and has declared that Iraq is prepared to withdraw from Kuwait. But in the same bulletin we also hear that the Americans are demanding the unconditional capitulation of Iraq. One of the cameramen, a serious man who has already filmed the poison gas attacks in the Iran–Iraq war, comments: 'We Arabs don't accept ultimatums. We'd rather die.'

The cameraman is right: our President refuses to capitulate. So it's clear that the ground offensive against our troops is about to begin.

There are additional clues about the coming American attack in the printed flyers that flutter down from the sky all along the road. They explain precisely how the Iraqi soldiers are to surrender. That nothing will happen to them once they are prisoners of war, and that thousands of our soldiers have already gone over to the Americans and the Saudis. One flyer even shows illustrations of the correct way to surrender.

We don't make it to the Republican Guard, but just spend around two hours at a base on a little hill not far from Safwan. We barely have time to shoot our photographs and films, as there are frequent raids on this region. The men only tell us that the Americans are even carrying out low-altitude bombing raids with B-52 bombers, because there are stationary Scud-firing bases near this hill. It's from here that the Iraqi missiles are being fired in the direction of Eastern Saudi Arabia.

The journey back to Baghdad is less arduous, although my arm hurts, and I'm absolutely exhausted. Two hours after our return the footage shot by our cameramen is broadcast. First I'm shown with the troops. The announcer explains that I have been boosting morale among the brave soldiers. There are no close-ups of me; the bound right hand that I have to wear in a sling is only shown once, briefly.

I'm surprised that the report isn't more detailed, because after all we did put our lives in danger to get the footage. A short time later I learn why my material wasn't broadcast quite as patriotically as usual: while we were travelling south, studio footage was being shot of the 'real Uday', who also had his arm in a sling and a bandage around his head, and declared firmly: 'The rebel bullets hit me, but only injured me slightly. As everyone can see, I'm not dead.'

I see this rotten piece of dramatisation in the hospital. The newspapers chew over Uday's resurrection *ad nauseam*. A pointless enterprise.

First, because hardly anywhere in the country has electricity, and people aren't going to see this television address anyway. And secondly because on 24 February 1991, at four o'clock in the morning, the ground offensive against our troops in Kuwait begins. The Allied military machine rolls over our proud army with breathtaking speed. On the first day almost 20,000 Iraqi soldiers surrender to the enemy. We hear nothing about that from our news reports. There is hardly any information about it: clearly communication between Baghdad and Basra has been broken. There aren't any more bombing raids on Baghdad itself, although US fighter-bombers are flying over the capital day and night, at a very low altitude. They fly in below the speed of sound, and crash through the sound barrier right over the city. It's a hellish noise – the crash of the sound barrier sounds like exploding bombs. The Americans are really playing cat and mouse with us.

State radio transmits a speech by Saddam Hussein every hour. He speaks in his whining voice: 'The contemptible Bush and traitorous Fahd began their ground offensive this morning. All along the front they are attacking our country and our people. Shame on them. But they will discover that the great and heroic people of Iraq are superior to them. Fight, oh brave people of Iraq. Oh you sons of the mother of all battles, fight to protect your wives and children, for you are on the threshold of the supreme renown, the glory of God. The weapons they have built to fight against us will slip from their hands, and then there will be only a battle between believers and unbelievers. Fight against them. Be ruthless towards them. Have no mercy for them. For God wants the believer to defeat the infidel.'

A shudder runs down my back when I hear that. The doctors who had, like myself, been waiting captivatedly by their radios (the speech had been announced beforehand) fall silent when Saddam finishes what he has to say and military music and patriotic songs ring out.

Saddam's 'rousing words' were no use any more. Four days later the Gulf War that destroyed our country was over. Sixty thousand men surrendered without a fight; in Safwan, in those positions on the Kuwaiti–Iraqi border which I had visited the first time I went to the front during the war, cease-fire negotiations began on 3 March 1991. Saddam sent the three-star generals Sultan Hashim Ahmad, Deputy Chief of Staff in the Defence Ministry, and Salah Abud Mahmud, commander of the 3rd Corps, there. Meanwhile another enterprise was under way: Saddam wanted to clear up, this time among his opponents.

Our army stationed in Southern Iraq suddenly seemed to be collapsing. There were no structures of command any more, formerly loyal officers were mutinying, and in the area around Basra, where there was violent resistance against Saddam even when the air raids were going on, and where the army suffered some of its severest setbacks, furious soldiers were tearing the huge portraits of Saddam Hussein from the walls of the buildings. Ba'ath Party headquarters were being attacked everywhere, and the mutinying soldiers were hunting down officials and secret policemen. For a few days it looked as though these uprisings could develop into a violent revolution that would sweep away the hated Saddam regime. In Basra the mutineers even managed to storm all the prisons and open the penal colonies. A kind of liberation movement was beginning, and the disturbances quickly spread. To everyone's complete surprise, the whole of the South and South-East of the country became the stage for a slowly spreading revolution.

The uprising in the South was led by the 'Supreme Council of the Islamic Revolution in Iraq'. The leader of this movement was the head of the Iraqi Shi'ites, Mohammed Bakr Al-Hakim. In Northern Iraq the Kurdish Peshmergas led by Massoud Barsani and Jalal Talabani were trying to bring Iraqi Kurdistan under their control.

But the situation was so widespread that hardly anyone can say which regions Saddam Hussein and his Republican Guard still controlled, and which areas were ruled by the insurgents and mutineers. Only one thing seems certain: the only people who still stood loyally behind the President were those garrisons that had been stationed around Baghdad throughout the whole war, as well as the bulk of the Republican Guard. When the disturbances even spread to the area around Karbala, Saddam Hussein called together the men in Baghdad whom he could still blindly trust, even in this situation: his sons Uday and Qusay; his sons-in-law Hussein Kamel Hassan and Saddam Kamel Hassan and Ali Hassan Al-Majid ('Chemical Ali'); and General Bashar Al-Sabani, the head of the elite secret service.

These six men and Saddam Hussein himself led the battle against the rebels. Their task was to use all the means at their disposal to put down the uprising. Qusay Saddam Hussein and Bashar Al-Sabani took command of all the secret services. Uday's father promoted him to the post of chairman of the journalists' association, which meant that he was in charge of all the media in Iraq. His first official act was to raise the wages of all journalists by 25 percent. He also made land available to all journalists to build houses on, and declared, 'My goal is the maintenance and protection of freedom of speech as well as the observation of unhealthy phenomena.' Everyone in Iraq knew very well what Uday meant by 'unhealthy phenomena'. Anyone who didn't keep to the rules laid down by the palace and unconditionally churn out propaganda for Saddam Hussein would be liquidated.

Hussein Kamel Hassan and Saddam Kamel Hassan each controlled ten intact divisions which were not involved in the Gulf War. Ali Hassan Al-Majid was in charge of the eight regiments of the Republican Guard. This army was enough to take successful action against the Shi'ites in the South and the Kurds in the North. The means that he used were of barely describable brutality. First of all the government newspapers *Al-Iraq* and *Al-Thawara* published communiqués that could not be presented more clearly: 'Warning to all those who think they can call the national unity of Iraq into question. The power of the state and the people will crush you! Anyone who tries to undermine the security of the Iraqi revolution is a traitor and a mercenary of the enemy. All traitors will pay, their punishment will find them wherever they may hide.'

Despite this appeal the disturbances continued, sometimes even spilling into Baghdad. Streets were blocked off, buildings were sprayed with anti-Saddam slogans. The counter-revolution wanted to mobilise Baghdad to topple Saddam from his throne. But Saddam struck back.

Units of the Republican Guard under Ali Hassan Al-Majid were wreaking havoc in Basra and Karbala. Low-ranking mutinying soldiers were shot on the spot while their leaders were either hanged in the streets or imprisoned in Baghdad. One hundred and six Shi'ite leaders, including Abu

Al-Kassem Al-Khawai, were given special treatment by Ali Hassan Al-Majid and Qusay Saddam Hussein. They paid particular attention to Al-Khawai, who was seen as the supreme religious head of the Shi'ites in Iraq. He was ordered to tell the Shi'ite rebels to submit to Saddam Hussein's regime and give up all their plundered weapons. The 95-year-old man refused, saying, 'I will tell my men, tear down the pictures of the tyrant. Smash his statues. Shut the infidels out of the mosques.' That was his death sentence. They poured petrol over him and lit it.

They wanted the other prisoners to tell them the names and command structures of the Shi'ite revolutionaries. They hit a wall of silence. Qusay Saddam Hussein made every tenth man step forward, and sprayed those men with a kind of nerve-gas that paralyses the lungs – a terrible death. Others had their eyeballs torn out, their ears and noses cut off, their arms and legs beaten to a pulp.

Saddam Kamel, who was married to the President's second-eldest daughter, Rena, was responsible for the prisons of Al-Daghil and Al-Raduanie. On 1 April, when fear of assassination had intensified into paranoia among the President's family, Uday's brother Qusay calls me in. Unlike Uday, who had completely withdrawn during this time, Qusay is actively participating in the battle against the insurgents. We travel together to Al-Radwania, the district in Baghdad that houses one of the most notorious secret police barracks.

Conditions in the prison there are absolutely appalling. The cells are crammed full of Shi'ite and Kurdish rebels. The men are scrawny, skin and bone, covered with lice, most of them can barely stand upright. It is stuffy, unbearably hot. I can't even guess how many people are being kept here like cattle to the slaughter.

The whole place smells of urine and vomit. A sweetish smell of corruption comes from several cells. Above all that there are the groans of the dying and the cries of men being tortured.

Qusay is sweating, and I notice that even he can barely stand the stench in the building. His hands are clenched into fists, he stares straight ahead. We march into the director's office. There sits Saddam Kamel. He looks bloated and is breathing heavily. When we enter the room he stands up; I see the rings of sweat under his armpits. Saddam Kamel briefly shakes Qusay's hand and hugs him; we go into the inner courtyard of the prison.

The director knows what is to be done. He has two upholstered chairs brought out and puts them in the middle of the dusty prison-yard. Saddam Kamel sits down, with Qusay next to him.

Then the director has a group of prisoners brought in. They are Shi'ites from Karbala, allegedly leaders of the revolution against the President. They are supposed to have had anti-Saddam slogans painted on the walls of buildings.

In his right hand Saddam Kamel has a pistol, in his left documents about the traitors who are to be questioned here in the yard, in the blazing morning sun. The questioning is a farce. 'Say that Saddam is the greatest,' he hisses to the prisoners. None of the men grovels to Kamel.

'You are craven cowards, beg for mercy and we will set you free!' Anyone who begs for mercy is shot on the spot. As he observes, 'The President doesn't like cowards.' That day he shoots 15 prisoners, from his chair.

On another day it is said to have been almost a hundred.

This repellent procedure, which enables Kamel to vent his accumulated hatred, his bloodlust, continues for four hours. For me it is a paralysing shock.

He has the corpses thrown into the mass cells along with the other prisoners. The bodies are only cleared away when they begin to rot and the stench becomes so penetrating that even the guards can't bear it any more. For every man murdered, Saddam Kamel is given a reward of 20,000 dinars by Ali Hassan Al-Majid. For his loyal service Saddam Hussein also gives him a Mercedes and several office buildings in Baghdad.

In mid-April 1991 Saddam Kamel, known as the 'butcher of Baghdad', was ambushed on his way back from a mass-shooting in the district of Al-Karada. Some young men tried to kill him with ordinary hand guns. Saddam Kamel was unharmed, and his bodyguards were able to arrest three young men. Saddam Kamel killed them while they were being interrogated, with electric shocks.

Saddam Hussein himself takes part in these orgies of killing. On one occasion I am an eyewitness. Uday has just had me picked up from the Al-Hayat building, which was undamaged during the war. We travel to Project 2000, Saddam's former grand palace, which is now nothing more than a ruin. Next to the rubble stands a convoy of Mercedes, the President's cars. Saddam Hussein is viewing the destroyed palace with his security officers Rokan Al-Tikritti, Chabib Al-Tikritti, Abd Hamid and Saddam Kamel. Qusay is there as well. The President is furious. For a few minutes he stands in silence by the rubble, then he orders Rokan Al-Tikritti to fetch prisoners.

More than 5,000 people are held in the prisons in the palace grounds. They represent a kind of protective shield against the insurgents. It isn't long before Rokan comes back with 30 prisoners. They are Kurds. Saddam shoots them one after the other, point blank. Uday, Qusay, Archad Al-Jassin, Abd Hamid, Chabib, Saddam Kamel and Rokan kick the corpses with their feet. They are wading in blood. Everything is red. The ones who don't die immediately are finished off by the security officers with a shot to the head.

But this massacre isn't enough for Saddam. He has 30 more prisoners brought in, and kills them as well. Every time he empties his magazine, he has Rokan hand him a new weapon. This bloodbath seems to satisfy him. He laughs loudly, the laugh of a madman. 'I feel better now,' he shouts.

I don't feel so good. Despite the fact that a few days after this butchery Saddam gives me a dark-blue 500 series Mercedes, 200,000 dinars in cash and a house that Saddam calls 'the hero's house' for my 'heroic deeds' during the war, I feel wretched. I hate Uday, I hate Saddam Hussein, I despise my life, I despise myself. I want to get away from this madness.

I can't say how many people were murdered, tortured to death by Saddam's thugs after the Gulf War. They numbered in their thousands, and barely a family in Iraq was spared. As a result of this murder campaign, Saddam was largely in control of Iraq again by June 1991. Uday returned to his old rhythm of life. Although he was now in charge of the journalists, he continued with all his other business as well. Through his companies he controlled almost all building work in Baghdad, as well as the supply of food and goods which were smuggled into Iraq from Jordan because of the sanctions. Children were dying in the clinics because there wasn't enough medicine available. Hundreds and thousands of wounded soldiers didn't know how they were going to feed their families. Uday didn't care, he went on celebrating anyway, openly, shamelessly, in front of everyone.

Eighteenth June 1991. Uday's 27th birthday. The clear-up operation in the palace grounds is still under way. The feudal swimming pools around the President's palace look as though there had never been a war: luxurious, exclusive, a kind of paradise. Uday has invited more than 300 girls and women to this party. And all of Uday's demi-monde friends are there again. His car dealers, his pimps and of course Abdel Akle, the singer. Just as though there had never been a war. Uday and his clan celebrate licentiously. There is champagne, whisky, French wines, even German beer; a fantastic buffet with every delicacy you could wish for. A dream world, a distorted reality – outside the palace the people are starving, inside the profiteers from the war are enjoying themselves. The cheats, the murderers, the unscrupulous exploiters. Alcohol flows, the party is noisy and vulgar. Everyone is completely drunk.

But worst of all is Uday. He jumps on to the stage, grabs the microphone from Abdel Akle and orders, with a filthy giggle, 'Heeheehee, all the women have to get undressed. I want to see the women naked. Stark naked.'

Some of them do as Uday says, others are coy. Watching from the stage, Uday takes the microphone again. This time he isn't grinning: 'I said, everyone. Without exception. Anyone who refuses spends the evening with my bodyguards.' They obey his order, like sheep. They peel off their outfits. Uday is royally amused when they are all naked. He lights a Havana, draws on it twice, then he adds, 'Now the men. Get undressed, you whoremongers.' They do so.

The rest of the party is one single great orgy. Writhing bodies, screeching women. They are coupling shamelessly, all over the place. In the pools decorated with mosaics, on the lush lawn, on the couches. Abdel Akle's music drowns the moans.

The next day Uday calls me in. He accuses me of

harassing Beida Abd Al-Rahman at his birthday party. Beida is an Iraqi television presenter, one of Uday's long-term girlfriends. She's a star, and a big cheese in the crazed mass-manipulation machinery of the Saddam clan, in which everyone knows the lies and yet no one says anything – out of fear and a lust for power. It is true that Beida spoke to me. She knows that I am Uday's double, and she also knows that I am strictly forbidden even to speak to Uday's girlfriends. At the party, she had asked me with a giggle whether I wanted to go out with her and her friend. A ludicrous question. 'No, I don't want to have any problems with Uday,' I replied.

Uday won't listen to me. I'm not sure, but I suspect he may even have set Beida on me in order to provoke me. He knows I hate him. It's obvious that I'm only doing my job because I have no other choice. 'Why do you harass my girlfriend, why do you run after her?' rages Uday. His hands are trembling with fury, he is gasping, screaming. 'I can sense that you despise me, that you want out of here. But you're under my control, you're my fiday, my serf. Never forget that. I'm going to have to re-educate you.'

'Education' means torture, fear, psychological terror. Uday discovered a long time ago that I'm yet another renegade. I'm finding it more and more difficult to hide my contempt for him, and my hostility is becoming increasingly apparent. There is no longer any hiding the fact that I despise him, and he me. I am sure that he is secretly planning to have me wiped out, because he can't simply let me go. I know too much about him, and he still needs me. But since he knows that I'm his enemy, his options are either to kill me – or make me submit to his will once and for all. He can't break my disobedience and resistance to him. So that business with Beida was just a pretext. He wants to humiliate me, to prove to me and prove to himself that he's got me under his control.

I am led away the same day. There is a special institution for 'education', a secret police camp, the desert camp of Al-Rashid outside Baghdad. More than 5,000 political prisoners are kept there. It's a nightmare. The whole complex is unprotected in the blazing sun, the temperatures in this part of the country rise to over 50 degrees in summer. The cells are small, they have no windows, just small barred slits. There is hardly any sanitation, the toilets are latrines that don't flush. My personal warders are two serious criminals who were condemned to death but pardoned by Saddam Hussein to work as torturers in this camp. They only have to obey a single order, and their obedience to it protects them from the gallows: 'You must torture anyone who is sent to you. Even if that person is the President's son.' Now I'm the one being brought to them.

Everything has its precise order in this appalling place. You get up at four, you report at five, bare from the waist up. Then it's time for punishment. From six until ten in the morning. They beat me with electric cables and leather whips. Twenty strokes on the back each time. Then a break. More whipping, another pause. Kneeling. My nostrils are plugged, I can only breathe through my mouth. They force me to do sit-ups until I can hardly move. If I collapse they stick needles under my fingernails and force me to do another ten sit-ups. There's a break from ten 'til eleven. More education from eleven 'til two in the afternoon. Break. Then more torture from three 'til six. The prisoner has to lie down with his stomach on the floor, then the torturers get to work on him.

Soon the skin on my back breaks. But the torturers have strict orders not to be held back by pain or infection. The open wounds are smeared with dirt. If I lose consciousness, I'm thrown into a tub of brackish canal water, into which my torturers generally urinate. For the first two days I try to stand up to my torturers. I want to be a man, I try to suppress the pain, not to give them the feeling that they could break me. They increase the dose. I'm not just beaten, they tie me to a kind of fan fastened to the wall. I hang there head down, and the fan is switched on. It turns around, first slowly then faster. Then they start hitting me with their electrical cables. I get a terrible blow on the nose and faint. My nose is broken. Another time they shut me in a kind of niche in the wall. The niche has no window. The temperature in that narrow space is incredible, I can't sit down, it's too small. I have to spend two days in the hole.

I share my normal cell with Sabah Merze Mahmud. He's been there for seven months, and he's completely broken. It takes Mahmud four days to trust me at all. At first he didn't talk to me. Now he pours his heart out to me: 'I was with Saddam in Samarra, at the age of sixteen. I was his friend,' he laments. Later Mahmud rose to the top of the Ba'ath Party in Iraq, and even became Saddam Hussein's first bodyguard.

He fell into disfavour after an argument in the exclusive Al-Said Club in Baghdad. Mahmud had attended a party for leading Ba'athists. The highlight of the party was an appearance by the Iraqi singer Mahmud Anwar. Anwar was just singing a hymn to Saddam Hussein when the then head of the President's Chancellery, Ahmad Hussein, suddenly leapt to his feet and gave the singer whole bundles of dinar notes. Mahmud was furious; he shouted to Ahmad Hussein, 'You can only throw money around like that because you've stolen it!' All at once the music stopped, and Ahmad Hussein's elder son threw himself at Mahmud, who drew his revolver and fired several shots into the air as a warning to Ahmad Hussein's son.

The next day Ahmad Hussein complained to the President about what had happened. Mahmud was summoned to see him, and Saddam ordered him to apologise to his adversary. 'I refused,' Mahmud tells me in our little cell. That was enough. Saddam had him brought to the Al-Rashid education centre. 'You'll stay there,' he was told, 'until you apologise.'

I ask Mahmud why he didn't do so ages ago. He says, 'Because I'd rather than die than go on serving that animal.'

For 21 days I squat in that miserable hole with Sabah Merze Mahmud. He tells me he used to be a street-thief in Baghdad, along with Saddam. He tells me how they stole from passers-by and used the money to visit a brothel in the Al-Rahmange district of Baghdad, which was run by Amira Al-Maslani and Manal Yunes. This house of pleasure was a popular meeting-place for all the Ba'ath Party leaders. When Saddam Hussein came to power, he made the madam of the brothel the chairwoman of the Iraqi Women's Association.

On the 21st day our torturers come into our cell. One of them grabs Mahmud, who is about to give up the ghost; the other injects something into the veins of his haggard right arm. They drag Mahmud from the cell. I remember his furious words: 'Why do you work with these criminals? Have you no honour? They will do the same thing to you as they did to me. They will throw you away when they don't need you any more.' They were the last words I every heard from him.

SIXTEEN

Escape from Hell

I remain alone in the cell; three weeks during which I ponder over my sufferings. They come every day to exercise their savagery on my body, leaving me hanging between life and death. I crawl to the corners of the room hoping that movement will alleviate my agonies. I am reduced to silence by the pangs of hunger, and my festering wounds make me weep inside. I long for a drink of water to relieve the scorching heat of the cell and the burning of the whips.

Fear starts to creep in on me. For a long time I have been fighting this, fighting to keep myself together, to be myself. I have been clinging to a thread of hope and promising myself that the nightmare will come to an end. But it becomes more difficult and the pain overcomes my will, killing the hope within me. I no longer have the power to resist. I have become a mere tattered rag of a man and surrendered myself to them without anger or hatred. I leave them to torture my body without a word or a groan. I have lost all sense of pain, just as I have lost the ability to sleep. Everything seems the same to me, sleeping and waking, pain and rest. I become a nothingness; nothing more than a mere remnant.

I can't think anymore. I have thought long and hard, but now that well within my head has run dry of all those black thoughts which I turned over in my imagination, 'They'll do the same to you, Latif, as they did to Mahmud. They'll repress you writhing in agony and then you'll die. They won't treat you any less severely. They'll shoot you and you'll die on the spot. You'll feel no pain as the dogs rip you to pieces. No, Latif. You've got to pull yourself together. Resist. Yes, they have power over your body, but your mind belongs to you alone.' In a moment of clarity I tell myself that I will not give in, that my loathing will see me through. I will rely on this to take me away from their world of brutality. 'Think of their crimes. You're not alone, thousands have tasted the torture of the gang, and they swallowed the bitterness and resisted.' I start to recall things. I organise my mind and imagine a stack of paper in there. I dip the quill in the inkwell of my tears and write a list of names – the victims who have fallen into the regime's dark pit: Ali Jaafar (poisoned), Mohsaen Al-Sahab (poisoned), Munem-Hadi (starved to death), Ahmad Saleh (beaten to death), Hamed Al-Dalimi (legs broken and left for the dogs), Saleh Al-Saa'idi (eyes gouged out then beaten to death), Sabri Al-Hadisi (hit in the head and died, and before they would let the family take the body they forced his brother to dance on it).

There is also the list of ministers: three men in charge of the Ministry of Trade were shot dead, as were two ministers of industry; three ministers of foreign affairs and three ministers of defense.

Fifty-nine government officials have been killed by the regime's indiscriminate bullets. The regime's mill never ceases to grind, consuming men at every turn, pulverising their bodies without mercy.

Even the Gulf war hasn't removed the regime's barbs and it becomes even more vicious. It slaughters thousands after the war ends, its knife cutting their throats.

The President's agents played havoc in the regions that the regime assigned members of the Party and the government to destroy. In the Kubise district, for example, many men fell in the service of the regime, and their reward was death without mercy: Khalid Abd Osman Al-Kabisi, a former minister; Rahim Al-Sattar Sulaiman Al-Kabisi, a member of government; and Abd Al-Hanan Al-Kabisi, an officer.

In the district of Hadisa there was a similar massacre: Kordi Said Abd Al-Baki Al-Hadisi, a Party member (hanged); Abd Al-Asis Al-Hadisi, a general in the army (executed by firing squad); Shokat Dakom Al-Hadisi, a member of government (executed by firing squad); Murtoda Said Abd Al-Baki Al-Hadisi, a former minister; Muhammad Sabri, a deputy minister; Nisan Al-Hadisi, an officer; Kasheh Al-Hadisi, a pilot.

All of these men were piled into a mass grave in the centre of the district.

Then my pen stops writing; I too am struck by a surge of pain.

Why did they all surrender themselves? They let the regime slaughter them like cattle. Is there no one brave enough in the country to say no, or to draw his weapon and sever the snake's head? I ask myself this question, but know the answer. I know that the clan is closely knit, that the reins are tight and that Saddam is sly and cunning. He cultivates love, but alongside hatred, and he subdues men as if they were horses or dogs.

Me too. Didn't I hate Uday? I detested every day that I spent in his company. I know that when he takes his father's place, he will be even more brutal and despotic. He had given me many opportunities to empty my bullets into his chest if I had wanted to. I had been with him many, many times, and watched him beat his women, had accompanied him as he tried out his new cars. Just one pull of the trigger would have been enough. But I did nothing. So I can't blame the others; we're all cowards, caught between fear and the desire to bask in the warmth of the regime. We love it and hate it equally. We revolve in its orbit. We have become puppets manipulated by the regime's wanton fingers.

The grey clouds of fear swirl long in the skies of Iraq; houses, people and stones all join in the game, some willingly and some in search of escape. Voices scream in praise of the regime to drown out the people whose hearts seethe with loathing.

The people went to bed at night hoping that the morning would bring them the long-awaited liberator. They watched the skies in the hope that some birds from Heaven would come and shower the clan with stones. But when they came, they showered their bombs on the people and not on the regime. They gave the regime its power back so it could attack and wander between the houses harvesting heads which were ripe for picking. The regime's grip became tighter, and the spoilt young man took up the thick stick to protect his father's back.

Meanwhile, Qusay sat at the head of the secret service charged with turning it into a more coercive and tyrannical instrument. The first deed of the agency in its new era was to kill First Lieutenant Solman Harb Al-Tikritti, accused of spying for the opposition. This was not true, but Qusay simply wanted people to know he was in control, to show the power of the new security system after he had re-organised it.

Previously, the security agency comprised four organisa-tions: the secret service, information service, military information service and national security service. When

Qusay's hands were free he took the best men from the other organisations for the secret service. He showered them with privileges and raised their salaries. Aside from this, all the other security organisations fell under Qusay's orders; all the competing organisations were in his grip.

On my 23rd day in the savage camp, the executioners come at four in the morning as usual to take me. This time, however, they don't lead me to the torture room, but to another one. They tie me to a chair fixed to the floor. I don't ask what they intend to do with me, but avoid looking at them and keep my eyes to the ground. Suddenly, one of them speaks to me, 'Do you want to know what we injected Sabah Merze Mahmud with?' I don't reply, but merely nod my head. He bursts into laughter. His face is ugly and his teeth are decayed. He saunters over to me, then squeezes my shoulder with his right hand, pulling a pen out of his jacket pocket with the other. He begins to draw it up and down my arm as if looking for a vein. He does this while laughing and muttering in my ear, 'Thallium. Do you know what Thallium is?'

My body, which up to know has been motionless, starts to tremble when I hear the man's words. Yes, I now what Thallium is. What a beastly man he is. Thallium is a substance that kills the body's cells one by one. One's hair falls out bit by bit, and the limbs start to shake. The body can no longer control itself. It loses its balance and senses. A man no longer has the power to eat and is transformed into a wild animal tearing at itself. Every moment is like death. I know that deadly poison; they had put it in the food of some of the officers during the first Gulf war to get rid of them without fuss. When the illness seized them their service came to an end. But they didn't forget to honour them as heroes who had dedicated themselves to the regime and the people.

He increases the painful pricks and I can feel the pen piercing my skin as the man's panting breath pierces my back. He repeats the word in his snarling voice, 'Thallium. Thallium.' He circles round me like a raging bull, brushing me with his stinking breath. If I had a little strength left I would spit in his face and kick him. The sound of footsteps in the corridor releases me from his breath. His companion tells him that they have come, and he stands away from me. The door opens wide and Azzam enters followed by Uday and 12 bodyguards, all wearing black suits and concealing their eyes behind Ray-Ban sunglasses.

Uday comes up to me and begins to wave his whip. Laughing, he asks me with his usual vulgarity, 'How did you find the disciplining? Have you had enough or do you need a few more weeks?' He looks at me with hatred, waving the whip in front of my face and cracking it in the air. He begins to walk around me, repeatedly asking, 'Have you had enough?' He waits for a reply as he repeats the question over and over again. Then he suddenly strikes me on the chest and yells 'Answer me!'

The answer is right in front of him: a skeleton, swollen lips, a back covered in sores and filth, my strength destroyed under the blows. Feebly, I ask him to have mercy on me, 'Sir, I can't take it anymore. Sir, I am your fiday and that's what I'll always be. You control me. I will be under your orders. May God preserve the President and his mighty son and protect them for everything.'

My entreaties have no effect on him, and he orders the guards to treat me like a monkey. 'Shave him like the African sons of slaves,' he tells them. By 'sons of slaves' he means the Shi'ite rebels, followers of the Islamic Al-Daawa Party; those rebels who after the war retreated to the swamps behind the Tigris and the Euphrates to re-launch attacks against

Saddam's forces. Confrontations with them became ever more vicious, with the regime's soldiers burning entire forests and combing the surface of the swamps searching for them. Then they led them away to be shot without mercy. Sympathisers were taken away and humiliated: they had their moustaches, their beards and their hair burned off.

The guard seizes my head and cuts off my hair and beard, rubs me with soap and curses me. The others, at the head of whom is Uday, dance around me laughing vulgarly.

Uday takes the razor from the guard and feels my throat with it. He lets it pass over my face until it reaches the crown of my head, and then starts to shave my scalp like a madman. When he has finished with my head he turns his attention to my eyebrows and beard. He looks at me and starts to clap, roaring with laughter, 'A Shi'ite monkey. Ha, ha.' This is how they describe me after my humiliation. In desperation, I say in a feeble voice, 'Sir, please kill me.'

Uday throws the razor to the floor of the cell and turns away without speaking. He leaves and the guards untie me. They pick me up like a tattered rag and hurl me on to the stony ground. Then they drag me outside and push me into the back seat of their car. The car takes us far from the camp, heading for the Al-Aadamiya district of Baghdad. We pass my parents' house and the car slows down a little. They shove me out a few steps from the door, then accelerate away. My debilitated body and my head, cut by the razor, hurt when I hit the asphalt and I lose consciousness. I try to fight it and crawl until I come to our door. Weakly, I begin to knock and knock striving to make someone hear me. I break down in tears, humiliated and sapped of strength. Blood mixes with my tears. Then the door opens.

My mother stands there looking at the heap in front of her. She steps back a little, then recognises me. She has stepped back in fear, thinking that the crumpled heap at her feet, a shaven head and bloodied face, was just one of the beggars which fills the streets of Baghdad after the war.

'Mother,' I say feebly. But she hears me and looks at me again, still not able to embrace me. She begins to scream and runs inside. I can hear her anxiously calling my brothers and sisters. They quickly come and carry me into the living room. Gallalha rushes to support my mother. She holds back her tears and they bring her a glass of water. 'We need a doctor for Mother and Latif,' my younger brother shouts, 'We've got to take them to hospital straightaway.' I lift my arm a little, and in a whisper say, 'No.'

'Why?' he asks.

'Don't ask,' I reply, 'Just help me.'

'I'll help you if I can,' he says.

He starts to try to bandage my wounds. He examines my back and says it is no use, that he has to take me to the hospital. I don't have the strength to resist, and they take me to a private hospital, registering me under an assumed name.

I am bed-ridden and in a terrible state. My vertebrae aren't where they should be. The festering sores on my back make sleep an unattainable dream. Scratch myself and make myself bleed trying to stop the pains which are caused by the dirty water. Long nights of suffering, pain and agony. If not for the extreme care which the hospital doctors give me it would have lasted longer than it did. I start to recover.

I am determined not to return to their world, to escape from their murderous embrace. But how? I have to think what to do, have to flee from all Iraq. I keep my decision to myself, conceal it deep within me, and begin to work out the details of my plan. I have to be extremely cautious and wary if I am to escape from their hell.

Once again, my family take me into the warmth of our

home after it had been extinguished for me. They surround me with the warmth of their feelings to wipe away my torment and the harshness of my days.

A few days later there is a knock on the door: Uday's men have come – Azzam Al-Tikritti, Salam Al-Aoussi and Ahmad Souleiman. They drive me to him in a special car. 'Uday is waiting for you in the headquarters of the Iraqi Olympic Committee,' they tell me. Uday shakes my hand warmly in welcome. He is effusive in his apologies for all the suffering that has been caused me. Then he looks into my face closely, and tenderly says, 'My dear friend, you were never far from our thoughts. I was always asking about as you were lying on your bed. I was worried out you and wanted you to recover and tell us what was bothering you. I've always believed in you. Throughout all your years with us I've never seen anything from you but goodness. I'm not only talking about the performance of your duty. In spite of everything, you'll always be my friend, and you'll always find me ready to help you. My door's always open for you. Whatever you want, I'll do.'

Uday waits for a moment, then looks into my face again. Emphasising his words, he suddenly says, 'From this moment you are free. I have released you from my service, and from every government responsibility.' Once again he stresses, 'From this moment you are free.' I am jubilant. Free. I take a few deep breaths, and must look relieved. Then, after the cunning young man gives me a few moments of exhilaration, he adds 'You just have to sign this pledge.'

Without thinking, my eyes pass over the lines on the paper which Uday is offering me. I quickly read what is written, what will free me from their hellfire.

I, Latif Yahia, the fiday, hereby confirm that I will not

*disclose any confidentiality or information or duty that I
have performed while in the service of Mr Uday Saddam
Hussein, also that I will not reveal any information
concerning any security zone that I have visited or in
which I have been trained during my service, also that I
will strive to conceal the names of any members of the
Intelligence Bureau and the Special Security Agency,
similarly the identity of any person with whom I have
worked during my service with Mr Uday. Any
contravention of this pledge by me will be punishable by
the death penalty.*

Despite the fear of execution which the pledge promised, I
sign. I don't even hesitate; the doors of freedom are waiting
for me and I pay little attention to their piece of paper.

Uday takes the pledge from me and carefully examines the
signature. He seems relieved. Then he slowly says, 'We
appreciate the efforts of those who service us loyally,' and he
tells me what my reward is to be: an import/export office on
Palestinian Street; a small farm with a fully-furnished
house; a Japanese Super car; 300,000 dinars; two identity
cards in his name which allow me to enjoy two suites – one
in the Babel Aubari and one in Al-Rashid hotel – which he
has relinquished for me.

I don't know what delights me the most, the gifts or the
freedom. It was now time for me to live a little, to swagger
around in happiness. I try to contain myself. I give him the
keys which I possess, the keys of my flats in the Qadisiyya
complex and the Hayat building. We embrace and I make
ready to leave.

Before we part he tell me that he wants to say something
to me, 'Latif my friend, when you see me coming into the
Miliya Mansur hotel or the Rashid or any other place, you

must leave immediately. Don't wait to be told.' Then he adds, 'From tomorrow, I'll be sending you two guards from the Olympic Committee to keep you out of trouble.' I am well aware that the object is to keep me under surveillance and not to protect me. But I don't care. 'I'll make my plans.' I tell myself, 'The important thing is that I'm now free.'

I go to our house and sit alone thinking deeply about what I have resolved to do; make plans to flee, escape from the cage. Early in the morning of the following day the two guards arrive, Taymur Muhammad and Marwan Hashim. I lead them inside having already prepared myself to meet them, and having decided how I should conduct myself in the coming days. They say that they are putting themselves at my service. 'And I need help,' I say and explain to them what I intend to do. 'In a little while you will accompany me to Al-Nahda where I want to put two cars up for sale, and I need some assistance.' They don't object, and leave me for the palace to pick up a Mercedes which Saddam had given me. Then they go to the headquarters of the Olympic Committee to pick up the car which Uday has presented me with. Finally, we go to Al-Nahda.

I drive my brother's car while the guards drive the other two. We park by one of the many showrooms there and I go inside to speak with the owner. I explain to him what I want and the man goes off to have a look. One of the cars packing the showroom catches my attention, a large black Cadillac. When the man returns I ask him about the car, saying that I want to buy it. Proudly, he says, 'That car belonged to President Al-Bakr. His son Haytham brought it to me.' We don't quibble much over the price which he wants for it. 'In an hour I'll come back with the money,' I tell him. The man doesn't have to wait for long. I return and pay him the money

we have agreed upon, 80,000 dinars. We draw up the contract of sale and I leave him with my two cars to sell.

I let one of the guards drive the small car while I drive the
large and luxurious Cadillac. A glass partition separates the
front from the back seat. The second guard sprawls in the
seat behind me. Perhaps he is dreaming, imagining that he
is President Al-Bakr. I smile to myself and speed to the
house. I go in hurriedly and gather my things together. 'I'm
leaving immediately,' I tell my family, 'I'm going to my farm
in Al-Rashidiyya.' I speak to them impolitely and my
behaviour towards them is rough, a roughness they are not
used to seeing in me. I don't want to be like this, but I have
no choice, the one living inside me has stamped me with his
uncivil behaviour. Has their Latif perished within me,
leaving behind his image and his disgraceful conduct? Uday
has made me his aggressive counterpart in arms and I had
become another Uday.

I order Taymur to take my things to the car and leave
without saying good-bye properly. In a hurry, I say 'I'll drop
by and see you from time to time. As often as I can.' Silently,
they sorrowfully bid me farewell; say good-bye to their Latif
for whose return they had waited so long – and now here
they are losing him once again.

I am uncivil with the two guards also. This is what I
intend; I have decided to be like this – impolite and severe.
I know that they are making notes of what I do, my every
movement. This is what they have been trained to do and
this is the task that they have come to perform. They have
come to be Uday's eyes; he has sent them to watch me and
not to protect me. I know his games. Now here I am toying
with him. He will learn from them that the Latif he knew has
disappeared and that another Latif is taking shape, a Latif in
the image of Uday, frivolous and wanton, with no care but to

drink the dregs from the cup of life. I reckon that to achieve complete freedom needs a certain amount of prudence and the cunning of a fox.

I have to continue behaving in this new way, spending my nights riotously. At the beginning of every evening I enter the doors of a different hotel. Every night I have a new woman who I take to my bed at the end of each evening. I spread my net out to catch many girls, some of whom had once had relationships with Uday.

A few months pass in this way, with me following the same frenzied routine. I have no care but to lead a dissolute and bawdy life.

I become even coarser. On the few occasions that I find my way to our house I make no attempt to curb my wilful arrogance. Many times my uncivil conduct drives my dear mother to tears; it is breaking her heart to see me in this way. And my father, that wise gentleman enveloped in silence, he avoids me, makes an effort not to show the pain which rages within him.

My re-entry into Baghdad society is no surprise to my acquaintances. Indeed, the people of Iraq are accustomed to this kind of pantomime, and they still remember news of my supposed execution broadcast by the regime's television.

I am still in danger. One evening, I come out accompanied by one of those young girls who spend the night with me, both of us reeling with drunkenness. We get into the car with the two bodyguards. We have only moved a few metres from the doors of the Babel hotel when we are startled to hear a shot breaking the quiet of the night. The bullet hits the front of the car, but we all escape unscathed. The shot has come from a car without a number plate which quickly pulled alongside us, the driver firing his Kalashnikov at us but missing his target – or perhaps not intending to hit us. We stop and are surrounded by cars of the secret service which were all over the place. The men recognise me and give me a salute.

I recover from the effects of the alcohol and the sudden attack and give my orders to the two guards. I tell them to take the car to the garage, and the other to escort the girl back into the hotel. I stand speaking with the men from the secret service. I ask them not to bother with it, to act as if nothing has happened. Then I return to my hotel suite. I throw water over my body and go to bed hoping to relax. What relaxation? The telephone rings a few times and that accursed young man is at the other end. His voice reaches me, him pretending to be horrified at what has happened to me. 'Thank God you're safe', he says, 'I'll send Numayr and my private chauffeur to pick you up. I'll wait for you in the Rashid.'

Uday once again. God help me. Why doesn't that wastrel leave me alone? Why? Why? I sit on the edge of the bed with questions revolving in my head. Numayr and the chauffeur arrive. I leave the girl stretched out in the bed and tell her to get some sleep. Then I leave with them for Uday. We go into the hotel and make our way to the large hall, the Thousand and One Nights' hall, the most splendid in the Rashid.

Uday is as I remember him, flirting with his young women and reeling under the effects of the alcohol. He rushes up to me, embraces me and says, smiling, 'Once again, thank God you're safe. You're a wolf and we need have no fear for you. A childish prank like that doesn't alarm you. You've experienced dozens of them. Come and enjoy yourself.'

I'm not that Latif who he was familiar with in the past. I don't hide away in a corner watching the riotous assembly as he was used to seeing me do. I say that I want to dance, and he comments 'You've changed my friend.' Laughing, I reply 'Birds of a feather . . .' I take a couple of girls into the middle of the hall and shout to the band, 'I want a special song which glorifies the President.' Uday comes over and dances with us. His delight in my behaviour makes him fire his revolver at the ceiling. I do the same. 'Excellent Latif,' I tell myself, 'Everything's going according to plan.' Then I add, 'You've got to keep fooling that Uday so that he relies on you and trusts you. He must believe that you've really changed, that you've become a mere loafer just out for pleasure, and that he isn't frightened for the secrets which you hold within you.'

'Uday, my friend,' I say, 'I'm tired out. I'm going back to bed,' and I say good-bye to him and return to the hotel. I give myself up to sleep until the afternoon of the next day.

I resolve to execute my plans quickly. I need to make dollars in preparation for my flight, so busy myself buying a few thousand of them on the black market, hiding them in a safe place in the farm house. I ask my two guards to put the Cadillac up for sale and bring me the money from the other two cars. For my own use, I buy an American Oldsmobile. I still maintain my new lifestyle, staying up late and partying every night.

I dial the number and speak to him. After a few pleasantries, I say laughing, 'Uday, my friend, I'm sick of being protected. Can't you release me from it? I want to be alone.' I was tricking him and prevaricating. He summons me to Project Number 7 and I go to him. We spend that evening chatting intimately. In response to my request, he says, 'If you really don't want protection, then so be it,' and he hands me a mobile phone. 'Whenever you need anything, just contact me on this. Always keep it with you to replace the guards.' I thank him and give him a hug.

What do I have to do? The days are flying by, and I have arranged the details of the plan in my mind. I certainly have to leave my money with someone whom I can rely on. I think of a childhood friend and speak to him casually about it. I entrust him with what I have, saying, 'Take care of my money for me. When I need it I'll send someone to collect it. He'll bring a letter with my signature on it.' I ask him to give the messenger the money immediately, and we agree on this.

I return to my night revels, my old friend always accompanying me. I tell him my story, give him an account of what has happened to me. I unburden some of my cares on him, and tell him frankly that I want to escape.

He is alarmed, is silent for a moment, then choosing his words carefully tells me that it is very dangerous. 'I've made up my mind.' I say, adding, 'I've got to try.' I attempt to convince him. 'This is a chance that won't come again. The regime is being convulsed in every direction, thinking about more important things than Latif.' Then I reveal to him the appointment time, 'I've decided to make my escape on New Year's Eve. I reckon it's the most opportune moment. The regime will be totally absorbed in parties and debauchery, and control over the road junctions will slacken off.'

'My friend,' I say, 'I can't back down now. I'm asking you for your help,' and I ask him to keep my secret and to repeat it as much as he wants only after I have successfully made my exit. That evening I go out for a stroll. I am slowly crossing the road in Al-Mansur district when I see a man in front of me, Adil Al-Janabi, Uday's new friend and a well-known pimp who occasionally fills the flesh-pots of Baghdad with young women from the countryside – a new type of woman to attract Uday.

Inquiring about one of my cars, the man says, 'I saw your

Cadillac in the showroom, but you're asking too much for it,' and he tells me of his desire to buy it. He offers me a lower price than I'm asking, but I tell him I'm not interested in selling it, and go on my way.

On the following evening, I find my way to the Thousand and One Nights' hall. I have just sat down to take dinner when Uday enters surrounded by a group of people – friends and women, among whom is Adil Al-Janabi.

I get up to leave, remembering what Uday had ordered me when he had set me free. 'Latif,' he asks, 'Where are you going?' I go over to him and shake his hand. 'You ordered me to do that,' I reply and remind him of what he had said. He laughs loudly and goes on, 'I'm glad you haven't forgotten and that you honour your pledges. But don't go. Come over and join us once you've eaten.'

I do as he requests, and the night is full of carousing which I join in with. Before I leave, he invites me to a party he is holding on the next evening in the large Miliya Mansur hotel. He says he is throwing it to celebrate his father's having awarded him with medals of valour for his efforts in Kuwait and in opposing the Kurds.

Once again, my head is wracked with pain. I drive the car slowly. What valour, you deluded fool? I was the one who faced death over there, while you were lost in your crudities and your frivolities. But there is nothing I can do to get out of it; I simply have to attend, have to wear an expression of happiness and delight, have to excel in the new role I have chosen as a means of escaping from their world.

Ninth December 1991. I arrive at exactly the time stated. It is precisely nine o'clock as I enter the Miliya Mansur hotel. I take the lift up to the top floor and go into the room where the party is being held. I nod a greeting to the partygoers around the table and take my place. I call the waiter over and ask for a bottle of whisky, some ice and a few salads. Before I can enjoy the first glass, Uday comes into the room and sees me. He is fuming with anger. He ignores me so I remain in my seat. I start to think, start to search for a reason for the change in him. Half an hour passes and I still haven't resolved my confusion. I pull myself together and go off to the toilet. One of his guards is there – Ahmad Souleiman. He shakes my hand and whispers, 'What have you done Latif? The young gentleman is angry with you,' 'I don't know,' I reply, 'Yesterday we were laughing and joking together . . .' Then he comes in. He stands in front of me and doesn't let me finish my sentence. 'Latif, what have you said to Adil Al-Janabi?' he yells. I tell him what had gone on in Al-Mansur, explaining that the man had asked me to sell him my car and that I had refused. He screams again, 'You're a liar. You told him you wouldn't sell a car to Uday's pimps.'

What a liar that Janabi is. He has managed to stir up Uday's wrath, has plotted to turn him against me.

Uday begins to shout again. He orders me to stay where I am until the party finishes. 'Don't move,' he says. 'I'll come to take you with me.' I understand what he means; his eyes are aflame. He turns to the guard Ahmad Souleiman and orders him to make sure that I do as I am told.

I am frightened. Pictures of the criminals in charge during my detention spring to my mind; Ghalib, Abd Al-Husayn and Abu Dhayba. Once again, I feel the blows of the black whip. You've got to get out of here Latif. But how? You've got to use your wits. I hide my heaving emotions and engage Ahmad in conversation. I talked with him for almost an hour to calm myself down. I realise that this is a good opportunity. 'Ahmad,' I say, 'Why don't we have a drink? Go and get us something to quench our thirst.' He overcomes his apprehension, laughs and goes off to get us a couple of glasses. Quickly, I press the button of the lift and throw myself in. It takes me down to the ground floor and I run to my car. I start the engine and say good-bye to Baghdad.

A few guards are attracted by the sound of the engine and their cars speed off in pursuit of me. I put my foot down on the accelerator, but they are still trying to catch up. Finally, I manage to lose them, tearing around the streets and side roads of Baghdad until they disappear. I breathe a sigh of relief and take the road leading to Nineveh province.

What are you doing Latif? I have to gather my thoughts. All I have on me is 3,000 dinars, my personal revolver, the mobile telephone and a few identity cards with assumed names.

My heart beats faster. I try to remain calm. Then a military checkpoint appears in front of me on the road. I stop the car and the guard bends down and asks for my papers. I turn off the light in the car. He has recognised me. He takes a few steps back and salutes me. I start to breathe again and speed off. I don't stop again until I reach the last checkpoint before entering Nineveh, arriving there at five in the morning. The guards hadn't checked on me, but had all waved me through.

Tenth December 1991. Now, I have to choose which friends I am to go to. I turn them all over in my mind, wondering who I can depend on. I settle on one whom I am certain will be able to keep quiet. I go to his house and knock on the door and ring the bell until he comes rushing. He finds me standing in front of him and embraces me warmly. I begin to relax, to shake off my fears and misgivings.

'Open the garage and help me hide my car,' I say. We drive it in and throw a cover over it so that no one can see the number plate. Then we return to the house and I fall into the first chair I come across. He disappears for a while, then returns with the cup of tea I had asked for. He starts to scrutinise me. I quickly tell him what I am planning. 'I must get to Kurdistan,' I say, 'and from there abroad. I need help.' He looks apprehensive. 'I don't want to cause you any trouble. If you're concerned then I'll leave immediately.' Putting an end to the matter, he replies, 'Don't worry, I'll sort everything out for you. Money can achieve the impossible.' I tell him what I have on me, saying, 'All I've got here is three thousand dinars and my revolver.' 'That'll get you to Duhuk,' he replies. 'You'll be safe there. There's no government there, only the Peshmerga.'

Under cover of night we take the car to the woods around Mawsil and dumped it well out of sight. I throw the mobile telephone as far as I can into the Tigris, and breathe a sigh of relief. We stand by the side of the road and hail a taxi which takes us back to the house. My friend sits turning over the names of those who help people escape, trying to find one of them who would escort me to Duhuk. When he have decided on a name, he leaves me outside, returning two hours later and saying that he has reached an agreement with two men who are to undertake the task. 'They'll be here at precisely ten in the morning to accompany you,' he adds.

I spend a sleepless night tossing and turning in bed; I can't rid myself of the fears that have started to assail me. The two men appear at the exact time they have said. I embrace my friend in farewell, tears forming in my eyes. I give him the pistol which I have, telling him that it is to remember me by. He hugs me again, I shake his wife's hand in gratitude, and we set off.

The driver takes the car over non-surfaced roads to avoid being stopped. One hour seems like an age. On the outskirts of a small village the car stops. We start to walk, leaving the car at the side of the road. For eight hours we walk along rough and unfrequented tracks and through mountain passes. In exhaustion we try to steady our feet; uneven mountain tracks covered with snow. We go into a safe cave to rest for a while, then travel on until we eventually reach a post of Peshmerga fighters.

They greet us warmly and I make an effort to speak to them in Kurdish. We are given an old battered car to see us on the rest of our journey.

Eventually the driver of the car says that we have now reached the land of safety. I look at the country in front of me and see the outskirts of Duhuk. I sigh with relief and all fear leaves me. There is nothing here to tell us that we are still in Iraq, everyone wears typical Kurdish dress, walking proudly in their loose-fitting trousers and all carrying weapons. There are different flags, and the pictures of the Kurdish leaders are displayed on the house doors and at the street corners. To the man with me I whisper the name of a relative whom I want to see and I tell him the address. He nods in agreement, and we begin to search for the road to the village I want to go to, asking passers-by. Eventually, we stop in front of the house. We knock on the door and wait.

My relative stands for a moment regarding me, then rushes to give me a very warm hug. He can't believe that the one he is embracing is Latif and can't let go of me. I feel warm inside, overflowing with a feeling of well-being at his deep love. We all sit together at the crowded table which the people of the house busily set for us.

Later, my two guides retrace their steps to Nineveh after I give them 1,000 dinars which we'd agreed upon, and I go back to talk to my relative.

*

Twelfth December 1991. I tell my relative's eldest son about my desire to go to one of the United Nation's headquarters to seek their assistance in leaving Iraq. 'The region is dangerous now,' he says', 'And you look like a stranger. We're afraid you'll fall into the hands of the rival groups here.' He asks me to tear up any documents I have which might reveal my connection with government circles in Baghdad. After we have turned the affair over together, he says, 'Tomorrow, I'll take you to a photographer who'll take a photo which we can use in forging nationality papers for you. It won't cost more than one hundred dinars.'

I receive the papers which that clever young man has made, and go with him to the United Nation's headquarters in Duhuk. I speak to them in English and they take me to the director to explain my situation. I stand in front of him, watching him as he notes down every word I say. He is very thin and his skin is somewhat dark. After I have told him the story, he mutters a few words. 'Come back in a week,' he says wearily. I try to persuade him with my fears, but he insists on the appointment he has made. I return disappointed and heavy-hearted.

Thirteenth December 1991. Before noon, the door shakes under continuous knocking; some men have come to question the people of the house about the stranger who is staying with them. I go out to the men who are asking after me and tell them what the situation is, then I accompany them to the headquarters of the Kurdish Front.

They interrogate me, but are amiable and treat me with no little respect. I stand before six men who represent the active political parties in the region, each man representing one of the opposition parties. They question me continuously to establish the truth of my story, and I am subjected to this interrogation until nine o'clock in the evening. I am exhausted.

Once again, I am afraid. The man who is obviously in charge of the inquiry and who it transpired is a representative from the Iraqi Communist Party, says, 'You'll stay here in prison until we can verify your story.'

Again, Latif. Prison follows you even when you're far from Baghdad and when you think you've said good-bye to hardships.

But my relatives manage to bail me out, assuring the man that they promise to place me at the disposal of the inquiry at any time if they convict me and find something in my story which implicates me.

They take me back to the house and I sit down exhausted from the long time I have spent under interrogation. I reveal to my relative that I want to retrieve the money which I had entrusted to my friend in Baghdad, and in their proficient manner they arrange it for me. They take me to a man whom they indicated would guarantee that the job was done without mishap, and I write a letter to my friend as we had agreed and sign it. I write down the address on a separate piece of paper. The messenger takes the letter and sets off.

Fifteenth December 1991. Sometimes coincidence plays a happy role in our lives. We are sitting in the courtyard of the house passing the time in conversation, when a knock comes at the door and one of my relative's friends enters whom I knew was from Turkey. After a little while, I tell him about my desire to go there. 'I don't think Turkey would suit you,' he advises me, saying that the squares and coffee houses are teeming with Iraqis, some of whom were working for Saddam. He adds confidently, 'The best thing for you is to go to the Military Coordination bureau of the coalition in the

Zakhu region. The Americans there will make things easy for
you. Don't depend too much on the United Nations, they
drag their feet too much.' I had already informed him that
they had told me to come back in a week.

I am overjoyed when he offers to take me in his truck. He
says, 'I've got this big truck to carry gas and the Coordination
Bureau will be on my way. I'll take you with me in the
morning.'

Sixteenth December 1991. I wake early and after getting
myself ready sit waiting for the anticipated journey. The
Turkish man arrives at the hour he states. I say good-bye to
the people of the house and direct my relative to look after
my money if it should come. I tell him I'll come and collect
it once he informs me that it has arrived. Then we set off in
the truck. Only a little time has passed when the man points
out a building which has come into sight. We have already
arrived at our destination. He stops the truck to get out, bids
me farewell and wishes me success.

I stand in the large yard; two big houses with satellite disks
on top and armoured cars and some normal vehicles parked
in front. I make my way to the first house, ring the bell on
the entry phone and someone comes to see who it is. I stand
in front of a man in Kurdish clothes. 'Yes?' he says abruptly.
'I want to meet the man in charge here,' I say. He answers
me haughtily, 'We don't have the time,' and makes to close
the door in my face. 'Please,' I say, 'I'm not from here. I'm
from Baghdad and I've got a problem.' He asks me to wait
and goes back inside.

I stand in front of the closed door hoping that someone
more understanding will come. Five minutes pass. Then the
door opens again and another man appears wearing a
military uniform and looking somewhat like an American. I

glance at the badge on his tunic, the letters showing that the man has a strange name. I speak to him in English, and he answers in Palestinian Arabic. Then his mouth widens into a broad and friendly smile. 'What can we do for you?' he inquires. 'I've got a problem,' I say, 'And want to try and solve it.' He then says something which he obviously repeats whenever he answers any knock at the door, 'The problems of the Kurds are never-ending.'

In clear and deliberate words I try to sway him, 'I'm not from here. I'm not from this region. I'm not from the north at all. I'm from Baghdad.' He turns to the Kurdish man standing next to him and orders him to go inside. When he is satisfied that we are alone, he says, 'But we're not a help agency. We're merely a detachment protecting the Kurds against Saddam's attacks. You need to go to the United Nations.' I explain my attempt with him. I had to get nearer to the goal posts. 'My problem isn't a usual one,' I say. 'My life's in danger.' He takes out a notebook and asks me to leave my name and address.

'Latif Yahia Latif. First Lieutenant in the secret service.'

The ball hits the back of the net! The man never finishes writing down the second half of what I say, but stares at me from the shock of my reply. He quickly takes me by the elbow with his right hand and leads me inside. We stop in the middle of a large room, and in disbelief he says, 'What did you say?'

I kick the ball in again, 'I told you my name and position. You heard me.' Then I add, ensuring that the ball is well and truly home, 'I'm more than that, I'm the private fiday of Uday Saddam Hussein.'

There is no room for hesitation, he warmly welcomes me into the large room, a room crammed with equipment, receivers, telephones, many different kinds which I knew well – just like the equipment packed in the Republican Palace.

The man tells me his name, 'I am Saad Al-Din Halim, but here they simply call me Din.' Then he asks whether I want something to drink.

Din leaves to return with a cup of tea as I had wanted. He is smiling broadly, he has become more friendly. He says that I should consider myself at home, then adds, 'Don't be afraid. When we've verified who you are we'll take you to the country you want.' Jokingly, I ask, 'Is this the work of the United Nations?' He bursts into laughter, understanding what I meant. 'Yes,' he says, 'I said the same in the beginning. I'm sorry, but every day dozens of people knock at the door asking us to help them get out of Iraq. It's like we're some kind of travel agency.'

Saad Al-Din picks up the radio and speaks to Colonel Nap, the man in charge of the Bureau. A few minutes later the man is in front of me; a man of medium height standing there looking at me. He is clearly a cheerful man. He reaches out to shake my hand warmly, then sits down inviting me to join him. He begins to get the broad outlines of the story. I repeat it all to him, speaking in Arabic with Saad Al-Din Halim acting as interpreter.

Before we get down to the details, he invites me to eat with him. After this, we go back to finish the session. There is a stream of questions, but I hide nothing. Colonel Nap follows me attentively, carefully writing down the details on the paper piled up on the small table. Whenever he fills a sheet he passes it to someone sitting next to a radio transmitter to forward it to Washington immediately. Hours pass during which I give my account and they write it down. I speak until eight o'clock, by which time I have said everything I have to say.

After a few moments of silence, Nap says, 'It's a strange tale, filled with terrible things and events,' and he holds out his hand to me with compassion. 'Now, you must rest a little.' He and Saad Al-Din accompany me to the other house and lead me into a private room. Nap smiles and says, 'The house is yours. Have a rest.' Then, correcting himself and laughing, he says, 'Or rather, not all of the house is yours, some of it belongs to the soldiers here,' and he points at some closed rooms. I nod that I understand and he leaves me to the hospitality of one of his officers, Captain Ted Jolly. Jolly is a very friendly person and I am captivated by his charm.

Twentieth December 1991. Four days full of questions, searching for every minute detail. They sit me down in front of three men dressed in civilian clothes. Nap tells me that they have been appointed to conduct the final interrogation at the request of the American Ministry of Defense. One of the three men keeps a camera trained on me the whole time.

Before the interview finishes they want to prove how powerful they are. One of them puts his hand in a bag, pulls out a number of photographs and tosses them on the table. He smiles, and points to one. 'This is a photo of Uday.' I begin to examine my photograph. I am wearing Uday's special suit. The man continues to smile, then addresses me again, 'We've known about you for some time, but we had to be sure. Thanks.' He stands up, followed by his two colleagues and they all shake my hand and leave.

Colonel Nap and Saad Al-Din go with them, leaving me, Captain Ted Jolly and an American woman officer called Julie from the Air Wing. We talk about nothing in particular.

Thirty-first December 1991. In the early part of the morning all the officers of the Bureau are busy preparing to say good-

bye to the old year. 'Of course, you'll join in the celebrations,' says Saad Al-Din, 'A lot of guests are also coming
from the American base in Turkey.' In the evening the
garden is full of celebrating; men and women officers mix
together and the bottles of whisky succeed in taking the edge
off the cold and warming the people up.

Fourth January 1992. While I am relaxing, watching the
television in the hall, Nap arrives and says, smiling, 'How are
you, Latif?' he sits down and we start to joke. 'What do you
think?' he asks, 'Would you like to go to America? We can
arrange for you to go there as a political refugee.' I realise he
is serious and that he is trying to find out my intentions. I
thank him but refuse the offer, saying, 'I've made up my mind
to go to Austria.' I couldn't even place the country on a map
of Europe. All I know is that I have a cousin over there who
is a doctor in Vienna. Nap says he will arrange things for me.

Sixth January 1992. I tell Saad Al-Din that I want to travel
to Duhuk, and he goes off to see Nap who comes
immediately. In amazement, the man says, 'Why do you
want to go there? We've sounded the Austrians out regarding
your request and the authorisation might come at any
minute and you'll be on your way.' I let him know why, 'I
have some money over there which I need to start my new
life.' I look into the man's face, waiting for his reply. 'OK,' he
says, but his face shows signs of worry. Perhaps he is
concerned, knowing that it is unsafe to travel there; he has
received reports of fighting between the Kurdish political
parties throughout Kurdistan. But he can do nothing but
agree to my request. 'We'll send you in a private car from the
Bureau which will take you to where you want to go in
Duhuk.'

So I return there again. My friends receive me joyfully and I say good-bye to the driver of the Porsche who had taken me there, asking him to relay my greetings to Nap and Saad Al-Din and to tell them not to worry. 'I'll be back with you at the Bureau in two days at the most,' I add.

It is afternoon as I sit with my friends around a large table playing Concan, talking and swapping stories. They are delighted when I inform them I am on my way to Austria and that the Americans are doing their best to help me arrange things.

My relative leads me to his own room and closes the door behind us. He takes a suitcase out of a wooden cupboard and says, smiling, 'This belongs to you.' I grip his arm with my right hand and breathe a sigh of relief. I give him the 10,000 dinars to pay the man who had brought the suitcase and return to our friends sitting at the table scattered with playing cards.

Seventh January 1992. At eight o'clock in the morning there come a few heavy knocks at the door. My relative rushes to see who it is and finds a group of armed men there. I hear them through the partly open door of my room mentioning the name of their leader. They say that they are men of Rasul Mamand, the leader of the Kurdish Socialist Party, and explain their mission by adding that their leader wants to meet me. He has ordered that I visit him and they have come to accompany me. My relative tries to fob them off, saying that I am still asleep. But they insist I go out to them and they repeat their request. They are all carrying Kalashnikovs. I don't think much of it, think that it is quite normal. No man in that area is ever without weapons. Indeed, it is their duty to oppose the regime, and I have to submit to their request; it appears to be an invitation that I can't refuse. I say this to myself as I get ready to climb into one of their cars which are parked in the area around the house. I get in still holding the suitcase of money.

They tell me that we are going to meet Mamand in the district of Raniyya in Al-Sulaymaniyya province on the borders between Iraq and Iran. Our convoy moves along rough and difficult roads, narrow and twisting and covered everywhere with snow. It is called the 'Road of Barzan'.

The man sitting next to me begins to speak. His name is Khalid. Filled with misgivings, I tell him, 'I want to go back to Duhuk.' He shakes his head, and from his rough expression I understand what is going on, I realise that I have fallen into a trap and that I am being driven into the unknown. Their voices, once gentle, change their tone.

Insolently, Khalid says, 'We're going whether you like it or not.' This is final, and his face is stamped with deceit and lack of remorse. He puts the muzzle of his revolver against me to intimidate me. Suddenly, he asks me, 'You're carrying a lot of money, aren't you?' He doesn't wait for a reply, but puts his hands in my pockets and pulls out the contents. He also takes my gold watch, a ring I am wearing and a chain. He does this brazenly. I tighten my grip on the suitcase of money, sensing the calamity which hovers on the horizon. Thieves, highway robbers, scoundrels. I am troubled by many thoughts, but keep quiet and do not reveal what is within me. If I did, perhaps my neck would be the price. I become increasingly frightened; maybe they are taking me to barter with me, delivering me to Baghdad and collecting the reward money – millions of dinars which Uday has probably set aside for the person who brought me in after I had fled from under his control. My imprisoned screams begin to burst from within me. I have to release them. Angrily, I say 'Who is this man called Rasul Mamand? Where is he? If he really is the leader of an opposition party, then you certainly aren't his men. You're nothing but thieves and highway robbers.' They pay no attention to my shouting. The one called Khalid simply strikes me lightly on the head as a warning because I am making so much noise.

I am debilitated with fatigue, but more so from fear of the coming unknown. The long journey over rough roads has exhausted me and the brutality of the men crushes my spirits. Fourteen hours seemed like an eternity.

At half past ten at night, we enter Raniyya province. They don't take me to the party headquarters as they had initially claimed they would, but to a ruined building. They throw me into one of its dark rooms and snatch the suitcase from me which contains my money. They strip me of everything, then leave.

Once again Latif, you've entered the desolation of prison. I sit in one of the corners of the room and try to collect my thoughts. My limbs stiffen with the cold. Snow falls on to the roof making me more ill at ease. I begin to think back, who are the leaders of the Kurdish opposition? Masud Al-Barzani, the president of the Kurdish Democratic Party; Jalal Al-Talabani, president of the Kurdish National Union Party; Rasul Mamand . . . Rasul Mamand? I had come across this name before, perhaps in official reports or the chit-chat of members of the secret service. What does he want from me? And why this rough treatment?

I have to find a way out. But how? And even if I find one, where could I go? It is a desolate place. You'll freeze, Latif, if you try to walk in this icy desert. I realise the futility of the attempt, and return to slump in the corner. I sit waiting for a miracle which fate might bring me. I surrender myself to an unknown destiny.

After a few grim days, I realise that I'm not the only one in this desolate place. I have found someone else, found him in another room suffering like me from the severe cold, the torments of hunger and isolation from the world. He is an old man. Feebly, I question him in Kurdish, and he answers me faltering in his words. He complains of violent pains in his chest, and says that we have fallen into the hands of someone without mercy, into the hands of thieves and scoundrels, the hands of the 'bandit' Rasul Mamand's gang. He tells me that Mamand was always called 'the bandit' because of the highway robbery and burglary engaged in by his men. He tells me some of the things they have done. Under his orders his followers used to rip up telegraph poles to sell to Iran. They plundered everything, agricultural equipment, road-making equipment, and whatever they could lay their hands on they would sell to whoever paid the price. 'I rely on your wisdom, Hajj Ibrahim,' I say, this being the name of my companion in that wild place, 'What do you advise me to do?' He bows his head for a moment, then feebly replies, 'Be patient. God will help us.' 'Why are you here?' I ask him. 'I'm not a member of any of the parties which swarm over the province,' he replies. 'What brought me here was merely an attempt to protest; a few angry words. Every week, some lorries come to this province carrying liquid gas and paraffin for the people of the region. Mamand's men control its distribution, giving some of the lorries' load to their friends and acquaintances and selling the rest on the black market for their own profit. It was my bad luck to wrangle with them. And now here I am, suffering from hunger, illness and the harshness of imprisonment.'

Twelfth January 1992. Eventually, they arrive. The come to me, their weapons drawn, and pull me out of the corner. They tie a blindfold firmly around my eyes and shackle my arms. Then they drag me to one of their cars and drive me to a region called Jar Qarna – another desolate place. I count 16 steps, after which they take my blindfold off and depart, leaving me a small dim paraffin lamp.

Khalid and his gang arrive again and direct a number of threats at me. He warns me to say nothing. 'Don't say a word,' he cautions, 'Don't tell anyone that we've taken something from you. If you do, I won't think twice about killing you.' In despair, I say, 'I'm not interested in the money. I just want to go back to Zakhu.' 'Not yet,' he replies, 'We're not going to let you go just yet. We haven't finished with you. We've still got a few inquiries to make about you, and after that we'll decide what's to happen to you.' I become agitated and scream inside again. 'Who are you? I want to see Rasul Mamand.' My words provoke them and they give me a sound beating. They strip my clothes off and throw cold water over me. Then they leave me, not forgetting to lock the door behind them. Every day for ten days they come and make me taste all kinds of torture.

On the morning of the tenth day, they take me outside, give me clean and pressed clothes and order me quickly to put them on. I do as I am told, the cold which has frozen my limbs making me submissive. Then they roughly shove me into their car and drive me back to Raniyya province. They take me into a house where a barber is waiting and push me towards him. He cuts my hair and trims my beard and moustache. After this, they lead me to a room in which a video camera has been installed. Khalid orders me to sit in front of it and to thank their party, to heap praise on their leader, to speak eloquently so that they can record it on a cassette and keep it.

Another piece of theatre. Another gang of scoundrels. They are doing just as Uday used to do, imitating the regime which they have rebelled against. There is nothing I can do. I have to follow their wishes. I sit down and repeat what they ask me to, putting on a false smile for the camera.

They take me back to the prison at Jar Qarna and put me in the very same room. This time, however, and unlike before, they give me a mattress and a cover and bring me some reasonable food. I'm not aware of the reasons for this novel treatment.

Twenty-fifth January 1992. The door of the prison opens. This time they have come with three men whom they fling inside, throwing them one on top of the other in the middle of the dark room. Then they lock the door. At first I am wary of talking to the newcomers, afraid that they might be accomplices whom they have sent to spy on me. For two days I watch them and they watch me. By the middle of the third day I am still reluctant to speak, but have to. I learn the names of the men and they learn mine. The first is called Bakhtiyar, the second Ahmad and the third Hasan Khushnaw. They get to know that I am from Baghdad. They ask me why I am here and I tell them that I don't really know.

Before the day ends on which we have got to know each other after so much hesitation, both Bakhtiyar and Ahmad are dragged out by the thieves, leaving me and Hasan Khushnaw. Hasan explains to me the circumstances which have led him to this place. He says that he had been a member of the Military Intelligence Bureau, the 'Department of In Depth Surveillance'. During the war with Iran he had infiltrated Tehran to plant bombs. He did this several times and was usually successful, receiving rewards from Saddam's regime as a result. The regime showered him with gifts. After Iraq's invasion of Kuwait he returned to Raniyya where his family lives, wanting to join the opposition. But he fell into their hands, the hands of Rasul Mamand's men. They accused him of still working for the regime in Baghdad, and wanted to sell him to Iran which would take him dead or alive. They had learnt that Tehran had set aside five million Iraqi dinars for the person who brought him to them. He was therefore valuable prey and a good opportunity for Rasul Mamand's gang. In despair, Hasan says 'They do this all the time. They hunt people down to get the reward – whether from Baghdad or Tehran, it's the same to them.'

I feel frightened again. Perhaps this is the reason they have been eager to sit me down in front of the camera. I can see the nature of their plan now, there is no doubt that they are wanting to sell me to Saddam's men. They are holding on to the video cassette so as to avoid the anger of the Kurdish parties, holding on to evidence that I have been their guest and that they have welcomed my arrival. I have left them of my own free will and the cassette is the best proof for anyone with doubts that they are completely innocent.

Twenty-ninth January 1992. Hasan Khushnaw and I don't sleep for long, they come and snatch him away just as they had with Bakhtiyar and Ahmad. They don't take him outside, but rather lead him to another cell which I can locate from his loud and agonising screams; through the solid walls I can hear the cracks of their whips as they beat the poor man.

Once again I am alone, overcome with fear and sunk in despair. The walls have been written on time and time again, and still show the faint outlines of Ba'ath Party slogans. Indeed, our prison had once been one of its headquarters, had been occupied by one of its organisations. But now, after these people have tightened their grip on Kurdistan, they have turned it into a prison to which they lead men who have committed no crime or offence. So, there is no difference between them; there is no difference between the regime and the opposition – they are all the same.

O country of my birth, you ancient land, it is as if you can grow nothing but satanic thorns. If it is my lot to flee from here, I will never return to you, you desert which holds nothing but injustice and tyranny.

Second February 1992. They come again before midnight. I hear them as they curse him and push him violently inside my cell. Then they leave him and depart. I look at him. Despite the faint light I can make out his features, a young man in the prime of life, no more than 18 years old or thereabouts. I cautiously start to speak to him, becoming certain that he isn't one of their men. He tells me that he is a follower of Masud Al-Barzani, the leader of the Kurdish Democratic Party, and relates to me how he has found his way here. We become friends. He says that he has told himself that he won't be here for long, that his problem isn't serious. I don't know why Muhammad Zirak, as he is called, is so confident that the men will release him soon, but I too cling on to hope, hope that Muhammad would help me if he is proved to be correct. If this were to happen I implore him to help me, and he confirms that he would. He says that as soon as he is released he will tell his superior who will relay the information to Masud Al-Barzani, the leader of the Party. To ease my mind, he says, 'Don't worry. I swear on my honour and on all that is sacred that I'll do it. I'll do everything within my power to have you released.'

My mind is set at rest; the clouds of fear, despair and hopelessness are dispersed. With all my heart I hope that he will be set free – for his sake and for mine.

*

Seventh February 1992. I believe Muhammad Zirak's appraisal of the situation. In the early hours of the morning they come again, and it seems from their manner that they have come to release him. He says good-bye to me and quickly whispers in my ear, 'Don't worry, I'll arrange things.' This is echoed by the look of encouragement he gives me as he is dragged outside. After he has gone, I sit in hope, sit on the edge of the mattress waiting for my salvation.

Tenth February 1992. Before the sun had reached its zenith, I hear voices approaching and the sound of cars. I jump up to look, to see what is coming – relief or torment? I can't believe what I am hearing, loud shouts repeatedly calling my name.

'Latif. Latif. Where are you Latif?' It is clear. No doubt about it. My name. They aren't calling for somebody else; they are calling for me, searching for me. Before I can shout out in reply, a familiar voice says, 'He's in the shelter.' The voice is distinctive and I recognise it immediately. It is his voice, the voice of that villain called Abd Al-Karim, Abd Al-Karim who had so expertly punished me when they had targeted me for their crimes.

I am overwhelmed with joy. You have escaped, Latif. You won't die here. You won't be consumed with loneliness or frozen with ice. I will continue the journey you have begun to flee far from the world of the wicked. The young man has done it. Muhammad has kept his promise.

I hear their footsteps as they come down. They stop before me and a young man in front of them greets me. With a broad smile, he says, 'I am Doctor Sarbast, from the Kurdish Democratic Party. Muhammad Zirak told us you were here and we came immediately. You are our guest now,' and he reaches out to shake my hand in friendship.

'You are our guest now,' he repeats amicably, as he leads me into the light. Then he starts to express his regret at what has happened to me and to apologise as if he and his party had caused it all.

The large courtyard is crowded with men attired in distinctive Kurdish dress. I see the two of them immediately, just as if I had been looking for them – Khalid and Adb Al-Karim. I rush up to them, anger and loathing vying with my joy at getting out of the prison. I spit in their faces with all the force I possess. Villains, murderers. I'll uncover you and your thieving leader. I want to grab them by the throat, to repay them for all the horrors they had inflicted on me. Nothing prevents me but the obvious friendliness on the faces of the other men who have come for me. Despite my fury, I don't want them to see an ugly side of me, but have to conduct myself with propriety and to leave it to them to settle things with those lying thieves.

Smiling and trying to calm my thoughts and my rage, Dr Sarbast leads me to his Land Cruiser. Our convoy drives for five hours, travelling along rough roads, until we reach the headquarters of the Kurdish Democratic Party in the district of Shaqlawa in the governorate of Arbil.

The cars stop in front of the large building and we all get out and go through the large gates. I see a large picture of Masud Al-Barzani hanging over the entrance. As we are sitting inside, Dr Sarbast assures me that their Party will not allow Mamand's Party to continue in its crimes which mar their struggle. As we go to eat the food spread on the table for us, he continues to welcome me and to apologise for what I have been through. I eat with great appetite, but it isn't hunger or the aroma of the food which makes me enjoy it so much; what has given me such an appetite even before they appeared and is more significant and momentous is my freedom after so many tormented and harsh days. To this is added the friendliness of the men and their warm reception.

I told my host of my desire to travel to Zakhu. Laughing, he says 'You never give up! We've been looking for you for ages and now finally we've found you. As soon as we received a cable from Colonel Nap we started to look everywhere. We asked all the Parties, including that of Rasul Mamand. Now you're with us. Early tomorrow morning we'll take you to where you want to go. Have an untroubled and carefree night. Take some rest and wash away some of your cares and worries of moving from pillar to post.' Then he leaves me at the side of the comfortable bed which he has led me to. I go into the bathroom to clean myself, let the water wash over me to remove the filth of the prison – the prison of those thieves, those scoundrels.

Before surrendering myself to sleep, I sit on the edge of the bed, trying to put down some of what I have heard recently, and don't forget to make a list of the things that those thieves and villains have stolen from me. This will be evidence to put before the leader of the Kurdish Democratic Party in his dealing with the crimes and transgressions of Rasul Mamand's Party. I also compose a letter of thanks and gratitude to Masud Al-Barzani. When I have finished, I feel a great sense of ease and surrender myself to a tranquil sleep.

Eleventh February 1992. I awake to the sound of gentle knocking on the door of the room. One of the men enters carrying my breakfast in his right hand. Putting the food down on the table next to my bed, he says, 'I hope you've slept well.' He then asks me to tell him what I want. With hospitality and great affection, he says, 'Don't be shy. You're at home now.' I am much cheered by his friendliness.

I get up and wash, get dressed, and eat with the same
appetite as before. As I am drinking the last sip of tea,
another man comes. He greets me and asks me to follow
him, saying that Mr Nijarvan is waiting for me. Then, in
explanation, he adds, 'Mr Nijarvan is Masud Al-Barzani's
aide and his nephew.'

We go to him and find him standing behind his desk ready
to meet me. He shakes my hand in welcome and apologises
and expresses his regret at what has happened to me. I thank
him and ask him to convey my respects to Masud after
learning that he is on a mission to Turkey. Smiling, he says,
'If he'd been here he would have met you himself,' adding,
'He was most insistent on the importance of rescuing you.'
Then, jokingly, we went on, 'Whatever your job in Baghdad
was, so long as you have fled from over there, we consider
you to be one of those opposing the iniquitous regime, and
it's our duty to forgive you and offer you every assistance.' At
the end of our meeting he bids me farewell in sincere
friendship.

Dr Sarbast accompanies me to the car which is parked by
the door and waits for me. I get into the Land Cruiser along
with the driver and four bodyguards, and we set off on our
way to Duhuk. The driver takes us along the 'Road of
Barzan', and at eight in the evening we are at the outskirts of
Duhuk. We arrive fatigued and exhausted from the rough
road.

They take me to a luxurious house where the owner gives
me a warm welcome. They introduce me to him, saying that
he is Mr Babakir, one of the officials in the Kurdish
Democratic Party in the governorate. With a broad smile on
his face, the man tells the guards, 'Latif's my guest today,'
then he orders them to return.

*

Twelfth February 1992. In the morning, Babakir knocks on the door of the room. Smiling, he says, 'You must get ready for your journey.' We talk a little over breakfast and when the car arrives he accompanies me to it in farewell. He shakes my hand and wishes me well.

At eleven o'clock and before the sun is at its zenith, the car engine stops and we are at the door – the door of the headquarters. At the sound of knocking the same man I had seen before comes out, that Kurd whom I had seen the first time I had come to them. This time he receives me with a smile, without the earlier sullen mood. He says that Colonel Nap isn't there, that he has gone out on patrol with Saad Al-Din. Captain Ted Jolly comes and embraces me warmly, then leads me inside. We sit and chat until Nap and Saad Al-Din arrive. They give me a big hug. 'We've been looking for you for a long time,' says Nap, 'We asked Al-Barzani and Al-Talabani to search for you throughout all Kurdistan. And now finally here you are in our house.'

He has much heart-warming news to give me. 'You'll stay here only until tomorrow,' he says, 'And in the morning we'll inform the United Nations that we've found you.' Then he adds, 'Austria has agreed to grant you political asylum.' He laughs loudly, ' We have exchanged you for a Christian family which lives in Vienna and which wants to go to America.' Apologising, he continues, 'Your room in the house is currently being used by guests who have come from America, but we'll manage,' and he immediately rings Jalal Al-Talabani, asking him to provide me with a temporary base in Zakhu.

They take me there. Waiting for me is a man called Husayn Agha in whose hospitable hands Nap and Saad Al-Din leave me. The man leads me into his house and we chat amicably. I learn from him that he lives in Europe and comes here a few times every year to help in the work of the Party.

I am the man's guest for ten days during which I am much cheered by his warmth, his kindness and his refinement.

Twenty-third February 1992. I return to the headquarters once again, Nap coming to take me there in his car. As we are walking to his office he tells me that all the procedures have been completed. Then, with deliberation so that it would register with me, he says, 'You'll travel next week.' I am overjoyed to hear the news for which I have waited for so long. 'You could have gone before that,' he explains, 'But I preferred to take my time to enable you to travel by air. We've arranged for you to be transported to Turkey by helicopter.'

Second March 1992. He stands at the door of my room and looks at me before saying anything. In turn, I look at him. What was Nap up to? I wait to hear what he is going to say, preparing myself for a shock. Then he starts to laugh. 'Come on,' I say smiling, 'Let's have it.' 'You'll fly to Turkey today,' he replies. Today? I rush to embrace him, tears immediately forming in my eyes. The picture of my family springs into my mind. I remember Baghdad in all its sweetness and all its bitterness. The dream has remained with me a long time, has lingered, but in the end has disappeared. I will leave my world, the pleasure and the pain, the loyal people and the villains.

Nap stands in silence. He respects the feelings in me which are suddenly released and leaves me to myself for a few moments. Then he returns to lead me to another room and show me the many gifts he has prepared for me, bottles of perfume and other things. He and his colleagues want me to remember them. He doesn't forget to take a camera from its case and to take a number of souvenir photographs. 'I'll come for you in an hour,' he says laughing, 'So that we can celebrate your leaving our headquarters.'

They all turn up, Nap, Saad Al-Din and the other officers – men and women. They crowd around me and we begin to laugh and joke. We clink our glasses together until the roar of the helicopter announces that it is time to go. I go with them to the small air strip and hug them all before climbing up and being swallowed in the depths of the helicopter.

I sit with mixed emotions, feelings of joy mixed with feelings of pain. The helicopter raises itself in the air, and through the small window I take my last look at the country of my birth.

The helicopter lands at one of the military bases in Turkey, and we find two cars waiting for us carrying United Nations' emblems. I shake the hands of the men from the international organisation who have come to receive me and go with them to their headquarters in Diyar Bakr.

After I have stayed there for a while, a driver takes me to a luxury hotel, making sure the receptionist understands that all my requests are to be attended to.

Third March 1992. On the following morning two men from the organisation come to the hotel and take me to Diyar Bakr airport, where there were many journalists waiting for me. They crowd around me and their cameras flash to capture my picture. They try to extract a few words from me but I refuse to say anything. Then the aeroplane arrives to save me from their insistent inquiries. I wave good-bye and fly off to Ankara.

I find him waiting for me at the airport. He introduces himself, saying that he is the United Nation's official there and that his name is Brian. He takes me to the Kunak hotel where I find similar attention to that I had found in Diyar Bakr. The man impresses on me that I am their guest, and before he leaves puts his hand in his attaché case and gives me $1,000, saying that it is for any unexpected eventualities. He leaves two men with me to look after my needs. He also leaves me his telephone numbers, saying, 'Maybe you'll need me. Get in touch any time you like.'

Sixth March 1992. Brian takes me to the Austrian embassy where they finalise my entry permit into their country. They do this with an international passport which Brian has arranged for me, a passport which is for one journey only.

Ninth March 1992. At ten in the morning, I go with Brian to the airport and we sit waiting for the plane which will take me via Istanbul to Vienna. The hands of the clock indicate that it is half past two in the afternoon when the plane lands in Vienna.

Now, I walk in the land of freedom. At last, I can breathe a sigh of relief. From now on, I will begin to settle my account with the regime in Baghdad. This is what I say as I walk outside the attractive airport.

The Turks broadcast the news after I have left for Austria. In its evening transmission, Radio Ankara says that the double for the son of the Iraqi dictator has successfully fled to Europe. The Turkish newspapers publish the same information, as do the world news agencies. At the doors of the airport someone from the Austrian news agency is waiting for me, waiting for the double who has come out from behind the walls of the kingdom of terror.

That date will always be engraved in my memory, 9 March 1992, the day when a new life began, a life without fear – life without Uday.

Dr Yahia is currently working on a sequel to *The Devil's Double*, detailing his life from the day he left Iraq to the day he saw Saddam topple from power.